# THE T[illegible]CATIONAL TECH[illegible]LOGY

Educational technology is controversial – some see it as essential to providing free global learning, others view it as a dangerous distraction that undermines good education. In both instances, most theories that have previously been applied to educational technology do not account for the distinctive nature and vast potential of technology. This book addresses this issue, exploring how education has been bound up with technology from the beginning, and recognising that educational aims have already been shaped by technologies. Offering a 'dialogic' theory of educational technology, **Rupert Wegerif** and **Louis Major** respond to contemporary challenges to education within this book, including, but not limited to, climate change, misinformation on the internet and the impact of artificial intelligence.

Chapters introduce, discuss and contextualise key theories and illustrate through case studies their uses within a diverse range of educational contexts, spanning from primary education to adult lifelong learning. Each chapter also concludes with a short summary, demonstrating how these theories translate to practical implications for design.

A fascinating response to current developments in educational technology, this is a crucial read for all involved in creating, researching or making decisions about the use of technologies within educational contexts.

**Rupert Wegerif** is Professor of Education and Academic Director of the Digital Education Futures Initiative (DEFI) at the University of Cambridge.

**Louis Major** is a Senior Lecturer in Digital Education at the University of Manchester.

# THE THEORY OF EDUCATIONAL TECHNOLOGY

## Towards a Dialogic Foundation for Design

*Rupert Wegerif and Louis Major*

Routledge
Taylor & Francis Group
LONDON AND NEW YORK

Designed cover image: © Xuanyu Han / Getty Images

First published 2024
by Routledge
4 Park Square, Milton Park, Abingdon, Oxon OX14 4RN

and by Routledge
605 Third Avenue, New York, NY 10158

*Routledge is an imprint of the Taylor & Francis Group, an informa business*



*British Library Cataloguing-in-Publication Data*
A catalogue record for this book is available from the British Library

*Library of Congress Cataloging-in-Publication Data*
Names: Wegerif, Rupert, 1959– author. | Major, Louis, (Louis Christopher), 1985– author.
Title: The theory of educational technology : towards a dialogic foundation for design / Rupert Wegerif and Louis Major.
Description: Abingdon, Oxon ; New York, NY : Routledge, 2024. | Includes bibliographical references and index.
Identifiers: LCCN 2023032208 (print) | LCCN 2023032209 (ebook) | ISBN 9781032051864 (hardback) | ISBN 9781032056371 (paperback) | ISBN 9781003198499 (ebook)
Subjects: LCSH: Educational technology—Philosophy. | Education—Effect of technological innovations on. | Education—Aims and objectives. | Instructional systems—Design.
Classification: LCC LB1028.3 .W3985 2024 (print) | LCC LB1028.3 (ebook) | DDC 371.33—dc23/eng/20230828
LC record available at https://lccn.loc.gov/2023032208
LC ebook record available at https://lccn.loc.gov/2023032209

ISBN: 978-1-032-05186-4 (hbk)
ISBN: 978-1-032-05637-1 (pbk)
ISBN: 978-1-003-19849-9 (ebk)

DOI: 10.4324/9781003198499

Typeset in Sabon
by Apex CoVantage, LLC

# CONTENTS

# FIGURES AND TABLES

## Figures



## Tables

# ACKNOWLEDGEMENTS

Although we take responsibility for the final text, this book has been a collective effort by a large community of fellow researchers who have generously given their time to read and comment on drafts and to discuss ideas with us in corridors and conferences. We see this book as a contribution to a much larger dialogue about the role of technology and the future of education, building on the work of many who have inspired and stimulated us; so many that there is not enough room to mention them all by name.

Working with colleagues including Genevieve Smith-Nunes and supported by collaborators in industry such as Nick Sample (Arm), in 2020 we established the Digital Educational Futures Initiative (DEFI) at Hughes Hall, University of Cambridge. A number of ideas in this book have been informed by many interesting discussions taking place since. This includes with collaborators Jude Hannam, Kevin Martin, Imogen Casebourne, Bryan Maddox, Mike Hogan, Wayne Holmes, Patrick Carmichael and Shengping Shi (Kevin and Shengping kindly provide case studies discussed in Chapters 2 and 8). You can learn more about DEFI at www.deficambridge.org.

Similarly, the Cambridge Educational Dialogue Research Group (CEDiR) at the Faculty of Education University of Cambridge has offered a valuable intellectual forum to discuss emergent ideas over a number of years. We would like to especially thank Sara Hennessy for her immense collegiality and critical friendship, and also Alison Twiner and all CEDiR's doctoral students, researchers, international associates and collaborators.

During the later stages of writing this book, colleagues from the Manchester Institute of Education (MIE) including Mark Carrigan and Drew Whitworth reviewed chapters, while others provided valuable friendship and support. The 2022 launch of the Digital Technologies, Communication and

Education (DTCE) Research and Scholarship group in MIE aims to provide a new forum to discuss many of the ideas discussed in this book, in addition to other emergent priorities in digital education.

We have been fortunate to work with many wonderful collaborators over the years and would like to acknowledge these. This includes the Digitalised Dialogues Across the Curriculum (DiDiAC) team discussed in Chapter 3, led by Ingvill Rasmussen and Paul Warwick. Indeed, the second author would like to extend special thanks to Paul for first sparking his interest in dialogic education, and to Sue Swaffield for her valuable mentorship in the years prior to this. Both are influences that will not be forgotten.

The research on Generation Global mentioned in Chapter 6 was a collaboration with Jonathan Downey, Ian Jamison and Phil Durrant as well as others. The Argunaut project summarised in Chapter 7 was a collaboration with a large team of researchers including Bruce McLaren, Ulrich Hoppe, Reuma de Groot, Maarten de Laat, Andi Harrer, Raul Drachman and Baruch Schwarz. The Thinking Together research described in Chapter 8 and at other points was led by Neil Mercer and included significant input from Lyn Dawes, Karen Littleton and many others.

Other colleagues have offered critical friend feedback at some point, whether drafts of chapters or otherwise. These include Mark Johnson, Jan van Aalst, Michael Baker, Arthur Bakker, Mutlu Cukurova, Ola Erstad, Thorkild Hanghøj, Steve Higgins, Rupert Higham, Simon Knight, Jeremy Knox, Kristiina Kumpulainen, Maria Beatrice Ligorio, Manolis Mavrikis, Aline Nardo, Martin Oliver, Rich Osborne, Manoli Pifarre, Ingvill Rasmussen, Baruch Schwartz, David Williamson Shaffer, Mike Sharples and Steve Watson.

In addition to thanking those who indirectly supported us to complete this work, for instance colleagues in the EdTech Hub, we would like to extend special thanks to Martyn Hammersley and Gerry Stahl for generously taking the time to offer such rich and thoughtful feedback as the book neared completion.

We are truly grateful to all.

# 1

# INTRODUCTION

## Why we need a theory of educational technology

There is nothing more practical than a good theory.

Kurt Lewin (1952, p. 169)

### Why do we need a 'theory' of educational technology?

Most educational technology research is done with limited or no reference to theory (Bodily et al., 2019; Bond et al., 2019). And when theory is mentioned, this is almost always educational theory without reference to the theory of technology (An & Oliver, 2021). This chimes with the frequently expressed view that teaching should be led by pedagogy and not by technology. This claim is often asserted as a truism, as if no one could possibly disagree. A great deal of the theoretical literature on educational technology reinforces this assumption by expressing the concern that technology and technologists, possibly backed by money from the 'EdTech industry', are taking over education (e.g., Selwyn, 2017). In other words, the underlying framing here often seems to be that human-led education is good and that a technology-led education is bad.

At first glance, this makes perfect sense. On the whole, we use tools to help us achieve our goals. We like to think that we are in charge of the plan, not the tools that we select to help us. It would be odd to think of the tools as having agency on their own. Odd and also uncomfortable, perhaps even a bit frightening. The idea of technology taking over and telling us what to do is a common plot of dystopian movies and TV shows such as The Terminator or Westworld. But if we step back from this surface way of seeing things, to take a more theoretical perspective, it is not so clear that we can separate people from technology in any simple way. In Chapter 2, we argue

DOI: 10.4324/9781003198499-1

that humans have always been entangled with technology. We establish how a lot of the teaching and learning that most people tend to assume as being central to education serves the needs of technologies, especially communication technologies. The focus in primary education is on learning how to read printed signs in books, writing similar marks with a pen on paper, and how to use mathematical notations including numbers and a specialised symbol system. Because they have been around for a while, we sometimes forget that literacy and numeracy are technologies just as surely as social media apps on mobile phones or artificial intelligence (AI) language assistants.

It is interesting that we do not tend to think of literacy and numeracy as technologies. They are clearly neither natural nor universal. It is quite possible to be human without knowing how to use written sign systems. It is not obvious that oral societies are helped by education into literacy, indeed much of the evidence seems to point the other way.[1] Perhaps literate people are incapable of distinguishing themselves from their particular kind of communications technology and so assume that education that preserves and expands literacy is a universal human good. Taking a theoretical perspective or stance means questioning this kind of assumption. After all, non-literate oral societies also have education, and future societies in which the means of communication might be very different from what we can imagine now will also have education. If it is true, as we argue, that being human means to be bound up with technology, then it follows that education needs to change as technology changes. This is because when our technology changes, then so do we.

An overarching theme throughout this book is that we need to develop the theory of educational technology as a new strand in the dialogue about education. This is because, so far, our theories of education have not taken the distinctive point of view of technology into account. Technology does not just do what it is told and help us to realise our independently arrived at ends. Technology shapes us from the inside, it is always already there influencing how we understand ourselves and how we make decisions. This means that thinking about how we use technology in education is thinking about how we want to shape the future of education and, indeed, future humans. Designing educational technology requires thinking about what technology is, and what it could be, as well as thinking about what education is and what it could be.

This book is not simply about the theories that can be applied when designing or thinking about the use of technology in education. This common approach implies that theory is something outside of practice, which can be thought of separately, and then applied to shape practice. In education we often find that theory and practice are closely bound up together. The content of the curriculum and the way that teachers teach imply a theory of education, sometimes several different theories of education, even when this theory aspect of educational practice is not explicitly articulated. The 'theory of educational technology' is, for us, a two-way street. We learn as much about theory from thinking about how it applies to the use of educational technology in practice as we do about the practice of educational technology from applying theory. If it is true – as Kurt Lewin said in the quotation beginning this chapter – that there is nothing more practical than a good theory, it also might be true that there is nothing from which theory can learn more than good practice.

To illustrate our argument that a distinct category of theory, the theory of educational technology, can be useful we offer two short case studies. These are very different accounts of practice with educational technology which are really stories about two different ways of framing educational technology (in Chapter 4 we refer to this kind of framing as the 'grammar' of educational technology). Throughout the book, we use case studies to illustrate the two-way relationship between theory and practice, and in particular how: (1) thinking about practice with technology helps us challenge and develop new theory, (2) thinking from a theoretical perspective helps us challenge and improve practice with technology.

### *Case One: Personal devices to accelerate learning*

A primary school teacher writing a guest blog on Larry Cuban's website describes how, after giving a class of eight-year-olds personal tablet computers, soon the teacher wanted to take them back.[2] Cuban is well known for his insightful criticisms of what he refers to as the 'tech industry', and how this has influenced education policy makers to invest in technology in ways which have few demonstrable education benefits (Cuban, 2009). This blog describes how the tablets were sold to the school board as a way to support greater student-centred (as opposed to teacher-centric) education so that each child could have a more personalised learning journey. They were also supposed to make education more efficient and more effective. In addition to technical issues, such as random alarms and the need to plan for contingencies in case some tablets were not working or if the broadband dropped, the teacher believed there was a more fundamental problem: the presence of tablets prevented effective collaboration. Specifically, the teacher felt students in her class needed more time to develop their oracy (spoken language) skills. However, after being given personal tablets, they interacted mainly with their screens. An example given was how learners no longer wanted to play together with LEGO on the carpet on a rainy day since now they each had their tablets to occupy them. The blog cited Sherry Turkle's book *Alone Together* (2011) as offering evidence that the use of mobile devices is preventing children and young people learning how to talk together. It also cited an OECD report (2015) suggesting that educational technology does not accelerate learning. The blog quotes a line from this report: 'Students who use computers very frequently at school do a lot worse in most learning outcomes, even after accounting for social background and student demographics'.

### *Case Two: Coding Pirates future island*

Our second example is from a Danish project called Coding Pirates Denmark[3] (Nørgård & Paaskesen, 2016). In an open warehouse-type space, up to 30 students aged 7–12, working with adult volunteer helpers, were given a variety of materials, glue guns, GoPro video cameras and variously coloured blankets and boxes with kit including LEGO programmable brick sets called WeDo. They were tasked to work in small groups of five or six to together design a 'future island' where they would like to live. After building a prototype with kit provided, they videoed their island explaining design decisions before posting the video on YouTube. This was followed by all groups collaborating to unite the best elements of their different islands into one big island. The exercise involved discussions about citizenship issues, what it means to be fair and what their ideal future society might look like. The authors describe how their 'open-ended' approach to education can help to foster and promote technological imagination, creativity, collaborative problem solving and critical reflection.

### *Commentary on these cases*

The author of the first account was not positive about the educational role of the technology. The authors of the second account were, by contrast, very positive. We do not know enough from these short cases to say if they were correct in their assessments. What we want to draw your attention to is the very different ways in which the role and nature of the educational technology is framed. By 'framing' we mean how educational technology is understood in relation to other factors. This framing of educational technology is not done by the authors alone. It is also embedded in the institutional contexts, the design of the spaces, the funding, the culture, the curriculum and other often invisible contextual factors.

In Case One, educational technology is framed as supporting individual learning as opposed to collective learning. In Case Two, by contrast, educational technology is used as a support for small group and whole class talk and collaboration. In One it is framed as working against the development of communication skills, whereas in Two it is a support for multimodal communication between groups and an audience beyond the class through using video. In One, educational technology is framed as against physical play with LEGO. In Two, building with physical LEGO blocks is key to the use of technology. In One, educational technology is framed as a (failing) supplement to an existing curriculum. In Two the technology – including use of blankets, tables and other building materials, along with digital – is framed as a central part of the educational activity. See Table 1.1.

**TABLE 1.1** Comparing frames in Cases One and Two.

| *Case 1: Personal tablet devices* | *Case 2: Pirates future island* |
|---|---|
| Individual | Collective |
| Support for curriculum | The main curriculum |
| Virtual play through static devices | Physical play with dynamic devices |
| Instruction | Play |
| Monologue | Dialogue |

Theory is valuable in unpacking and examining all the implicit frames that underlie practice but have often come to seem natural and so are 'taken for granted'. Using theory also allows us to get a handle on the assumptions that lie behind practice so that we can challenge and develop these in a conscious design-focused way.

The contrasting ways of framing in Cases One and Two are not new. A quite similar contrast between ways of framing the use of technology in education was seen in classrooms in the 1970s when Papert's constructionism clashed with 'instructional technology' based on Skinner's behaviourism (a struggle described in Chapter 4). The contrast between Cases also illustrates how writing about educational technology often seems to be either announcing the next best thing that will transform education (Case Two), or condemning the negative impact of technology on 'proper' education (Case One). Applying theory to reflect on different framings of educational technology might be useful in helping to transform the common, unproductive oscillation between these two opposed positions towards a more constructive dialogue, one that can perhaps deliver progress.

### What do we mean by the words 'theory', 'educational technology' and 'design'?

Definitions of key terms are often useful for thinking things through together. When definitions seem surprisingly slippery, however, this does not necessarily mean that they have been misunderstood. Indeed, such slipperiness might be a side effect of ideas that really are intrinsically ambiguous and impossible to pin down. As discussed below, we take a dialogic perspective, one consequence of which is that we believe the meaning of words is not fixed or final. Words acquire meaning through the differences they make in conversations, and conversations always happen in contexts in which different kinds of differences need to be foregrounded. This means that a single word can have many meanings, and that the meaning of any word is continuing to evolve even as we write and think about it. Fortunately, this slipperiness does not prevent us from being able to discuss and develop our shared understanding. This is because, in practice, key concept terms can be held to a number of relatively stable uses in specific contexts. When used by teachers in classrooms, for instance, 'educational technology', or 'EdTech', usually refers to digital technology. This does not mean that teachers are ignorant. They likely appreciate that books and whiteboards, pens and desks are also technology. But as the term 'educational technology' would not be useful if it referred to everything in a classroom, it is helpful to make a distinction between the normal activity of education and new digital tools brought in to support that activity.

However, educational technology also has a second relatively stable meaning in the context of theory. To say what that is we first must define theory. We consider theory to be the process of stepping back from practice to reflect on that practice by connecting it to other practices in other times and places. In this way, theory can be considered as a long-term dialogue, where the meanings of concepts evolve over time as they are used in relation to each other in a network of interconnected ideas. This evolution of meaning is driven by a process of questioning and answering, where new ideas are proposed and debated in light of evidence and experience. Importantly, theory is needed if a discipline is to learn from successes and failures and grow as a cumulative shared body of knowledge carried forward in a continuous dialogue between practitioners and researchers.

If we step back from everyday classroom practice to take a more theoretical perspective on educational technology the close association of technology with physical machines, particularly digital machines, turns out to be quite recent. The Greek word 'techné' that lies at the root of the modern word technology was used to refer to techniques rather than to machines. Interestingly, efforts to define educational technology by the Association for Educational Communications and Technology (AECT) have apparently taken the root meaning of techné into account in their current definition:

> Educational technology is the study and ethical application of theory, research, and best practices to advance knowledge as well as mediate and improve learning and performance through the strategic design, management and implementation of learning and instructional processes and resources.[4]

This definition can be used to begin the enquiry into educational technology that is the main content of this book. The idea that educational technology includes the design of learning has been in the AECT definition since at least

1994 (Seels & Richey, 1994). From the perspective of theory, it seems that technology is not so much a class of things or technical objects, but more a way of thinking about things in terms of how they work as well as a way of acting on things to design them to work differently (Dron, 2022).

It follows from our definition that pedagogies, methods of teaching intended to produce learning, are technologies just as much as computers or textbooks. What makes any technology distinctively educational is the presence of a pedagogy or pedagogies (Dron, 2022). Some technologies are designed and sold as being educational, learning management systems for example, meaning that they include in the design some idea of how to use them to support teaching and learning. Many more technologies become educational technologies when combined with pedagogies. Excel spreadsheets used to teach functional programming, or LEGO bricks used to teach arithmetic, might be examples.

Things that we take for granted as already established in education, such as the use of books and desks, are not always seen as technology because they have become naturalised or taken for granted as part of the context within which we teach and learn. However, when something new comes along, like chalkboards which arrived in classrooms in the early 19th century, then the question of function and design is raised for practitioners. Shifting from only having individual slates to using a wall mounted chalkboard was a particular challenge for practice. When first introduced, the chalkboard went unused until teachers realised that it could be used for whole group instruction. Specifically, teachers had to change their thinking from individual slates to classroom slates (Slade, 2001 quoted in Russell, 2006). When the chalkboard first arrived at Yale University in the 1820s, a rebellion ensued as its introduction meant students were expected to solve problems at the board without the help of books (Frankel & Kerr, 2020). Over 40 students were expelled. It seems then that new tools in classrooms are technology not because they are digital, but because decisions have to be taken as to how best to use them.

Following Diana Laurillard – and colleagues including Mike Sharples (Sharples, 2009) – we think of education as a 'design science' (Laurillard, 2012). The idea of design science was introduced by Herbert Simon in his influential book *The Sciences of the Artificial* where he writes that 'the natural sciences are concerned with how things are . . . Design on the other hand is concerned with how things ought to be' (Simon, 1969, pp. 132–133). Design sciences involve solving problems where there is no single optimal solution that could be found by the application of a rigorous method. Because design finds creative ways to resolve tensions between different drivers in the context of real constraints, it is often associated with natural evolutionary processes (Crilly, 2021). The biggest difference between design and evolutionary emergence is the involvement of humans. And this involvement of humans means the involvement of the future. Humans bring anticipation into the design process, informing designs with a vision of a preferred outcome. Design can therefore be described as creative problem solving informed by anticipation of the future.

In Chapter 10, we discuss how research on educational technology might be best approached as a form of design-based research, in which design frameworks are tested and refined iteratively, evaluating the outcome and refining the design based on evidence (Bakker, 2019). Design frameworks are made up of sets of often related design principles which take the general form of the claim that 'if we do *x* under circumstances *y* then *z* is more likely to happen'. For example, the claim might be that if we teach basic arithmetic to six-year-old students using an interactive video game then they are more likely to be engaged and motivated.

Design principles and design frameworks have to come from somewhere. They build on assumptions about the nature of technology and about what is important in education. We subtitled this book 'towards a dialogic foundation for design', rather than 'towards a dialogic framework for design', because we are not offering very specific guidance or a 'how to guide'. Rather, we outline an orientation or way of looking at technology and education which we believe can provide a good basis for generating effective design frameworks.

## Educational technology and the big challenges we face

In Chapter 2, we consider how the first schools were developed to transmit the then new technology of inscribing signs in clay. This new technology of cuneiform literacy and numeracy was, some argue, a response to larger numbers of humans than before living together in one space; a challenge which required recorded contracts and written law codes (Pea & Cole, 2019). In a similar way, it is possible to argue that our current system of mass compulsory education into literacy and numeracy was developed as a response to the needs of industrialisation and to the challenge of maintaining discipline and identity in nation states. The theory of educational technology is not about stepping out of time, therefore, but about understanding education in the context of history and in relation to developments in technology. In this book, we do not offer an ahistorical theory of educational technology but one that is a response to the challenges that education faces now, offering a way forward to design the future of education as a response to those challenges.

The advent of the Digital Age in a cultural-historical timescale and the advent of the Anthropocene in a geological timescale both raise serious challenges for humanity; challenges to which technology-supported education might be a response. The internet, which has emerged in recent decades as the new dominant mode of communication,[5] now connects the majority of the human race.[6] Despite efforts to filter the internet in some parts of the world by blocking access to specific websites and services, the internet remains one technology. The advent of a global internet is an extraordinary development which has brought with it many challenges. Initially seen as a potential support for democracy, the internet is now more commonly referred to as a threat to democracy with global social media platforms such as Facebook accused of encouraging extremism and the spread of 'fake news' (Fisher, 2022; Geeng et al., 2020; Oliver, 2020). Recent advances in artificial intelligence (AI), which are widely seen to challenge existing practices in education, are also related to the rapid globalisation of the internet. The Large Language Models (LLMs) which now enable the writing of convincing examination responses in almost every area of knowledge are based on data gleaned from the internet using web-crawlers. One big challenge of our time, it seems from these pointers, might be seen as managing the transition from multiple separate print-based cultures to a more global internet-based culture.[7] It is true that the internet has been around for a few decades and there has been no simple switch to a single internet-mediated global culture. Nonetheless, there are many signs of a – sometimes slow, sometimes uneven – direction of travel towards more internet-mediated practices and identities which tend in the direction of being transnational and translingual.

The Anthropocene is the idea that planet Earth has moved into a novel geological age characterised by human impact on the planet. Effects like global warming show that human actions are impacting on the quality of our environment such that collective self-regulation on a planetary scale has become essential if we are to continue not only to thrive but also, many would argue, simply to survive. The Anthropocene offers challenges to the future that imply the need for us to design education that might support the possibility of a future characterised by global collective thinking and collective action. In this book, we argue that designing educational technology is about designing for the future, and that a better theory of education with technology might help us address the challenges posed by the Digital Age and Anthropocene, as well as many other challenges both known and as yet unforeseen.

## Dialogic educational theory

Our approach to theory development is interdisciplinary. This is inevitable since we incorporate insights from the theory of technology into the theory of education to produce a hybrid which we call an investigation into the theory of educational technology. Many, perhaps most, theories applied to education originate in disciplinary areas other than the academic discipline of education. Psychology is a source of influential theories in education with behaviourism, constructivism, social constructivism and many more. Sociology also has an influence through functional theories, which emphasise basic socialisation and meeting the needs of the political economy, as well as critical theories, which highlight education's hidden role in reproducing social inequality. Physics has always enjoyed high status in interdisciplinary thinking and recently theories from physics, especially drawn from quantum theory, are being applied to education in theory often labelled 'new-materialism'. We take all these theories seriously as voices in the dialogue. Like other researchers, we consider that interdisciplinary research can help us to understand a great deal about education, and as a result are able to develop improved understanding about how best to design teaching and learning (Luckin & Cukurova, 2019). In Chapter 7 we also give a prominent place to theories that have come out of technology such as information theory, systems theory and cybernetics. However, despite being interdisciplinary, we remain rooted within education.

We think it is possible to be both interdisciplinary and rooted in the discipline of education because educational theory is always already interdisciplinary, incorporating many strands of thought. What makes educational theory coherent and distinct is not the origins of the ideas that it brings together but a focus on the two fundamental educational questions: '*What should we teach and learn?*' and '*How should we teach and learn?*' Implicit in these two questions is a third even more fundamental philosophical question: '*Why should we teach and learn?*'[8] Education, as a discipline, has not always enjoyed high status. However, there are reasons to think that it might perhaps be the most important discipline. After all, it lies at the beginning of all the other disciplines and includes them all within itself. It is noticeable that every human culture understands the concept of education and engages in educational practices. However, very few non-modern cultures would recognise physics, psychology or any other current university discipline. This is possibly because education is an essential precondition of human culture (Tennie et al., 2009). The relationship between education and other disciplines is perhaps like that in biology between stem cells, which have the potential to develop into any type of cell in the body, and specialised cells that only have a specific function. Most academic disciplines are specialisations dependent upon, and contained within, the larger human activity of education.

Our issue with most educational theories, theories that attempt to provide answers to the questions of what we should teach and learn and how we should teach and learn it, is that they do not sufficiently consider the role of technology. We think that education has always been bound up with technology. In investigating the theory of educational technology, and developing a dialogic theory of educational technology, we are therefore also interested in proposing a new theory of education, one that takes the voice of technology seriously.

The dialogic theory of education that we often call upon in this book is a distinctively educational theory. It has emerged from decades of practical research with learners and teachers that addresses the two big educational questions (Mercer et al., 2019). Although dialogic theory is often attributed to sources in philosophy such as Bakhtin and Buber, and it is influenced by the ideas of psychologists such as Vygotsky (all thinkers we discuss later in this book), the recent dialogic education theory that we build upon is a distinctively educational theory.[9] This theory is based on observations of how students learn, as well as the findings of multiple research projects that explore how to teach more effectively using a combination of dialogue and technology (Major et al., 2018; Wegerif, 2007, 2013).

Dialogic educational theory begins with the observation that learning is not only 'transmitted' explicit curriculum knowledge but nor is it only 'constructed' by the learner: learning requires dialogue and so is first called into being by someone or something outside the self, perhaps a peer, parent or a teacher, or perhaps just an interesting event in the world that makes the learner want to find out more. The dialogic relation that makes learning possible is one in which the learner is already partly outside themselves entangled up with the other. The 'other' here might be a person or it might be an environment. A key question for the design of education, and education with technology, is how to establish the kind of relationships and dialogic encounters which will enable students to respond and be drawn into participation in educational dialogues.

In everyday speech, the term 'dialogue' can be used to refer to almost any kind of social interaction where words or other signs are exchanged between people. However, the term 'dialogic' is typically used in at least three different ways in education which we think broadly correspond to three 'levels', the first more superficial and the last more profound.

### *Level 1: A dictionary definition*

The term 'dialogic' is defined by dictionaries like the Oxford English Dictionary as an adjective applied to describe anything 'relating to or in the form of dialogue'. This is the first level of definition that can be applied to dialogic education. Where there is group work, or a high level of open-ended teacher–student interaction, this might be referred to as 'dialogic education' without specifying any more technical meaning for dialogic than that the teaching and learning takes the form of a dialogue.

### *Level 2: Epistemological definition*

Dialogic is often used in a more technical way to refer to the idea that the meaning of spoken words or utterances is constructed within a context that includes more than one voice. The meaning is not determined by a dictionary, but rather depends on the position and role of the words within a larger dialogue. Words spoken are a response to previous utterances and also have an impact on future utterances (Linell, 2009; Rommetveit, 1992). To put this another way, if a friend sends a message with a happy face emoji, the meaning of that message does not stand alone but depends on the previous message and also on how you respond to that message.

This focus on how we construct meaning from a play of voices in a context gives a second or epistemological level of definition for dialogic education. It suggests that education should be understood as engaging students in an ongoing process of shared enquiry taking the form of a dialogue (Linell, 2009; Wells, 1999). For example, the Dialogic Teaching approach developed by Robin Alexander (2020) is epistemological in focus and involves drawing students into the process of the shared construction of knowledge. A similar epistemological focus can often be found in the community of enquiry approach in Philosophy for Children (Lipman, 2003), in the promotion of Exploratory Talk (Littleton & Mercer, 2013), and in the promotion of Accountable Talk (Michaels et al., 2008).

### *Level 3: Ontological definition*

Epistemology is about how we know things. Hence, any purely epistemological approach in education does tend to assume that there is a knowing self on the one hand, and an external reality that is known about on the other. However, taking dialogic seriously as a theory of meaning implies that it is not just a means to knowledge construction mediating between selves and reality, but that selves and reality are also part of the dialogue. Applied to education, this more ontological interpretation of dialogic suggests that dialogue is not only a means or tool to be used in education to help construct knowledge, but more than that, engagement in dialogue is a way to change ourselves and to change our reality.

Different versions of ontologic dialogic education focus differently on either understanding and transforming (1) the self, (2) reality or (3) social reality. Understanding the self as a kind of dialogic author, and education as developing both the freedom and the responsibility of this authorial self, seems to be a focus of one strand of ontologic dialogic educational theory (Matusov, 2009; Sidorkin, 1999). Another strand puts more focus on the transformation of reality, seeing education and science understood as dialogue as a journey of discovery from the naturally occurring illusion that selves and objects are separate substances within an external fixed reality, to the realisation that all identities are aspects of a kind of universal dialogue that we can learn to participate in more fully and more compassionately (hooks, 2014; Kennedy, 2014; Wegerif, 2007). A more political interpretation of dialogic education can be seen in the vision of Freire (1970), and those influenced by Freire (e.g., Flecha, 2000), of dialogic education as a way to empower the oppressed such that they can learn to 'name' their own reality in a movement that is both an expansion of consciousness ('conscientisation') and at the same time a transformation of social reality.

In practice, despite some claims to the contrary (e.g., Matusov in Matusov & Wegerif, 2014), these three levels of definition are not mutually incompatible. Most approaches to education that describe themselves as dialogic incorporate some element of all three levels. It is not uncommon for approaches to dialogic education to combine a focus on facilitating dialogue where all participants have opportunities to contribute ideas, promoting knowledge age skills through shared inquiry, and fostering dialogic dispositions while valuing dialogue as an end in itself (e.g., Flecha, 2000; Lefstein & Snell, 2013; Nystrand, 1997; Phillipson & Wegerif, 2016).

Not all interactions lead to learning. Bakhtin distinguishes dialogues from the larger category of social interactions or conversations through the fact that dialogues involve a chain of questions and answers where each answer gives rise to new questions (Bakhtin, 1986). In other words, dialogues are where people learn together through a process Bakhtin refers to as 'inter-illumination'. Education takes place through dialogues and dialogues require the opening of dialogic space. Dialogic space, which we explore in Chapter 8, is the space of possibilities that opens when two or more perspectives are held together in the creative tension of a dialogue (Wegerif, 2019). Externally a dialogue might be bounded within a classroom, at a particular time, taking place through audible words that can be recorded as sound waves and correlated with measurable neural changes. Internally, however, it opens up an invisible space of meaning that is unbounded and might range freely across many spaces and many times. Technology, we argue, plays a crucial role in opening, widening, deepening and sustaining the dialogic spaces which make learning possible.

## Theory and practice as dialogues at different scales

Plato and Aristotle understood theory (theoria) to be contemplation of timeless truths as opposed to the more engaged stance of techné (technology) which was about making things within time. Techné was not simply the practice of making things but referred to the type of close-to-practice theory or knowledge required for making things. Epistemé (science) was said by Aristotle to refer to eternal knowledge whereas techné, he claimed, referred only to knowledge of things that change in time (Aristotle, ca. 350 BCE/1925). This distinction between timeless truths and temporal practice has continued in the Western tradition of thought. This can still be seen today in the way in which fundamental science is contrasted to engineering and technology as if the one was finding timeless 'laws of nature', and the other was about translating these into real-world contexts where they are applied to change things within time.

We agree with Aristotle that there is a useful distinction to be made between a theoretical perspective and a more practical perspective. Nonetheless, we disagree that they are fundamentally different in nature or that the theory perspective is outside of time: we claim that both are carried by dialogues within time but that they refer to dialogues operating at different scales of time (we say more about this in Chapter 9). The term 'theory' does not refer to stepping outside of time but, more simply, to stepping back from the surface way of seeing things – stepping back from the immediate activity in a local context – to try to see from a larger perspective. Conceptual understanding of the term technology from a more theoretical perspective still refers to the use of this term to signal a distinction within a dialogue. However, the dialogue of theory is longer-term and more global in its referencing than the dialogue of everyday practice.

Understanding theory and practice as the same type of thing, types of dialogue, just operating at different timescales, enables us to understand the role that theory plays in relation to practice. Any practice which requires design requires a close-to-practice theory to inform the design. If you are teaching, for example, you use some sort of theory to tell you what to teach and how to teach it. Also, probably, this theory comes with stories as to why it is a good idea to teach whatever it is that you teach. This close-to-practice theory implies assumptions about reality and values that come from – and belong in – the longer-term dialogue of theory. Theory then provides foundations for the design of practice. This is why theories are potentially very useful.

Of course, it is often true that the two loops of theory and practice in education do not always work well together: theory can be out of sync with practice, or vice versa. Sometimes practices might continue with no theoretical reflection and development, repeating what has always been done and what has always been believed. The danger of this is that they fail to keep up with changes in the larger environment around them. This makes them at best increasingly irrelevant and, at worst, harmful. Or, sometimes, theory may run in a big loop of high-level concepts that does not connect to everyday practice and so does not learn from it. The risk here is that practitioners do not find this kind of out-of-sync theory useful and so become disconnected from the value of high-level or big-loop theory in general. Ideally theory needs to be constantly tried, tested and challenged through engagement with everyday practice. It is true that high-level theories of education cannot always be directly tested, but there is good reason to think that they can be indirectly tested through a kind of evolutionary competition between different approaches. We say more about how this can work in Chapter 10 when we look at research as a way of keeping the big-loop of theory and the smaller loops of practice in a constructive relationship. In this book, we aspire to produce new theory that is both high-level and long-term in vision and yet also grounded in practice and useful as a tool behind the design of practical educational interventions.

## A summary of what this book is about

This book has a twofold purpose: to provide a broad introduction to the theory of educational technology and to offer a new 'dialogic' foundation for the design and practice of educational technology. Since we think that theory is practical, and that practice is a way of trying out and developing theory, we include many short descriptive case studies of educational practice that illustrate the two-way relationship between practice and theory. We have drawn these examples from the whole history of educational technology and not only from the use of the most recent technologies. This is a field in which memory often seems to be in short supply as the latest flashy technological innovations distract attention from general educational principles that have been learnt already long before. We use these case studies drawn from many contexts to exemplify the application of theory to practice in addition to exemplifying what theory can learn from engaging more closely with practice.

To understand the role of technology in education it helps if we step back from our current education system and look at it from a larger perspective. This is what we do in Chapter 2, which considers the history of educational technology and argues that there is an interdependence or entanglement between technology and education that goes back to the origin of humanity. We find that while educational technology is now commonly seen as a supplement to the main business of education, the first recognisable schools emerged to teach how to use educational technology as the core curriculum. The complex demands of teaching how to use stylus and clay to record trade deals and collective stories led to the emergence of formal schools in Ancient Sumeria. The need to teach the communication technologies of literacy and numeracy drove the spread of schooling after the development of printing and national education systems emerged closely dependent on, and influenced by, print literacy.

Investigating the difference between ways of understanding knowledge and education in majority oral societies and in majority print literate societies leads us to refer to the 'cognitive affordances' of different media. Oral societies vary in their approaches to education but one kind of education that oracy tends to make easy (or 'afford') in some contexts is a vision of thinking and learning as a dialogue between voices, often between human voices and 'spirit' voices. This was, for example, how the oral thinker Socrates is often presented by Plato as describing education. Print literacy, by contrast, tends to make it possible and perhaps plausible to picture reasoning as like making a proof in geometry. In Chapter 3 we trace the idea of affordances to the perceptual psychology of James Gibson, and we investigate the influence on Gibson of Maurice Merleau-Ponty. For Gibson, perception was not best thought of as a product of 'information processing in the brain', as much cognitive psychology still claims. Rather, he saw perception as an aspect of the relationship between a 'body' and the world. Bodies perceive directly if a surface affords walking or if a bench affords sitting. But how we see the affordances of things depends not only on the physical possibilities of the body-world coupling but also on the meaning that a thing has (which is of course shaped by the culture and education). Whether or not a bench affords sitting or stepping, for example, might depend on whether you encounter it in a park or in a gym, and also on what kind of gym training or park induction you might have had.

Affordances turn out to be about meaning, and design of the affordances of educational technology turns out to be design for meaning. We locate meaning in the tension between the event of what a user actually does with a tool, and the horizon of possibilities around that event – all the things that the user could imagine doing with the tool and all the associations that it has for them.

In Chapter 4 we look at what, following Wittgenstein, we call the 'grammar' of educational technology: the ways in which this has been conceived and applied as 'teaching machine', 'tool to think with' and 'learning environment'. These ways of framing educational technology are theories that shape the design and use of educational technology. However, they are not precise enough to be the 'close-to-practice' theory we call design frameworks because they could each support a wide variety of designs. Thus, they are examples of what we call 'foundations for design'. This raises the question of how we select the best foundation for design. We see these different 'grammars' as competing for attention in the long-term dialogue of the theory of educational technology. Empirical research as to how effective they are in achieving their goals is certainly relevant, and we cite this when we can, but such evidence is – on its own – not enough to help us choose because each 'grammar' defines its own criteria of success and failure. We therefore offer a modest form of what could be called a 'grammatical' analysis exploring the coherence and implications of these different ways of framing educational technology.

In Chapter 5 we continue to explore theories and approaches to educational technology by looking at 'online mediated communities of practice', 'online multi-user role-play games' and 'connectivism'. Our analysis of the strengths and weaknesses of these grammars leads us to propose a new dialogic grammar or foundation for design. This new foundation for the design of educational technology builds on the connectivist theory of learning as a form of networking, but adds the importance of consciousness and identity. Dialogue, we claim, is needed to turn external networks of nodes and links into an internal space of resonance: learning is not just adding nodes and links, it is also expanding the dialogic space needed to make sense of each new node by bringing it into dialogic relation with all other nodes in the network. From connectivism, we draw the idea of learning as connecting a network of relationships. From considering the value of online mediated communities of practice and of future-oriented role-play games, we highlight the importance of anticipation of the future, or being pulled forward into the expansion of knowledge, through a dialogic relationship with the horizon of all that which is as yet unknown.

Heidegger's discussion of the way that tools and technology enter into experience has had a profound impact on the philosophy of technology. In Chapter 6 we consider implications for educational design that follow from his account. We go further to interrogate his apparent criticism of modern technology as something that 'enframes' us in a way that cuts us off from a more authentic and nourishing relationship with the world. We find that while Heidegger described modern technology as a great danger, he also recognised it as an opportunity for a different kind of human future. His analysis of the potentially world-creating and world-revealing effects of inhabiting technologies from the inside turns out to be relevant not only to understanding the use of everyday craft tools like hammers, but also for understanding more modern tools like Generative AI and the internet.

In Chapter 7 we respond to the critique of modern technology from Heidegger and investigate how meaning relates to technology and, especially, to educational technology. It is common to contrast human meaning with technology in a way that poses the use of technology in education as a threat to human meaning. We challenge this view claiming that meaning, the sort of meaning that provides motivation, is an effect of 'anticipation' in self-organising systems. Meaning of this kind is therefore not exclusively human. Human meaning, the experience of meaning and purpose is tied, we argue, to a feeling that we get when we participate in larger systems. These larger systems that, in a sense, call us to meaning, always have a technological aspect, if only in the medium of communication that supports these dialogues and makes them possible. Education for meaning can then be understood as part of the self-organisation of bio-socio-technical systems. We introduce ideas from a philosopher of technology, Gilbert Simondon, who argues that dialogue with technology is needed for what he calls 'transindividuation' – the creation of collective forms of identity. We illustrate the argument with examples of how educational technology can be designed to support education as induction into larger, culturally mediated kinds of meaning.

In Chapter 8 we look at technology in relation to the idea of dialogic space and explore education as the expansion of dialogic space. Dialogic space expands when 'voices' that were previously not heard or understood become heard and understood, and when things that were previously unthinkable become thinkable. Technology, we argue, has a key role to play in education understood as the expansion of dialogic space. The resonances between voices in dialogue together occur over time as much as over space. One aspect of education is the bridging together, and bringing into dialogue, different timescales through the mediating means of communications technology. In Chapter 9 we argue that new digital forms of educational technology can offer a particular affordance for inducting learners into participation in dialogues over longer-term timescales.

Research is essential to the development of theory. And the development of theory is essential to the development of practice. In Chapter 10 we offer a critical history of research on education and educational technology, arguing that changes in technology make new forms of research possible and necessary. We put forward a version of educational design-based research (EDBR) which is a form of action research and, potentially, a form of participatory action research. We call our version of EDBR 'double-loop' as it uses data and dialogue to reflect not only on the achievement of initial educational goals, but also to reflect back upon and change those initial goals in the light of the evidence. Finally, we relate double-loop EDBR to Merleau-Ponty's idea of meaning as 'Chiasm', proposing that one way to do research on and with educational technology is as a dialogue that systematically inter-reacts and inter-illuminates 'inside' points of view, accounts of experience for example, with 'outside' points of view such as statistical patterns in the data.

Strands from all the previous chapters are brought together in Chapter 11 to outline a dialogic theory of educational technology. Education, we claim, is about drawing students into participation in ongoing cultural dialogues. These dialogues are mediated by communications technology in various forms from words, through books, to the internet and AI language assistants. Technology in various forms is, therefore, at the heart of education. However, the distinctive role and impact of these different technologies need to be examined and better reflected in theories of education. Our dialogic theory of educational technology corrects this imbalance. It is intended to serve as a foundation for design. The usefulness of the theory can be tested, or at least explored, by building designs based upon it and testing how they hold up. We discuss the ethics of design, and propose dialogue, however difficult and messy this often is in practice, as the only practicable way forward. The kind of designs our proposed dialogic theory of educational technology grounds are combined pedagogical and technical designs to facilitate the dynamic inter-weaving of educational dialogues at different spatio-temporal scales, often linking short-term face-to-face dialogues to long-term global dialogues. Educational technology, we propose, should (1) engage students, providing opportunities and motivations to draw them into participation in educational dialogues; (2) connect students with others in wider learning networks; (3) expand dialogic space and time by building bridges between short-term dialogues and longer-term larger scale dialogues; and, finally, (4) support students into forming a constructive relationship with the radical open-endedness and uncertainty of the surrounding horizon of all that which is unknown.

# 2

# AN ALTERNATIVE HISTORY OF EDUCATIONAL TECHNOLOGY

> *Writing, Phaedrus, . . . is very like painting; for the creatures of painting stand like living beings, but if one asks them a question, they preserve a solemn silence. And so it is with written words; you might think they spoke as if they had intelligence, but if you question them, wishing to know about their sayings, they always say only one and the same thing.*
>
> Socrates according to Plato (approximately 370 BCE/2008)

> *If you want to hide something, put it in a book.*
>
> Alphaxus Kimani, farmer in central Kenya
> (see the case study in this chapter)

## Introduction

Histories of educational technology often limit themselves to recent innovations, especially the introduction of different digital technologies into schools (Weller, 2020). Those few histories of educational technology that take us a little further back continue to focus on the impact of technological innovations introduced into the classroom, for instance the educational use of film around 1900 (Cuban, 1986) and the first so-called 'teaching machines' in the USA in the 1920s and 1930s (Watters, 2021). The field of educational technology as a discipline has been described as waves of research responding to new devices: for example, there were waves related to computers in classrooms, then CD-ROMs, the internet, mobile learning, cloud computing, and more recently, AI and 'big data' (Oliver, 2016). These histories of educational technology assume a distinction between 'normal' education and education supported by new technology. This distinction can

DOI: 10.4324/9781003198499-2

be seen in the way educational technology is referred to as Computer-Aided Instruction (CAI), Computer-Assisted Learning (CAL), Computer-Aided Learning (also confusingly CAL), Technology-Enhanced Learning (TEL), and a host of other related terms and phrases.

We pointed out in the previous chapter that taking the perspective of theory is about stepping back from the surface of obvious things to question how these apparently obvious things came to be there. That educational technology is technology used as a support for education seems obvious. But how did this distinction between education and technology used to support education arise? Educational technology is, by definition, understood not as the main business of education but as a supplement to education, servicing educational ends, a support, an aide, assistance or, perhaps, an enhancement. In Chapter 4 we look in more detail at how digital technology has been applied to education in the last 50 or so years. However, in this chapter we offer a more extensive alternative history of educational technology. This argues that what we think of as 'education' is always already technology, it is just a kind of technology that has become so familiar to us through use that it is seen as natural.

## The first schools

Perhaps the first formal schools that we know about were founded around 4000 years ago as a support for a new information and communication technology: cuneiform writing and reading of signs standing for numbers and words (Harris, 1986). Cuneiform writing, which consists of scripts depicting logos and symbols, was used to write languages of the Ancient Middle East between the Bronze Age and start of the Common Era (CE). A good understanding of how these schools worked has been gained from excavations. In a schoolhouse in the Ancient Sumerian city of Nippur, for example, rows of benches were found along with baked brick boxes containing hundreds of fragments of stone tablets in addition to dried piles of clay. We can reconstruct that students would take lumps of clay from the box, mould them into a tablet shape and then press them with a stylus – a sharpened reed – to form letters in the cuneiform system of writing (Robson, 2001).

The tablets found in Nippur and other sites have allowed the school curriculum to be reconstructed with some confidence. The first phase taught students writing techniques beginning with the most basic sign form, a single wedge, from which the word cuneiform takes its name (cuneus being the Latin word for wedge). The second phase involved basic lists of nouns. The third phase featured more advanced lists and mathematics. The final phase introduced more complex compositions, poems of the doings of Sumerian heroes and gods, as well as model legal contracts like the sales agreement in Figure 2.1.

FIGURE 2.1 A cuneiform contract.

Schools were called *Eduba* meaning 'tablet house'. Each Eduba employed several people. First there was the head teacher or 'father of the tablet house'. Then a deputy head, called 'supervisor of the tablet house', who enforced the rules and regulations. Teaching assistants were called 'older brothers'. Their jobs were to write new tablets for the students to copy, to check students' work and to listen to memorised lessons. Other members of the faculty included 'the man in charge of Sumerian' (already a dead language by 1800 BCE when the school found in Nippur operated but still the main language of instruction) and 'the man in charge of drawing'. Mathematics was taught by the 'scribe of accounting', the 'scribe of measurement' and the 'scribe of the field'. Finally, there were men in charge of attendance and discipline, including a 'man in charge of the whip'. Students were punished for poor class work and penmanship, sloppiness of dress, speaking without permission, not speaking Sumerian with the Sumerian instructor and a variety of other faults.

We know about these schools from descriptions found in the clay tablets. The students were set practice writing exercises such as 'describe your day'. One well-preserved tablet is the story of a student who gets up early to go to school, comes home at lunchtime where his mother packs him a lunch of 'two breads', and then goes back to school again. His schoolteacher recites the tablet for him to copy. He gets into trouble for having bad handwriting and is beaten (Cromwell, 2019).

Such stories bring this world to life. They resonate with the experiences of anyone who has been through formal education. If you are reading this, you are literate which probably means that you have been to school and so can perhaps relate to having to get ready to go to school early in the morning, possibly eating a packed lunch and then facing the threat of getting told-off and sometimes even punished for having bad handwriting. However, the vast majority of humans who lived at that time and in all the centuries since did not go to school. An experience of childhood that has come to seem almost natural to many of us was previously far from normal. Those who went to school to learn to read and write in Ancient Sumeria, as also in the similar scribe schools of Ancient Egypt, were a tiny minority of the population.

Formal 'tablet schools' represent an investment of time and resources. Cuneiform writing in clay is clearly a form of communications technology and it seems that this technology, which provided a capacity for collective memory that endured across generations, was considered valuable by those in authority at the time. This technology could not run on its own but required skilled human operators. Scribes were needed to keep accounts, to compose contracts and to write the stories of their ancestors. It is not unreasonable to claim that the first schools were built to service a new technology.

## The literate human

It is common to hear that education should be about the method and practice of teaching (pedagogy), not technology (e.g., Tsui & Tavares, 2021). There are many practical contexts in which this makes perfect sense. Indeed, there have been numerous high-profile instances when technology has been 'parachuted' into educational contexts without sufficient – if any – consideration for how this might be done in an effective and contextually appropriate way (Cuban, 2009; Reich, 2020). As we saw in the first case study offered in Chapter 1, simply adding tablets into the classroom is not a substitute for teaching and learning. However, taking a more theoretical perspective, we believe that this would-be truism overlooks the extent to which humans are already entangled up with technology. The contemporary call might often be 'pedagogy first!' (Fawns, 2022), but as our analysis below shows, the reality of education has arguably perhaps always been 'technology first'. To be a literate person means that you have internalised a technology so thoroughly that, for you, it has become natural. Non-literate unschooled people are human too. Schooling is required not to make people human, but to make humans into a particular kind of 'human plus technology' combination.

The neuroscientist Stanislas Dehaene did extensive research on the difference that literacy makes to the brain and found many significant effects relating to how the demands of literacy colonise the visual cortex (Dehaene, 2009; Dehaene et al., 2015). These effects include a decrease in a capacity for face recognition and for holistic thought, correlated with an increase in capacity for recognising the perceptual differences associated with letters and for analytic thinking. What really makes the difference is the way that literate humans can see words and so are able to analyse them as separate things in the world. For non-literates, words do not usually exist as separate things to be held in the mind's eye and examined, they are experienced as part of the flow of meaning in a context. Literates, by contrast, not only hear words, they also see them. We know this from experience but also from fMRI brain scans (Dehaene, 2009). When literates listen to spoken words, activity is often found in the parts of the brain that process vision. This shift from only hearing words to also seeing words is very significant for thought, giving the impression that we can pin down and analyse meanings themselves simply by holding words in our inner visual attention (Goody & Goody, 1977). As Olson and Oatley (2014, p. 4) put it: 'When writing turns words and sentences into objects of analysis, it facilitates distinctive modes of discourse such as extended prose and distinctive modes of thinking such as formal rationality'.

Talking about the effects of literacy as if this only had one kind of impact on the cognition of all literate people has rightly been criticised as overly simplistic. There are, of course, many kinds of literacy practice doing different kinds of things in different cultural contexts (Street, 2006). Reading a book out loud together for example, which was a common practice in the Middle Ages and is still found in many religious education contexts, has very different effects from reading a personally owned book silently to oneself (Ong, 1972/2013). Scribner and Cole (2013) researched the cognitive impact of different uses of literacy (using this term to include numeracy) in a range of contexts. They found that only schooled literacy offered the increase in abstract rationality that Olson and Oatley described. Specifically, Scribner and Cole found that literacy used to support trading in a marketplace did not have measurably significant cognitive effects. But learning to read and write in a school did change ways of thinking. From more concrete and metaphorical thinking situated in contexts of use, to the more abstract, general and universal kind of rationality valued in formal education.

Cole and Scribner's research interestingly points to the pairing that is formed between a communications technology, in this case literacy, and a particular type of education, specifically formal schooling into literacy. The schooling system can be argued to exist to service the technology. Without the schooling system the technology can exist, but is potentially far less powerful in terms of transforming society and transforming selves. Evolutionary psychologist Geary (2008) argues that the connection between literacy and schooling can be explained through making a distinction between what he calls biologically primary learning, which we have evolved to engage with naturally such as learning to speak or walk and biologically secondary learning, such as learning complex mathematics or learning to write. This distinction should not be taken to mean that spoken language is biological and therefore not a technology. Even if we are, to some extent, hardwired for oracy, that does not mean that oracy is not also a communications technology. Words can be fashioned as cognitive tools to support us in many activities. Adults actively induct children into speaking words and listening to language, and children actively learn how to get better at speaking and listening. It would be wrong to oppose the technology and the biology here by suggesting that we do not need to teach oracy. Nonetheless, what we can learn from Geary's main argument is that we have clearly evolved to find the initial teaching and learning of language easy and to even enjoy it. Geary references research supporting what we all already know which is that, on average, students enjoy talking together with peers much more than they enjoy doing homework or learning linear equations (Geary, 2008). Hence, Geary claims, schools have emerged so that societies can transmit more complex 'biologically secondary' types of skills such as writing and arithmetic. Because we have not been designed by evolution to learn these skills naturally the extra social support of schooling is required. After all, he is saying, the *edubas* of Ancient Sumeria included a 'master of the whip' for a reason: young students did not always find learning literacy and numeracy fun and they had to be forced to do it.

## Cave paintings, perhaps the first educational technology

In the curriculum in the *edubas* of Ancient Sumeria we know that, as well as topics such as coding, decoding and basic numeracy associated with accounting, there was also a focus on learning to read and write collective stories. These were stories of the gods, origin stories and great deeds of the ancestors as well as triumphs of the current rulers. Yuval Harari, in his contested but often insightful account of human history, claims that what makes humans different from other animals is the capacity to tell stories that people unite behind (Harari, 2014). Shared stories are required, he claims, for the shift we have made from being an animal species living in biological kinship groups to a human species living in shared cultures. Perhaps, as Geary claims, schools arose because the technology of cuneiform literacy was too complex for everyday informal learning. However, once schools were in place, they incorporated elements of the oral education that already existed: stories of gods and ancestors.

Every oral society inducts its members into the shared stories that define the identity of the collective. This is often done with specific rituals of initiation involving different forms of communication technology. Such initiations typically involve artefacts like masks, sculptures and paintings representing cultural voices (Phillips, 1978). These voices need to be internalised by an individual for that individual to become a 'full' member of the community.

The initiation rites of Pende youth in the Democratic Republic of the Congo offer an example which is illustrative of such ceremonies. After a lengthy ordeal of teaching and initiation, a Pende youth will appear in a distinctive colourful mask indicative of his new role as an adult (Gilombe & Yeoman, 2010). The mask is later cast aside and replaced by a small ivory duplicate, worn as a symbol of adulthood. The masks and amulets are 'epiphantic' signs that evoke the presence of ancestors (Leiman, 2002). One becomes an adult in this society by connecting to the sacred stories and the voices of the tribe.

According to the first professor of neuro-cognitive-archaeology, David Lewis-Williams, the cave paintings made and used by San bushmen in Southern Africa served a similar function to the masks of the Pende. Some of the cave paintings of the San bushmen are up to 40,000 years old. While Pea and Cole (2019) argue that cuneiform writing in Ancient Sumeria was driven forward by a need to keep records of goods, another lineage for some forms of early writing has been claimed that is linked to cave paintings (Von Petzinger, 2017).

Cave paintings are a global phenomenon, pre-existing the first writing. Paintings showing similar abstract patterns, hands and animals are found all over the world. Initially these paintings were widely thought of as a kind of magic intended to increase the number of animals and improve the hunt.[1] Of course, there are many kinds of cave paintings in many contexts and so there is no need to suggest a single explanation. Nonetheless, the universal applicability of the 'sympathetic hunting magic' theory of cave painting was challenged by Lewis-Williams (2002) and others who highlighted that some of the animals painted in the caves did not reflect local diets at the time. Lewis-Williams presents ethnographic evidence based on transcribed notes of interviews with San hunter-gatherers from the 1870s to conclude that the cave paintings of the San were, in effect, a form of educational technology. He suggests that the San used the paintings to record visions and evoke them later. One way of evoking the spirit represented was by touching it with the palm of the hand. Hence, Lewis-Williams claims, the many hand paintings found in caves. See Figure 2.2.

Cave painting has been suggested as a way of offloading cognitive processing onto features of the environment to extend the mind. Andy Clark refers to it as 'the early signature of cognition enhancing technology' (Clark, 2004, p. 176). However, we need to be cautious about extending literate ways of thinking about cognition to non-literate oral societies. Lewis-Williams gives the example of an Eland painted by San bushmen at full-moon using a mixture of hematite and blood. This Eland was not just a sign for the San people, it was also a living presence that sometimes spoke to them. During rituals in the caves, painted walls became permeable membranes that the San could

FIGURE 2.2 Hands at the Cuevas de las Manos.

*Source:* Mariano, licensed under CC BY-SA 3.0.

cross through into a shared cultural space where they would encounter the ancestral spirit voices (Lewis-Williams & Pearce, 2004). Gray (2010) concludes that the painted caves were not so much an extension of cognition on Andy Clark's model, but rather should be seen as epistemic niche construction. Many organisms alter their environment to construct niches that last longer than their individual lives and aide the reproduction of the species. These are called 'ecological niches', an idea we look at again in the next chapter. An example of this kind of ecological niche construction is the way that bees build beehives. An epistemic niche is, Gray argues, a kind of collective support for the continuity and development of the shared thinking of a people over time.

## From relationship to representation

The way of thinking found in oral cultures is different from literate ways of thinking (Goody, 1986; Goody & Goody, 1977). An example of this difference is the nature of the 'song lines' of Australian Aborigines. Song lines, or sung stories of journeys through the landscape around them, have been said to map the territory and encode knowledge essential to survival. These songs include information about animals, plants and water holes, for example, but all embedded in sung stories about the doings of mythical ancestors in the 'dreamtime' when the land was created. This knowledge is not a classification nor is it a representation. Song lines are experienced as a relationship with the ancestors who created the landscape. That is, cognition is experienced not as something that humans impose on the landscape but as coming from the landscape. The collective stories are called 'song lines' because the land sings its stories as an individual journeys across its lines.

One way to illustrate the shift from an education for relationship, to an education for representation, is to consider how the meaning of the word 'knowledge' has changed since this concept was first recorded in pictographs to how it tends to be used in Europe today. In the Bible, including parts like Genesis (first written around 1200 BCE), the word knowledge refers to an intimate relationship. Indeed, the English phrase 'knowledge in the biblical sense' is sometimes used as a euphemism for sexual intimacy. This phrase draws attention to the contrast many readers find between the concept of knowledge in everyday use around them and the concept of knowledge that emerges when reading the Bible. Tracing the roots of the Hebrew word for knowledge found in the Bible, Da'at (דעת) from the verb Ya'da (ידע), to know, we find that the original pictographs behind the two letters used in these words combine the image of a tent door flap (Dalet) with the image of an eye (Ayin). To know, for the Ancient Hebrews, apparently involved moving a seeing eye through the tent door flap to enter inside a previously hidden space. Knowing, according to this metaphor, involves the difference between an outside view and an inside view. Not just, for example, what someone looks like from the outside, but also effectively 'moving inside' them to know what it feels like to be them (Benner, 2021). See Figure 2.3.

| | Ancient pictograph | Modern Hebrew |
|---|---|---|
| Dalet (tent door flap) | 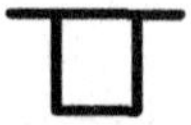 | ד |
| Ayin (eye) |  | ע |

**FIGURE 2.3** Knowing as the eye passing through a tent door to see inside the tent.

In moving from an understanding and experience of knowledge as relationship, to knowledge as representation, something might have been lost. Plato attributed a powerful critique of writing on these lines to his mentor Socrates (Plato, 370BCE/2008). Socrates was an oral thinker who lived and taught during a time when there was transition to a new communications technology, the technology of alphabetic writing. This came to Greece through the Phoenicians in the form of pictograms related to those used by the Ancient Hebrews. This new technology was impacting the nature of education in a way that troubled Socrates. Somewhat ironically, however, we only know this because Plato wrote down Socrates' reflections. In a story told by Socrates to his friend Phaedrus, the technology of writing is said to have been offered to man by the god Thoth as a 'pharmakon', meaning a remedy for the problem of humans having poor memories. Socrates then argues that far from being a 'pharmakon' as remedy, literacy is a 'pharmakon' as poison (the same word is used for both meanings). Socrates claims that literacy is a poison to humans for educational reasons. Being able to appear intelligent by reading from a scroll means that people will no longer need to be actually intelligent, which is something only learned in dialogue with other voices. Like the teacher quoted in Case One in Chapter 1 complaining about tablet computers, Socrates was concerned that this new educational technology would get in the way of learning necessary oracy and communication skills. Real intelligence, Socrates says, is relational. The written word, he claims, is no more than an image or representation of the real thing. Instead 'real' words are living oral words with meaning carried by the warm breath of people in dialogue. They are not representations of external things, so much as aspects of a living relationship in which meaning is experienced. Socrates is reported as describing written words as like 'orphans', 'ghosts' and 'dead seeds put out on flagstones in the heat of the sun' (Plato, 370BCE/2008). This is because they are abstracted from any particular relationship. This is a version of the idea of knowledge evoked by the image of an eye passing through a tent door. To know something is to enter into it and to feel what it means from the inside.

## How literacy universalised

As with most new communications technologies, literacy was an augmentation and not a replacement. Speaking and listening continue to exist in parallel to writing in literate societies. Throughout the 5000 years since the first invention of literacy, relatively few children went to school or learnt to be literate. Even in China, for example, a civilisation which so valued literacy that it introduced a national written exam system in 605 CE, literacy rates in 1950 were estimated at only 20% (Jowett, 1989).

The story of the universalisation of schooling to serve the communications technology of literacy is a complex one. Technological determinism, often associated with Marx, is the claim that technological development drives social change. It is common to reject technological determinism as reductionist and an affront to human freedom. In the history of literacy, it seems clear developments in communications technology did have a role to play. However, whether these developments were taken up or not depended on apparently contingent cultural contextual factors which could also be seen as cultural choices. One might say that for every 'how' coming from developments of the technology, there needed to also be a 'why' coming from the culture that enabled this new technology to be taken up[2] (Mumford, 2010). Nevertheless, in this story of how modern education came to be, developments in technology appear to play a significant causal role within what can be called a complex integrated bio-socio-technical system.

In Europe, the expansion of literacy was associated with the development of moveable type and the printing press by Gutenberg in around 1440, which brought down the cost of books and made mass schooling possible. However, moveable type alone was not a sufficient cause for the rapid development of printing, literacy and schooling. In fact, moveable type printing had already been developed around 1100 CE in China. Because of the many letters needed in the Chinese ideographic form of writing, however, it proved expensive to print in this way. Preparing and printing whole page blocks was cheaper and became more popular (Tsien, 1985). Gutenberg, using the Latin alphabet, had fewer characters to worry about. He was also doubly lucky because monks copying manuscripts such as the Bible had developed a way of writing Latin letters that was easy to imitate with moveable type. Gutenberg's first printed Bibles looked remarkably like handwritten Bibles but were up to five times cheaper to produce.

In Europe, the Protestant religious reform movement, which stressed the importance of everyone reading the word of God for themselves, supported the spread of literacy. Previously most books had been written in the dead languages of Latin and Greek that only priests, monks and members of the elite were able to read. Many Protestants were taught that it was important for them to read the Bible for themselves if they were to gain personal salvation. This religious motivation, coupled with the greater availability of texts due to printing, contributed to an increase in vernacular literacy rates and the founding of many new schools throughout Europe focusing on literacy and the fruits of literacy.

The connection between the printing press and the foundations of the modern mass schooling system is clearly made by Comenius, a leader of one early Protestant movement, the Hussites. Comenius was perhaps the most influential educational visionary during the age of enlightenment. In 1657,

Comenius's *Didactica Magna* (*The Great Didactic*, 1657/1967) proposed universal education for all, boys and girls, rich and poor, with teaching in vernacular languages and using textbooks. He was actively involved in organising school systems for European governments, most notably the Swedish government, and proposed the system of schools now found in the USA with kindergarten, elementary school, secondary school, college and university (Gilman et al., 1905). Comenius's vision of education built heavily on the potential of the printing press to produce school textbooks. He went further to explicitly link his proposed schooling approach to the technology of printing, commenting: 'we might adapt the term "typography" and call the new method "didachography"' (1657/1967):

> Instead of paper we have pupils whose minds have to be impressed with the symbols of knowledge. Instead of type we have the class books and the rest of the apparatus devised to facilitate the operation of teaching. The ink is replaced by the voice of the master, since this is what conveys information from the books to the mind of the listener; while the press is school discipline, which keeps the pupils up to their work and compels them to learn.
> (p. 289)

Comenius's vision included the need for feedback from students to show that they are now 'possessors of knowledge' (p. 293) and a requirement for end-of-year examinations ensuring that 'subjects have been properly learned' (p. 293). Comenius's model of nationally based phases of schooling was adopted by the whole of Europe and the USA during the 19th century (Barsky & Glazek, 2014).

### The unintended consequences of literacy

In Chapters 3, 6 and 7 we explore the idea that technology has agency in human affairs. By this we do not mean the kind of conscious agency, or intentionality, which individual humans appear to exercise when they look forward and make decisions. The kind of agency that technology shows is often unintended and hard to see because it frames the possibilities of human actions rather than determining those actions. We begin to look at a form of this kind of agency, 'affordance', in Chapter 3. In addition to what might be called the external constraints and guiding nudges of technology, there are also internal constraints and influences. Humans are always already shaped on the inside, in their desires and the choices that they make, by the technology that they use. This kind of agency is pointed to by the well-known saying that a person whose only tool is a hammer is likely to see every problem as a nail.

In Chapter 7 we explore the idea that motivation might be best understood as a by-product of self-reproducing feedback loops. If this is true, then it may make sense to think of technologies like literacy developing the motivation to universalise as a by-product of the processes required for their reproduction. It is noticeable how literates tend to find themselves motivated to spread this technology to others, not just specific others, but to all others. Might it be possible that this is not only, as advocates for literacy programmes claim, because literacy is just a very good thing? May it also be because, in some way, literacy cannot thrive without readers and writers, and the more readers and writers there are the more that literacy thrives?

## Nationalism

To promote universal literacy, Comenius advocated writing textbooks in vernacular languages like German, French and English. He himself, like most educated people of his time, wrote his books in Latin. Education into vernacular languages, that is those spoken by people inhabiting a particular country or region, coupled with the origination of popular literature and newspapers in each language, laid the ground for the rise of national movements in Europe. According to Benedict Anderson, sharing reading in the same language led to the feeling of belonging to the same imaginary community (Anderson, 2008). German speakers, in the 18th century, inhabited many kinds of political units and spoke many different dialects. What Anderson refers to as 'print capitalism' created and stabilised a single German language as part of creating a market for books and newspapers. One of the consequences of this print capitalism was, according to Anderson, to create and support a single shared sense of German identity. Those who read books and newspapers in German felt that they shared a world of experience with all others who did so. This kind of print-mediated identity became so real for many that they were prepared to die for it. In the nationalist wars of the 19th and 20th centuries, many Europeans did die for their nations in much the same way that they had previously, in the 16th and 17th centuries, fought and died for their religions. Promoting and supporting print-literacy-based nationalism became a key function of the new print-literacy-based education systems that spread throughout the world in the 19th and 20th centuries. The history curriculum is different in every country. One thing it does, however, tend to have in common, in continuity with the scribe schools in Ancient Sumeria, are stories about the ancestors who founded the nation, the greatness of the nation, its values and its virtues (Bullock & Bullock, 2020).

Comenius experienced the destructiveness of the religious wars that blighted Europe in the 16th and 17th centuries first hand, losing close family members and all his possessions. He advocated universal education as a way to create world unity and peace. He saw that, to spread enlightenment in the form of knowledge and reason, it was necessary to teach in the vernacular languages of Europe. This meant printing textbooks in these languages and making local mother tongue education a cornerstone of each national curriculum. For Comenius, at least, the print-based nationalism that ended up being supported by his universal education movement was an unintended consequence. It is extraordinary how quickly this nationalism took root and came to seem natural. When Comenius was born very little of the world was parcelled up into nation states with clear borders. Now every bit of usable land belongs to one of less than two hundred nation states. Every human also, on pain of real excommunication, must belong to one of these states, each with its own school system and maintained in existence by multiple print literacy practices such as visas, identity cards and passports (Wimmer & Feinstein, 2010).

## Monologism

The philosopher Toulmin noted that something happened to the dominant way of thinking about thinking when print literacy spread throughout Europe in the 17th century. Before mass print-based education, culture everywhere was largely oral, and thinking was mostly understood in terms of dialogues. According to Toulmin, the tradition of thinking about reason as a type of dialogue was maintained up to the 16th century by humanist writers such as Erasmus and Montaigne. However, Toulmin points out, there was a major shift in Europe in the 17th century with thinkers such as Spinoza, Descartes, Leibniz and Newton. This new generation of thinkers, at the beginning of what became called the Enlightenment, replaced the perception of arguments as utterances in dialogues with the perception of arguments as propositions in proofs (Toulmin, 2003). Reason in the form of a dialogue is reasoning in a context in which there is uncertainty and creativity. Each 'voice' has personality and a perspective which they bring into the dialogue. Reason in the form of a proof is closed down and eternal. It is meant to be true in an abstract and universal way outside of any context (Nikulin, 2010).

This decontextualised way of thinking began with diagrams and can be found in the mathematics and some of the logic of Ancient Greece. It requires visual rather than aural thinking which is perhaps why dialogue continued to dominate as the model of reason in Europe until the mass printing of textbooks.[3] Euclid's *Elements*, for example, was one of the first books printed in large numbers after Gutenberg's development of a printing press in the 15th century. Spinoza used Euclid as a model for his type of reasoning which he called 'geometrico'. Spinoza was perhaps reflecting his experience of learning with textbooks such as Euclid's *Elements* when he put forward his apparently one-way model of education as moving from the uncertain process of thinking within time, constructing a proof for example, to a viewpoint outside of time when the proof was gained, a viewpoint he called 'sub specie aeternitatis' (Spinoza, 2006).

This timeless contextless view can be called monologism, meaning the ideal of a single true perspective, as if everything was laid out clearly in front of us on a table. This way of imagining cognition is a product, Toulmin suggests, of print literacy, particularly the printing of maths textbooks like Euclid's *Geometry*. The alternative to monologism is the dialogism of thinkers like Bakhtin who would argue that every book is written in a place and at a time that shapes its meaning. Every word even, he argued, is given meaning by all the ways in which it has been used, and so each word and each book is a situated perspective on reality within an always open-ended dialogue with other situated words and situated books.

### Individualism

Oral people tend to think mainly in the context of talking with others. The self-identity that emerges from the kind of technology of spoken words, pictures in caves, masks and small statues of the kind described for initiation of the Pende and San is identity as part of a community: the self is affirmed only insofar as the tribe is affirmed. And without the tribe there is, in the extreme, no sense of self. According to Ong (1969, 1972/2013), one of the consequences of the printing press, especially the printing of novels in the vernacular, was the development of individual literacy practices in which people read silently alone. The practice of reading and writing alone created a new kind of private space that appeared to be outside of any specific community. From this space one could imagine a freedom to stand back from, and question the views of, the community. Individual reading and writing, made possible for more people due to the spread of printing and education into literacy after the Gutenberg revolution, led to the ideal of the autonomous rational self. This ideal is central to an enlightenment view of education for freedom of thought, the aim of teaching students how to think for themselves without need of what Kant referred to as the 'crutches' of tradition (Kant, 1803).

### Case study: 'Building up' new models of digital education in Rural East Africa[4]

'If you want to hide something, put it in a book'. This comment by Alphaxus Kimani, farmer in central Kenya and programme leader for the afforestation programme TIST, succinctly captures the challenges facing learning with mobiles approaches in many rural communities across the Global South where print-based approaches to learning can be ineffective.

Kimani is an expert small group trainer, and for 15 years he has been helping adult learners across East Africa use dialogue to facilitate learning within non-formal small groups. Building from long-standing oral traditions of learning, Kimani and his colleagues have honed a set of ground rules for supporting dialogue: rotating leadership at every group meeting, a focus on facilitation and servanthood, and a unique pedagogical construct known as Kujengana ('to build up' in Swahili) which is the act of small group members verbally recognising the positive contributions of the current leader.

Kimani's point is that traditional approaches to learning with mobiles are derivatives of formal classroom environments and do not meet the needs of rural adult learners accustomed to educational models based in non-formal small group dialogue. These approaches fail to employ community-based ground rules like Kujengana and miss an opportunity to root the pedagogy within the lived experience of the small groups.

Kimani is part of an educational design-based research project called the TIST Learning Centre. It is accessible across Kenya, Uganda, Tanzania and now southern India. With a focus on offline access, low bandwidth functionality, economic resource constraints, diversity of participant educational background and face-to-face small group dialogic pedagogy, this project breaks away from past forms of knowledge production and content delivery by reinterpreting how to support and facilitate learning. The TIST Learning Centre is a free-to-use suite of educational content for rural adult East African learners. The platform is developed around a 'bring your own device' approach to scalability and requires no additional hardware to operate. Learning content is available in English and Swahili, with translation into indigenous tribal languages ongoing, and presented in text and aurally through recordings in local dialects. Current content, developed by TIST participants, is primarily focused on agricultural education, the carbon cycle and carbon markets, and programmatic information. Efforts to expand the range of content are ongoing, and there is an expressed desire from learners for a greater range of topics such as theology, literature and science.

Driving the content creation are face-to-face interactions between peers within a small group. A hallmark of non-formal small group education is the ability for group members to share knowledge through demonstration, such as a local farmer showing fellow members how to create green manure. These demonstrations are traditionally done in situ at a small group member's local farm. The TIST Learning Centre enhances this peer-to-peer exchange by capturing demonstrations from participating farmers via a mobile video recording which is shared via WhatsApp. These videos are then incorporated into the modules within the TIST Learning Centre, expanding the reach and scope of these peer-to-peer demonstrations. It is an opportunity for farmers to share knowledge beyond the geography of their respective rural community, and it has become a valuable repository of local knowledge capture and dissemination.

Instrumental to the functioning of peer-to-peer exchange are the suite of small group ground rules established by TIST farmers. As stated, these ground rules support rotating leadership (leadership rotates to new members at each group meeting), servanthood (leaders serve the group by facilitating group dialogue rather than dominating conversation), and the indigenous pedagogical practice of Kujengana (rooted in the belief that each person within a small group has unique talents and gifts to contribute to the community). Kujengana is the act of small group members verbally expressing specific and positive contributions made by the small group leader. The act of rotating leadership allows each member to experience this positive feedback in the form of Kujengana. As a practice, Kujengana is meant to encourage confidence and foster a sense of purpose by celebrating the contributions of each group member.

The focus on a learning with mobiles approach rooted within community-developed small group practices and adapted to the technological affordances of rural learners has fostered the growth of a new approach to mobile learning, called the 'Hub Model'. In the Hub Model, a single user in a small group (the Hub) accesses learning content on the learning with mobiles platform before downloading this to an Android mobile device. The content is then passed to other learner handsets using a technological affordance colloquially called 'side-loading'. Side-loading enables offline sharing of content within the group. When the side-loaded content is shared amongst small group members the material acts as a catalyst for dialogic interactions of the small group. As a pedagogy, this leverages indigenous oral traditions along with simple technological affordances to overcome pernicious digital infrastructure challenges: entire groups of rural learners can access digital content through a single member, sharing costs and minimising the need to travel long distances to obtain connectivity. This is, to again use the words of Mr Kimani, how to make education 'sticky' in rural East Africa.

The learning with mobiles platform has 800 active users, with 60% of these users using the Hub Model on behalf of a small group of 5–11 other learners. The project has yielded a set of 'design principles' for use in learning with mobiles approaches in rural communities in the Global South. Findings suggest that adoption of indigenous approaches to dialogic learning can be effective for learning with mobiles in rural East Africa whilst also providing a mechanism to mitigate the digital divide.

### *Commentary on the case study*

This case study offers a practical reflection on the limitations of the kind of formal schooling, developed in Europe and based on print literacy, that has for many become synonymous with 'education'. But before schools existed there was education. Oral ways of teaching and learning did not disappear just because schools were built to teach literacy. Informal education in many workplaces and areas of collective life in literate societies continues to be shaped more by talking and listening than by reading and writing. These more oral ways of doing education are not always simple, for example they often involve socially shared 'ground rules' like the practice of Kujengana or 'building up' described. What we see in this case study is how learning through dialogue in small local groups can be extended by new digital technology, mobile phones plus the internet, to connect learners in larger networks without breaking the dialogic sense of relationship and community that is so important to oral education. Here, for example, short videos of farmers demonstrating useful techniques can be shared. This extends the kind of in-person peer-to-peer teaching and learning of small communities. But all content is not self-generated, there is also knowledge coming from outside that is mediated by leaders within the community. In this project, the combination of dialogic pedagogy and the use of mobile technology leads to an interesting new model of education which we will revisit throughout the book. This model of education has at least three key elements: firstly, empowerment to actively participate; secondly an online platform accessed by mobile devices supporting a peer-to-peer learning community; and thirdly the extension of learning that comes through interaction with larger external knowledge communities.

## Discussion

Most accounts of educational technology assume that technology is there to support education. In this chapter, we reverse this understanding to consider the argument that education is there to support technology. Humans are technological from the beginning. The history recounted in this chapter suggests that one aspect of education is tying new biological bodies into the technology that they need to become fully functioning persons in their cultural context. Humans become conscious, self-reflective individuals only after education through which they are led to internalise the local communications technology. Without a language, for example, one does not have a voice. And the language that equips people with a voice is a form of communications technology which, even though some facility for spoken language is hardwired, still must be actively taught and learned. Where, as with oracy, the technology has been around for a long time, the biological body has already evolved to prepare for the technology, meaning aspects of the process of education can seem effortless. But technology has its own timescale of evolution which is different from, and usually much faster than, biological evolution. When there is a mismatch between the separate biological and the technological evolutionary strands of development, then formal education systems emerge to patch over the difference and bring biological bodies up to speed with the latest technology. Formal schooling was developed as a technology to support the technology of literacy which includes numeracy. What we currently call our education system is still largely focused on creating people according to the logic of print literacy outlined by Comenius in the 17th century. The main skills taught are reading, writing and arithmetic, followed by knowledge in the form of representations of the world found in books. The accurate acquisition of this knowledge is tested orally by educators in classrooms and then in paper-based examinations at the end of each year or at least at the end of a course.

We began this chapter challenging the widespread claim that education needs to be led by pedagogy not by technology, a claim often connected to the view that education is about furthering human interests rather than technological interests. There are many practical contexts in which this stance makes sense. However, our alternative history of educational technology suggests that what we take to be education is always already technology on the inside (Dron, 2022; Fawns, 2022). Formal schooling began as a support for literacy and spread to global ubiquity as a support for print literacy. When people argue for 'pedagogy not technology' in education, therefore, what they may sometimes inadvertently be suggesting, without necessarily realising it, is 'let us stick with what we know best: the latest technological innovations of the 17th century'.

### *Prompts towards a dialogic foundation for the design and practice of educational technology*

We understand theory as a guide to better practice. At the end of each chapter, we bring out the implications of the theory discussed for the design and practice of educational technology and, more specifically, the contributions that discussions in the chapter make towards our emerging dialogic foundation for the design of educational technology. These prompts for educational technology design are not intended as a new orthodoxy but more as thought experiments to stimulate dialogue and prompt reflection.

Discussion of the history of education in relation to communications technology raises questions that relate to the foundations on which we can design educational technology for the future. Our short alternative history of educational technology suggests that we inhabit a world so shaped by print-based education that the side effects of this technology, particularly the educational ideals of abstract decontextualised thinking and free autonomous individual selves, seem so natural to everyone who has been properly schooled (a category presumably including all the readers of this book) that they are hard to question. Questioning these guiding ideals of education does not mean rejecting them, it just means trying to become more aware of the extent to which our ideals have been shaped by existing technology and through this becoming more able to reflect on the alternatives that might be possible with different technology.

Digital technology, including the use of AI language assistants, brings with it new possibilities for education which include a return to some aspects of oral education. Educational technology in oral societies, cave paintings, masks and sculptures, for example, are often used in support of education into relationship. Education into relationship is about changing identity and expanding the range of possible ways of being. In addition to designing educational technology for knowing about the world, it is also possible to design educational technology for relating to aspects of the world in a way that helps students to experience and understand. For instance, the use of oral podcasts, video communication and immersive virtual reality can be designed in a way that supports education for relationship and community. And the use of immersive virtual reality can help students to experience the sensation of being what they are studying, thereby enhancing more 'internal' intuitive and empathetic understanding to complement a more external print-based cognitive approach; perhaps experiencing travelling at near the speed of light, or embodying a cell in a growing plant, or directly experiencing the birth or death of a social institution.

The deep existing interconnectedness of human beings with communications technology suggests that education can be thought of as a way to support technology, rather than technology only being thought of as a tool to support education. This suggests new educational design principles. Currently much education about social media, AI and the internet focuses on protecting school students from dangers. While this is obviously very important, it might also be valuable to design education to show students from an early age how to best use mobiles and social media to learn together with others and to enhance their lives.

Where print-literacy-based education has tended to promote a monological world view with a focus on learning correct answers, the use of multimodal and globally networked digital technologies could augment this focus with a greater awareness of the multiplicity of perspectives existing on every topic globally. In doing so, this might foster greater intellectual humility and an orientation towards learning from inquiry and from dialogue with others.

Where print-literacy-based education has previously promoted nationalism with a focus on inducting learners into one language and one culture, new multimodal digital media on the internet, perhaps especially platforms like YouTube and TikTok, could be used to augment print-based induction by promoting greater and more diverse engagement with others around the planet. And where print-literacy-based education and individual assessments have become associated with the promotion of intellectual autonomy and individualism, new digital technologies might be used to augment this focus with support for induction into collaborative learning of a kind that could lead to the development of more effective collective intelligence both locally and transnationally.

The case study of Dr Kevin Martin's research on Kujengana in rural East Africa illustrates one way in which the combination of mobile phones and the internet can support a model of education integrating what is most effective in traditional oral education with what is most effective in print-literacy-based education. Expressed schematically this new model consists of:

1 Engaging and empowering new voices into the dialogue of education: any farmer can record their practice and share this on the platform to become a teacher as well as a learner.
2 Connecting people together in peer-to-peer learning communities: the TIST platform supports farmers from villages across rural East Africa to share their knowledge, ask questions and learn from each other.
3 Expanding local knowledge with more global 'scientific' knowledge: the educational platform does not only host discussions and local examples of good practice, but also more 'authoritative' open educational resources derived from the global and very long-term dialogue of science, agriculture and economics for example, where expertise in more global and longer-term dialogues are desired and called upon by the community.

# 3

# AFFORDANCE THEORY

> *... relata do not precede relations.*
>
> Karen Barad (2007, p. 136)

> *... the world is the ensemble of my body's routes.*
>
> Maurice Merleau-Ponty (1962, p. 247)

## Introduction

In the previous chapter we offered an alternative history of educational technology. Focusing on the impact of literacy as a contrast to oracy, this explored the way in which different communications technologies lead to different ways of thinking about knowledge and different ways of doing education. That oral people think differently from literate people implies that communication technologies have different 'cognitive affordances'. The theory of affordances has been very influential in educational technology. It is sometimes applied to claims that different technologies have different affordances for teaching and learning. For example, Diana Laurillard's conversational framework outlines what her work suggests are the main types of learning: acquisition, collaboration, discussion, investigation, practice and production, proposing that we match the affordance of any technology used to the desired type of learning (Laurillard, 2002). Interactive simulations might be good for investigation, whereas PowerPoint might be good for production, and an online argument-mapping tool like 'Pol.is' might be good for supporting discussion.[1] In a similar way, Richard Osborne developed what he and colleagues called a 'top trumps' approach to mapping the affordances

DOI: 10.4324/9781003198499-3

of different educational technologies in a way that can help match these affordances to different educational tasks (Osborne et al., 2013).

Laurillard is not suggesting that teaching and learning are radically changed by digital technology. The types of learning she proposes are drawn from recognisable types of classroom teaching and learning that can occur without the support of digital technology. For example, investigating can be done in a physical science lab, presenting can be done with a written essay or poster, and discussing can be done orally in small groups and then in whole class plenaries. Conole and Dyke also adopt the affordance approach to mapping educational technology, but they go further to suggest that new digital technology does have general affordances that change the nature of education. They mention affordances for immediacy, communication and reflection as well as what they see as less positive potentials like the potential for surveillance (Conole & Dyke, 2004). This suggests that different technologies can offer new pedagogical affordances. Or, put another way, that new digital technologies can enable ways of teaching and learning that were either not possible or more difficult to implement before these digital technologies became available. There are many examples of this, but an obvious affordance of networked digital technology, following on from the Kajungana Case Study at the end of Chapter 2, is the pedagogical affordance of the internet combined with smart phones for peer-to-peer learning between learners situated at a geographic distance from each other. Although only the synchronous peer-to-peer learning element is strictly a new affordance of digital technology – after all people could write letters to each other – the combination of mobile phones and internet learning platforms has made peer-to-peer distance learning generally easier and more accessible to all. The idea that different technologies can offer different affordances for teaching and learning, therefore, seems relevant to the theory of educational technology. In the remainder of the chapter, we investigate the origin, significance and spread of 'affordance theory' before giving an example demonstrating how this can be used to support educational technology design.

## James Gibson's theory of affordances

During World War II, following completion of his PhD over ten years earlier on visual memory, Gibson directed a psychology unit in the US Army. Part of his role involved developing tests to predict the performance of Army Air Force crew on tasks like night-time landings and firing on enemy planes. This led Gibson to realise that the then dominant theory of perception in psychology was inadequate for understanding fast-moving perception in the real world. The then dominant theory, which remains quite influential today, is a representational account of perception involving three entities: a subject, an object and an internal mental representation of the object within the subject.

Gibson rejected this representational model in favour of what he called direct perception. Essentially, his direct perception model posits a coordination between the features of an observing organism and the features of an observed environment such that perception emerges directly out of the relationship between the two. An antelope running on uneven ground responds to cues in the landscape about which way to swerve without needing to consult an internal representation of any kind. Similarly, fighter pilots do not represent the trajectory of the enemy and work things out inside their heads before firing, they learn to recognise when and where to fire responding to cues in their perceptual field (Gibson, 1977).

Gibson called his account of perception 'ecological' because it applied the ecological niche theory to the creation of an epistemic niche, an idea mentioned in the previous chapter. A niche, the environmental conditions that support the life of an animal, is, according to Gibson, a system of affordances. These affordances are features of the environment that connect with features of the animal. He wrote: 'the *affordances* of the environment are what it *offers* the animal, what it *provides* or *furnishes*, either for good or ill' (Gibson, 1979, p. 127). For humans, for instance, a flat surface provides the possibility of walking forward, something physically shaped like a chair provides the affordance of sitting, steps provide the affordance of stepping and so on. Gibson writes that:

> the composition and layout of surfaces *constitute* what they afford. If so, to perceive them is to perceive what they afford. This is a radical hypothesis, for it implies that the 'values' and 'meanings' of things in the environment can be directly perceived.
>
> (Gibson, 1979, p. 127)

### Affordances and technology design

The fact that the term affordance is so widely used in educational technology design today owes more to American researcher Don Norman than to James Gibson. Norman's influential (1988) book originally named *The Psychology of Everyday Things*, later retitled *The Design of Everyday Things* (2002), can be credited with popularising the term affordance. Norman knew Gibson and discussed the theory of affordances with him but nonetheless used the term in a new and different way that he later came to call 'perceived affordance' to distinguish it from Gibson's original concept (Norman, 1999).

Norman was frustrated with the poor design of many new everyday objects such as programmable watches and video recorders. Their designs were not intuitive for many users. He applied the concept of affordance to refer to the *perceived* possibilities for action of objects, a button could be seen to afford pressing, a handle to afford turning and so on. But unlike Gibson (1977), who stated that 'affordances of the environments are facts of the environment, not appearances' (p. 70), Norman focused on the visible properties that could communicate to a user how to use the object properly. For Gibson, many objects might afford pressing and turning regardless of the intentions of the designer. For Norman, by contrast, the use of the term affordance was applied to the design of common objects such that they showed the user how to use them. Whereas Gibson focused on the environment, Norman looked at the design of tools and how they could be designed so that they were easier to use.

For Norman affordances are perceived action possibilities for an agent. The design of a door handle can imply that it can be turned or, if designed differently, that it can be pulled. That is the perceived affordance. The physical affordance, on the other hand, is the actual action that is possible regardless of what the door handle looks like. To illustrate the difference let us take the example of a computer with a mouse. Physically the mouse affords clicking and moving around. The perceived affordance of mouse clicks and movements, however, depend on the user's perception of the action possibilities. In this case, the user's perception of the mouse goes beyond simply moving and clicking on a table surface. They expect that by moving and clicking the mouse on a surface, they can move a cursor around on a computer screen and perform actions that impact the computer's processes. So, whereas Gibson's version of affordance theory focuses on what is possible physically, Norman extended this to focus more on what was perceived to be possible and how to design for this perception. This seems an appropriate move for educational technology design. Once we acknowledge that how users respond is part of the affordance of educational technology, then pedagogy that shapes expectations becomes important to the overall design as well as any actual physical possibilities built into tools.

## Gibson's radical empiricism

Gibson's concept of affordance is sometimes criticised for being vague (Oliver, 2005). Part of the issue with making the concept of affordance more definite and useful is that Gibson, although identifying as an experimental psychologist, was also deeply engaged with theory. Gibson was using the psychology of perception as a base for a radically new theory of meaning (Chong & Proctor, 2020). One of the reasons the theory of affordances can seem confusing is because it tries to go beyond everyday thinking about the relationship between people and the world. Gibson wrote that:

> an affordance is neither an objective property nor a subjective property; or it is both if you like. An affordance cuts across the dichotomy of subjective-objective and helps us to understand its inadequacy. It is equally a fact of the environment and a fact of behavior. It is both physical and psychical,

> yet neither. An affordance points both ways, to the environment and to the observer.
>
> (Gibson, 1979, p. 121)

This claim that affordances are 'both physical and psychical, yet neither' (i.e., both 'material stuff' and 'mental stuff' at the same time) is influenced by William James' theory of radical empiricism (Lobo et al., 2018). This suggests that reality is both material and mental, and that these two aspects are inseparable. Experience of the world always means a response to our actions. For example, actions like reaching out and touching a door handle and sensing how it responds to our touch or turning our head and focusing the eyes to seek out and follow the movements of a bird in flight. James' pragmatism combines an epistemology of radical empiricism with a metaphysics of neutral monism. Radical empiricism suggests that experience is all we have: there is nothing outside of experience. James claims that we can describe the world of pure experience either from the side of the object (the sense datum) or from the side of the subject (the experience). This gets called a 'neutral monism' because James argues that there is only one kind of substance in the universe, experience, which can be described in both 'physical' and 'psychical' terms (James, 1895, p. 110).[2] As we elaborate below, ideas of a 'self' on one side and of a 'physical world' on the other are interpretations made out of a more original uninterpreted experience which is neither self nor world, or perhaps is both self and world. As an experimental psychologist it appears Gibson was trying to apply this theory with his concept of affordance, echoing James by suggesting this was 'both physical and psychical, yet neither'.

### Gibson and relational ontology

Gibson wrote notes in the early 1970s on Merleau-Ponty's (1945/2013) *Phenomenology of Perception*. He did not cite Merleau-Ponty as an influence on his ideas, although some claim he really should have done so given that what is distinctive in Gibson's ecological theory was already present in Merleau-Ponty's work (Chemero & Käufer, 2016, p. 67).

Maurice Merleau-Ponty, a professor of psychology at the Sorbonne University in Paris and a philosopher in the phenomenological tradition initiated by Husserl, focused on understanding perception as embodied knowledge. He saw the body as our access to all knowledge and the perceptual field as the original form of knowledge. The world, for Merleau-Ponty, was never simply objective but was always the world as experienced. He called the world 'the ensemble of my body's routes', meaning not only how the physical body moves in a landscape, but also how the eyes explore depths and how the ears and nose pick up clues that are brought together to create the experience of a world (1962, p. 246). Against the dualism of Descartes, who claimed that there is a world of mental stuff and a separate world of physical stuff with no obvious link between them, Merleau-Ponty's careful analyses of perception suggest that the physical and the mental, the 'physical and the psychical' in Gibson's phrase, are so closely bound up together in each act of perception that they cannot be disentangled.

Merleau-Ponty suggested an experiment we can all do to explore how subjectivity and objectivity (the mental and the physical) are bound up in even the simplest experience. If I touch my left hand with my right hand, I find myself on both sides of the experience. On the one hand, as I touch with my fingers, I experience my right hand touching something external much as it would feel to touch a tabletop or a plastic prosthetic hand. On the other hand, if I shift attention a little, I can relocate my attention inside my left hand and feel what it is like to be touched, as if some 'other' was touching my hand. If you are able to, try this simple experiment: as right hand feel the touching and, as left hand, feel the being touched. You are now on both sides of this double-sided act. This raises several questions. Are you now an object or a subject? Sentient or sensed? Mind or matter? Agentic or passive? And where exactly in this experience is the gap between these two sides?

Merleau-Ponty was writing before personal computers and the internet. An updated experiment for the Digital Age can illustrate the profound point his experiment makes about where space comes from. Anyone learning basic HTML website coding will find that it is possible to change the background colour of a website by typing in a short hexadecimal string, for instance, Hex Code #000000 for black. You type this code in the script variable that defines background colour, save it, then re-load the site and look at it through a web browser to find that the background colour has gone black, or golden, or aquamarine. On the one hand, as designer, you see the code. Then, on the other hand switching to the perspective of a user, you see the colour. The two are inseparable. But the two sides, code and experienced colour, do not meet in any shared space. Either you are on one side viewing the code as a designer, or on the other, viewing the experience as a user. Again, where exactly is the gap between these two experiences?[3]

Merleau-Ponty's point in his experiment with right hand touching left was that while each experience we have seems to take place in a pre-given world of space and time, if we ask 'where is the world?', we see that it is generated out of thousands of these kinds of mini touching and being touched experiences. When I touch the table, the table touches me back. I am on both sides of the experience. The same happens when I look at the horizon: the horizon looks back at me and locates me in the centre of it. The world of space and time that we experience, Merleau-Ponty is saying, is constructed through many perceptual acts and does not exist separately from them.

Merleau-Ponty's phenomenology of perception, first published in 1945, describes the body's experience of the world in a way which fits very well with Gibson's affordance theory. His later work draws out the implications of this for a relational ontology, and this can be helpful in clarifying the kind of non-dualist but empirical position that Gibson advocated. Merleau-Ponty, like Gibson, distinguishes between the body and the external world. He argues that the world is experienced in two ways: (1) as the body experiences it, and (2) as the body image is experienced in those interactions. This position, like that of Gibson, leads to the apparent vagueness and confusion of saying perception is both subjective and objective. In his later work, Merleau-Ponty tried to address this problem by articulating a new kind of understanding described as the intertwining of body and world, the sentient and sensed, as being already wrapped up inextricably together in what he called 'the chiasm' (Merleau-Ponty, 1968). His point was, like James's, that we do not start with a body facing a world. Rather, we start with perceptual experience and construct a body and world within experience. His account of experience was different from James's in including a certain necessary dualism or perhaps a kind of dialogue between 'inside' and 'outside' perspectives. Possibly the clearest way to make his point is to say that for every inside there is an outside, and for every outside there is an inside. These two perspectives, the inside and the outside, go together as two aspects of the same thing.[4] We say more about this ontology or way of thinking about reality in Chapter 10.

Karen Barad, building on her PhD research in quantum physics, seems to have drawn similar conclusions to those of Gibson and Merleau-Ponty. Her relational ontology suggests that the world is not made up of separate things, but rather that it is a network of relationships. Barad explains this relational ontology by invoking experiments in a quantum physics lab, arguing that relata – that is the things that come together in a relationship – do not precede relations (Barad, 2007). Applying this to Gibson's account of perception, we can consider how active perception may precede the model of an 'objective' world on one side and a 'subjective' person on the other. William James's idea of neutral monism that Gibson references, the idea that reality is neither just 'world' nor just 'mind', but always both together wrapped up in experience, is relevant but not sufficient to capture what Gibson is trying to say with the idea of affordances. Merleau-Ponty goes further than James in pointing out the dynamic nature of this monism. In place of a kind of universal 'stuff' of experience, Merleau-Ponty posits a kind of gap, what he calls the 'ecart' between sentient and sensed. His point is that this relationship is not a kind of identity but a kind of difference. Barad makes a similar point when she replaces the idea of 'inter-action' – as if two separate things touched each other – with the idea of 'intra-action', meaning that the world is always already inseparably entangled up together such that all we have is best understood as one thing that can only be known through events or 'enactments' that occur within it. Barad echoes Merleau-Ponty when she refers to intra-actions as the universe touching itself.[5] After the event of a touch, for example, perhaps a right hand touching a left hand, then it seems that sentient (subject) touched the sensed (object), but the roles of who is on one side and who is on the other are potentially reversible. The only thing constant in the structure of perception is the apparent gap around which sentient and sensed can reverse in this way. The gap between skin and skin for example, or between skin and a tool such as a hammer, or the gap between the fingers on the keyboard typing in hexadecimal code and the changing colours on the screen.

## From perceptual world to technology

Neither Gibson nor Merleau-Ponty wrote much about technology. However, their perceptually based relational ontology has implications for educational technology. The Gibson/Merleau-Ponty theory of affordances can be seen as a theory of how tools and technology come into being that gives us insight into the ontological status of tools. Take the example of words that become conceptual or cognitive tools. Spoken words like 'in' and 'up' and 'there' emerge from, and give voice to, affordances experienced directly in perception. As words abstracted from immediate perceptual contexts, and applied to other contexts, they form what has been described as the metaphorical basis for cognition (Lakoff & Johnson, 2008). Ideas of being inside or outside, of being above or below, of being closer to 'here' or being further away over 'there' are, in this 'embodied cognition' theory, the basic tools of all thought which can be thought of as like can-openers, screwdrivers and hammers used for constructing shared meanings (Coeckelbergh, 2017).

The antelope we described earlier swerving to avoid hills and holes to find the best way through a landscape might well, if she comes back that way every day, find herself making a path. Over years the path becomes a way of shaping the environment, a kind of tool. In a very similar way, for the ancestors of Homo sapiens, we can imagine that using stones to bash nuts open might lead naturally to the best stones being carried around to new sites to bash new nuts, before finally stones are fashioned to make them better tools for the jobs required. In this way technology emerges from, and remains within, the body-world interface.

Gibson (1979, p. 122) writes that over the last few thousand years 'man' has changed the world to make 'more available what benefits him and less pressing what injures him'.[6] However, he points out that:

> This is not a *new* environment – an artificial environment distinct from the natural environment – but the same old environment modified by man. It is a mistake to separate the natural from the artificial as if there were two environments; artifacts have to be manufactured from natural substances. It is also a mistake to separate the cultural environment from the natural

> environment, as if there were a world of mental products distinct from the world of material products. There is only one world, however diverse, and all animals live in it, although we human animals have altered it to suit ourselves.
>
> (p. 122)

Merleau-Ponty gives an example of tool use when he describes how a blind man with a cane can use it to feel the world, but in a way that is like an extension of their body.[7] He argues that such tools enable not only extensions of our bodies, but also extensions of our naturally given body-world. He generalises to suggest this creates an 'interworld' of shared culture, which is not separate from the perceptual world but an extension or augmentation of it (Merleau-Ponty, 1962, p. 146).

Merleau-Ponty is saying that cultural ideas expressed in language, in songs, in music, in dance movements and in tools, originate in perceptual affordances, in the pre-conscious and pre-objective dynamic structures of the perceptual body-world. If so, the songlines of Australian Aboriginals previously discussed are not just a curiosity on the fringes of knowledge, but they are central to understanding culture, cognition and technology as emergent phenomena – affordances – that arise naturally within the reversible gap or 'hinge' between body and world.

## Action possibilities and enacted affordances

While Gibson inspired by Merleau-Ponty might have been concerned with affordance theory as a way to re-think everything, Don Norman's main intention was to apply this theory to improve the design of user interfaces. The widespread take up of his ideas suggests that an interpretation of affordances as action possibilities is perceived by many to be helpful when designing new technology or when considering the potential implementation of a specific technological tool in new settings. Indeed, one way affordance offers a distinctive perspective on the use of technology in education is because it can be used to consider possibilities for action. However, focusing on action possibilities alone can lead to a fixation on the functionality of technology 'as tools, "things" to be prodded, pushed or pulled' (Osborne, 2014, p. 412) rather than exploring 'the meaning that is provided by the environment with respect to a specific individual and at a specific moment in time' (p. 69). In education, Osborne suggests, we need to look at the affordances offered by technology for new meaning-making as well as affordances for pushing and pulling things.

Krippendorff similarly argues that affordance theory is a theory of meaning (2005). Affordances, he claims, are the meanings that things have for users. But in the theory of how meaning works from Husserl, which we discuss in Chapter 7, meaning is never fixed but emerges from out of the dynamic tension between actual events and a 'horizon of meaning' that is unique to each event. In using tools, for example, meaning emerges out of the dynamic tension between how a thing is actually used in the present and the horizon of possibilities relating to how it could be used. Reflecting on Gibson's seminal notion of affordance, Krippendorff argues that directly perceived affordances in the Gibson sense need to be distinguished from enacted affordances, as the anticipation of action possibilities may fail or be disrupted. Enacted affordances might therefore be thought of as manifested possibilities.

## Understanding affordance as a relationship between technology and users

The concept of affordance is significant when considering the role of technology in education. In previous work we have advocated a view of affordance as acknowledging 'action possibilities', but additionally highlighting the value of recognising the closely related idea of 'enactment'; that is, how affordances are specifically implicated in promoting learning (Major & Warwick, 2019). Variables such as the educator, learners, educational setting, resources, subject norms (i.e., rules, routines and expectations), task sequence, activity type, technical arrangements and institutional context all influence what and how learners learn (Seidel et al., 2016). We also concur with others who suggest that the affordances of technology are inextricably bound up with specific, historically situated modes of engagement and ways of life (Bloomfield et al., 2010).

From this, it will be clear that which action possibilities become evident as enacted affordances, and in what form, depends on pedagogy as well as technology. It is not only the technology that is important; it is how the technology is used in a particular educational context. Acknowledging this is central to applying affordances in educational technology settings; and it is central to the work of educational practitioners and designers, since knowing that the pedagogy is supposed to inform technology use frees them to consider not how 'whizzy' a technology may be, but rather how it might become a 'participant' in teaching and learning. In this sense, then, an affordance can be considered not as a feature of educational technology alone nor of the user alone, but something that only exists as an emergent feature of the relationship between the two.

## Designing for affordance

Osborne (2014) proposes extending the notion of affordance to give agency to both learner and technology, thereby recognising the important contribution of the digital environment to the learner experience. This approach is compatible with a view of material-dialogic intra-action inspired by Karen

Barad (Hetherington & Wegerif, 2018). A material-dialogic perspective does not view digital technology as separate from the activities of the educator and/or learners: rather, it envisages a 'voice' for the technology within intra-actions and focuses on the meaning provided by the environment (Hetherington & Wegerif, 2018). An understanding of action possibilities and enacted affordances, therefore, provides two appropriate lenses for considering if (and how) digital technology acts as a constructive partner in enabling and constraining learning.

In recent years, interest in the applications of educational design-based research (EDBR) has increased (see Chapter 10). EDBR can be used as an approach to technical as well as pedagogical development and aims to develop theories about domain-specific learning as well as the means that are designed to support that learning (Bakker & van Eerde, 2015). Thus, in addition to producing useful products (e.g., educational software), broader insights into how these can be developed and used are generated. An understanding of action possibilities and enacted affordances as interlinked 'design principles' may, therefore, be used to inform external partners. The interconnected nature of action possibilities and enacted affordances also resonates with the idea that 'enacted affordances are often quite different from the features imagined by the designers and can only be discovered through analysis of actual usage' (Stahl, 2007); both can be considered in the iterative phases of design, development and further testing that are a key feature of EDBR.

At the heart of the idea of enacted affordances lies the question of how are affordances implicated in actual learning processes and outcomes in specific technology contexts? In the next section, we illustrate some of these ideas by reflecting on empirical research involving analysis of the Talkwall classroom microblogging tool.

## Case study: Using affordances in teaching and learning

Talkwall is a freely available browser-based tool designed to support classroom dialogue and interaction. Secure and local to each classroom, during a lesson involving Talkwall, a main Talkwall is displayed at the front of the class on a projector or large screen (e.g., interactive whiteboard) and is typically controlled by the teacher; learners have their own individual or group Talkwalls that are accessed and controlled using any device with a web browser. The teacher presents the class with a question or a challenge (also displayed at the top of each wall), before learners engage in dialogue in small groups and contribute ideas in response (using short, microblog-style messages). These contributions appear on a class 'feed', similar to Twitter's timeline, which is constantly available and shared across all devices. Once posted, contributions on both teacher and student walls can be interactively sorted and arranged in a number of innovative ways. The software is one outcome of the Digitalised Dialogues Across the Curriculum project (DiDiAC)[8] undertaken by researchers at the University of Oslo (Norway) and University of Cambridge (UK) led by Professor Ingvill Rasmussen and Paul Warwick. Building on over a decade of EDBR undertaken in partnership with educational practitioners (Smørdal et al., 2021), DiDiAC involved the alignment of theories related to educational talk, a cultural-historical approach to understanding mediating technology, and a situated understanding of limitations and opportunities in the classroom (articulated by teachers during Talkwall's development process).

The DiDiAC research demanded the development of an 'enacted' affordances framework to examine how dialogue was mediated (enhanced, modified or replaced) as students used Talkwall. To do this, the team set about establishing a way to conceptualise the relationship between action possibilities and enacted affordances. As summarised below, they came up with the idea of 'affordances for dialogue' that encompasses these two elements. This approach is significant as it exemplifies how the affordances associated with educational technology, particularly that which mediates classroom dialogue given the focus of the research, can be specifically, as well as broadly, considered by designers and analysed by researchers.

Various sources may inform an initial consideration of action possibilities related to the use of a digital technology. These include Bower's (2008) work matching learning tasks with learning technologies, Jeong and Hmelo-Silver's (2016) analysis of affordances in the context of computer-supported collaborative learning, and themes identified by previous systematic literature reviews (e.g., Major et al., 2018). It might also be possible to work with technology developers to determine their perspectives on various 'built-in' functionalities intended to provide action possibilities to support desired pedagogical intentions.

With this understanding of the action possibilities that a technology might bring, an examination of lessons – through analysis of classroom video or live observation – can be undertaken to ascertain the enacted affordances evident during actual use. The first stage of enacted affordance analysis involves independently examining classroom data (e.g., video and transcripts) before reviewing, and developing, an initial framework of emerging ideas related to the affordances of the technology. Following this, the second stage of affordance analysis involves specifically coding for what we call 'enacted affordances' (i.e., in the case of Talkwall, how the tool's affordances are directly implicated in promoting dialogic interaction). After further discussion amongst researchers and teachers, and subsequent refinement of themes, a framework of enacted affordances can be agreed for the analysis of additional lesson episodes. Table 3.1 outlines the enacted affordances identified in the case of Talkwall.

**TABLE 3.1** Illustrating the 'enacted affordances for dialogue' identified for Talkwall.

| *Enacted affordances identified* | *Description* | *Illustrations* |
|---|---|---|
| Posting | The creation of a new contribution and any subsequent edits (in conjunction with dialogue). | Students discussing their ideas before deciding as a group a joint contribution to post to Talkwall. |
| Browsing | Review of Talkwall contributions (possibly with subsequent action). | Browsing Talkwall's feed exposing learners to other groups' ideas. Enactment can occur over a prolonged period, the effect of which may be felt for longer than the affordance is enacted (e.g., learners continuing to discuss an idea). |
| Selection | Selection of Talkwall contributions (possibly as a basis for dialogue, where it is often strongly linked to elaboration and reasoning). | A learner browsing the contribution feed and reading another group's post before selecting and 'pinning' this to their own group Talkwall, backing up their selection with a reason. |
| Positioning | Orientation/arrangement/prioritisation of contributions in relation to task requirements. Using hashtags (#) to categorise posts. | Learners' (re)positioning contributions to categorise them (e.g., placing 'for' and 'against' statements on the left and right of the screen respectively). Positioning may afford a visual representation of the current state of learners' shared thinking and can potentially replace spoken dialogue. |
| Support/ Challenge | Group member may find support for position, or have position challenged, from contributions posted to Talkwall rather than from within their group. | When a learner uses a contribution posted to the Talkwall feed by another group to support what they are saying. |
| Shared spaces | Revisiting/reference back to previous contributions available in a shared space. A potential source of evidence. | Learners revisiting previous walls or feeds to remind themselves of another group's idea to create a new contribution on a second wall of their own. This may also enable dialogues to progress over time. |

(*Continued*)

**TABLE 3.1** (Continued)

| *Enacted affordances identified* | *Description* | *Illustrations* |
|---|---|---|
| Orchestration | Deliberate manipulation by the teacher/Talkwall leader to delimit or manipulate the activity. This includes the choice of wall titles, backgrounds, and the ability to delete other people's posts. Includes focusing, via magnification and filter functions, to create an object of attention (potentially for dialogue to emerge around it). | A teacher filtering the Talkwall during a whole-class activity to focus on a particular group's wall only, followed by them asking the group to explain the positioning of their contributions. |
| Provisionality | Tentative selection or positioning of items indicates possible intention, which may be modified based on challenge/ dialogue. The ability to edit posts may also make a post provisional. | The provisional nature of positioning combined with a group's exploratory talk enabling learners to create and place contributions without final commitment. Such contributions may be viewed as dynamically constructed, easily and infinitely manipulable by teachers and learners. |

As reported elsewhere, Talkwall's enacted affordances were repeatedly, and directly, implicated in the dialogic interactions that occurred in classrooms where the tool was used in combination with a dialogic pedagogy (Major, Smørdal et al., 2022). This analysis process is cyclical and iterative. It is unlikely, once enacted affordances are initially observed and categorised, that further iterative analyses would not be undertaken. Through this process, rigor can be demonstrated and enhanced until a level of saturation and/or analyst agreement can be demonstrated. Such a strategy for determining enacted affordances also considers the wider ecology of learning, including the 'voice' or role of the technology in the interaction. The enacted affordances identified for Talkwall are interconnected and interrelated, with several of them also in play at the same time. For instance, learners' browsing and selecting from the Talkwall feed may be followed by creative engagement within a 'material-dialogic space', facilitated by the intra-action of positioning and provisionality with their dialogic co-construction of a particular concept. Action possibilities and enacted affordances are thus interconnected and interdependent and operate in a dynamic relationship that can inform and feed into one another.

## The complementary idea of constraint

Both affordances and constraints support particular actions. In doing so, they may also inhibit other actions that are more desirable. As Kennewell (2001, p. 106) writes:

> Constraints are not the opposite of affordances; they are complementary, and equally necessary for activity to take place. Of course, by virtue of their support for particular actions in a setting, the affordances and constraints may inhibit other actions which are more desirable.

A constraint may be perceived negatively as a barrier to action, but it may also be positive. For example, where guidance structures constrain the parameters of action in order that specific learning outcomes might be achieved. Like enacted affordances, enacted constraints may be an additional unit of analysis depending on the focus of the research.

To give a specific example involving Talkwall, it appears that the enactment of 'browsing' identified in Table 3.1, whilst affording access to a range of ideas from around the class, can inhibit exploratory talk. This is something described by Victoria Cook and colleagues (2019): where browsing was enacted, the size of contribution feed sometimes restricted exploratory talk as the desire to address all contributions posted to Talkwall's feed curtailed discussions. Further, when students browse the feed, it might also be easier for them to ignore certain contributions because the digital nature of these contributions arguably does not command the same level of respect as a human interlocutor physically present. This might lead to learning itself being constrained.

Don Norman talks about three main types of constraint in his book on design (1988): physical constraints, cultural conventions and logical constraints. The constraint to dialogue offered by browsing in Talkwall is perhaps a combination of a physical constraint ('too much content') and a cultural convention ('got to read all the stuff'). A design response against these constraints could be either to address the physical issue – by reducing the number and length of messages that could be browsed for instance – or to address the cultural convention, potentially by further pedagogical intervention to guide students to focus on one or two particularly pertinent messages to discuss together, temporarily putting the other messages to the side.

### *Constraints as a danger of affordances*

The simple example we gave earlier of creating a path by walking in a landscape shows how what can begin as an affordance might, over time, turn into a constraint. In Devon in the South of England there are many old country roads that, because of use over many generations, seem to have been cut into the landscape with such steep banks that no deviation from the path is possible. What began as one possible route amongst many has become, over time, the only possible route. There are many examples in technology design of this sort of process. The QWERTY design of English-language keyboards is a well-known case where an initial design that placed the keys frequently pressed together as far apart as possible (to solve the problem of mechanical typewriter keys sticking) is a feature of every laptop keyboard even though the problem it solves is long gone and QWERTY is a sub-optimal design for typing speed (Noyes, 1983). In Chapter 6, we discuss Heidegger's account of modern technology which makes a similar case that the whole of modern technology is a constraint on human freedom. Technology which began as an affordance for relationship with nature has, Heidegger claims, become a constraint limiting that relationship to one where nature is only now experienced filtered through the needs of technology. Heidegger's critique is general to technology but in some ways is particularly relevant to educational technology. In designing technology to support an affordance for a particular learning goal, we perhaps inevitably constrain the possibility of realising other learning goals.

Affordances often seem to come with constraints. Some may use this to argue that progress is illusory because any technology that enables us to do new things or see new things will be balanced by an equal and opposite constraint such that things that we used to be able to do we can no longer do and things that we used to be able to see we can no longer see. We remain optimistic. Progress, we claim, is possible not simply as achieving more efficiently whatever learning goals we have but also, more significantly, as progress in expanding degrees of freedom of thought and action by increasing the space of possibilities available (see Chapter 8 on education as expanding dialogic space). While every affordance may bring with it complementary constraints, we still consider that by designing for the affordance of reflection and dialogue we can design educational systems that promote greater awareness of human possibilities and perhaps also what some might call post-human possibilities. In Chapter 10 we argue for a double-loop educational design-based research (EDBR) methodology, of the kind earlier discussed in relation to Talkwall, that reflects on and deepens its assumptions even as it researches and develops better practice. In Chapter 11 we propose a dialogic foundation for design that is about designing for increasing dialogic space which means increasing the degrees of intellectual freedom or the range of perspectives that are possible. Our overall argument includes the claim that new communications technologies associated with the internet have been designed with functionality that we could use to expand the space of dialogue for learners. However, we can make this more likely to happen if we adopt careful and engaged design practices.

## Discussion

First attributed to perceptual psychologist James Gibson in the 1970s, the notion of affordance is a key theoretical concept for those interested in technology's role in education. It appears useful to claim, as Laurillard (2002) does, that different educational technologies afford different kinds of learning. It is also plausible that new digital technologies may offer new pedagogical affordances or new ways of thinking about and implementing teaching and learning (Conole & Dyke, 2004).

The original affordance theory was part of a theory of perception, not a theory of technology design. As a theory of perception, it was informed by the philosophical perspectives of William James and Maurice Merleau-Ponty and offered insight into the origins of meaning and technology. The world, Gibson claimed, is always already rich in affordances which offer us values and meanings as well as possibilities for action. Thinking about the origins of affordance theory reminds us that designing educational technology is not just designing action possibilities, it is also about designing for meaning making. We explored in this chapter the complexity of how technology enters into and shapes the meaning that we make. Although many factors interact, it is reasonable to claim that different media have different affordances for thinking which impact on how we understand the world and how we understand ourselves.

### *Prompts towards a dialogic foundation for the design and use of educational technology*

Our case study suggests a focused and practical way to apply the concept of affordances to educational technology design. This is to use observed enacted affordances, what we see people actually do, dynamically as a potential basis for revising a design. This idea of observing enacted affordances is not simply looking at what people do with technology, it is looking at what they do as an instantiation and illustration of an affordance which can then be used to revise the overall design. The Talkwall research we described offers an example of how educators and students used a new technology to support the learning goal of greater educational dialogue in classrooms. In this example, as is typically the case through EDBR, the pedagogy and the technology were iteratively designed together to strengthen that enacted affordance.

The idea of affordance has typically emphasised a focus on features of technology. However, the affordances for action and for thought of any technology depend on how the user responds. An important implication for the design and use of educational technology, therefore, is to recognise that affordance is not a feature of technology alone – nor of the user alone – but is an emergent feature of the relationship between the two. To design effectively for affordances, there is a need to design the cultures and norms that shape user responses in addition to designing the technology itself.[9] The nature of designing for learning thus should be seen as a dynamic iterative process weaving together the design of tools and the design of the pedagogy shaping expectations as to how to use the tools. A practical application of this general principle is the way in which almost any activity that requires groups to work together with technology can be enhanced by combining this activity with a pedagogy for developing and maintaining shared ground rules for exploratory talk (Wegerif & Dawes, 2004).

# 4

# THE 'GRAMMAR' OF EDUCATIONAL TECHNOLOGY

> *In many schools today, the phrase 'computer-aided instruction' means making the computer teach the child. One might say the computer is being used to program the child. In my vision, the child programs the computer . . .*
>
> Seymour Papert (1980/2020, p. 5)

> *. . . grammar tells us what kind of object anything is.*
>
> Ludwig Wittgenstein (2009, p. 373)

## Introducing the idea of 'ontological grammar'

In the previous chapter, we established that educational technology can offer particular affordances for different ways of teaching and learning. We found that affordances do not only lie in the technology, but also in how people can envision using the technology. In this way an affordance is not a feature of the technology alone, nor of the user alone, but is an emergent feature of the relationship between the two. To help us describe the different ways of imagining and enacting the role of educational technology, we borrow and adapt the idea of ontological grammar proposed by Ludwig Wittgenstein. Wittgenstein, one of the most influential philosophers of the 20th century, wrote that 'grammar tells us what kind of object anything is' (2009, p. 373). This idea of grammar does not just refer to language, but also to what Wittgenstein called 'language games', which are examples of language use and the actions into which language is woven. He proposed that the meaning of words depends on their use and that their use depends on the rules of the

DOI: 10.4324/9781003198499-4

language game being played. Language games are not just about words, but are about activities embedded within what Wittgenstein calls 'forms of life'.

Wittgenstein suggests 'water' as an example of how meaning depends on the 'game' being played and the form of life that is the context of the game. Depending on the context in which the word 'water' is uttered, it might be an urgent request (perhaps to dampen a fire), an exclamation (possibly surprise after encountering water in a desert), a response (perhaps an answer provided to a quiz question that asks what the chemical symbol $H_2O$ represents), and so on. The definition of 'game' is another example Wittgenstein uses. There is no characteristic that is universal to what we might call a game: board games, betting games, card games, Olympic games, team games, war games, etc. Conceptual analysis, understanding the meanings of words like 'game' or terms like 'educational technology', became for Wittgenstein a 'grammatical' investigation. To understand concepts, he claimed, meant to see more clearly what role they played in language games within forms of life.

Central to the idea of ontological grammar is the insight that the meaning of words, what they really refer to, is to be found in the way that they are used: '"How is the word used?" and "What is the grammar of the word?" I shall take as being the same question' (Wittgenstein et al., 1979, p. 373). This is an idea introduced in Chapter 1 as key to dialogic theory and, indeed, Wittgenstein's account of language games is often cited as a source for dialogic theory in education (Shotter, 2008). Concept words do not work like signposts pointing to stable areas of reality, Wittgenstein writes, but they are better thought of as tools which are used to get things done in a range of contexts. By extension, what 'educational technology' is can only be determined by exploring how this term, and the words and technologies associated with it, are being written about and are being used in different contexts. This grammatical analysis of educational technology reveals an expanding range of grammars or ways in which the role of technology in education is being imagined and enacted. Philosopher of technology Mark Coeckelbergh uses Wittgenstein's grammatical approach to understand not only words but also how technologies are thought about and used in different social contexts (Coeckelbergh, 2022).[1] In this chapter, we apply the same approach looking at educational technologies.

In everyday language the ontological grammar normally applied to tools and so, by extension, to technology in general is that of being a mediating means for a subject acting upon an object. The idea implied by the grammar here is that there are active agents who use tools to impact upon passive objects. Sentences like 'Jane used an axe to chop the wood' seem to have the same essential ontological grammatical structure as a sentence like 'Jane used an app to teach multiplication'. The idea that technology can be used as a tool to support teaching seems natural in everyday language use. This simple grammar remains very common in education. Perhaps it is still the default or dominant understanding of educational technology. However, as we will show, there are a number of alternative grammars including variants in which the tools themselves take on a certain agency.

## Educational technology as a 'teaching machine'

Although some teaching machines were used in classrooms in the 1920s, the first widespread use of the term educational technology came with the application of B. F. Skinner's behaviourism to US classrooms in the 1950s. Skinner saw education as being about achieving a measurable change in student behaviour in the direction of achieving pre-defined learning goals. The most efficient way to achieve this, according to Skinner, was through positive and negative reinforcement of behaviours. Where learning goals are complex, the role of instructional design is to break this complexity down into manageable smaller steps (Skinner, 1968).

Skinner believed that the traditional classroom model had disadvantages because students learn at different speeds and reinforcement is often delayed due to a lack of individual attention. His 'teaching machine' sought to address these problems through a programme which combined teaching and test items to support a student gradually through the material to be learned.

**FIGURE 4.1** Skinner's teaching machine (students responded by 'filling-in-the-blank').

*Source:* Silly Rabbit, licensed under CC BY-SA 3.0.

This 'machine' was initially conceived as a tool to help teachers teach, although Skinner also considered that it might one day be possible to develop a similar approach that could ultimately replace the need for teachers. The machine was composed of a fill-in-the-blank method (see Figure 4.1). If the student was correct, positive reinforcement (praise) was given before moving on to the next question. If the answer was incorrect, the student was given the correct answer to study to increase their chance of success and getting positive reinforcement next time (Watters, 2021).

The metaphor of technology as a teaching machine informed the first use of computers in schools in the form of 'computer-assisted learning'. Although the technology has of course improved since, this way of thinking about the role and use of computers, this ontological grammar, remains popular. More elaborate versions of these early teaching machines are now being widely used. As mentioned earlier in this book, today a range of different terms are used to reflect educational technology which might be argued to resemble the original teaching machines. This includes terms such as 'computer-assisted learning' (CAL), 'computer-aided learning' (also confusingly sometimes referred to as CAL), 'computer-aided instruction' (CAI) and 'cognitive tutoring systems' (CTS). Our own research highlights how differences between these terms are often subtle and used interchangeably (Major & Francis, 2020). These contemporary teaching machines are often promoted as the 'future of education', exactly the language used by Skinner in the 1960s (Kabudi et al., 2021).

### *An illustration of the computer as teaching machine model*

Sparx Maths[2] is a personalised learning platform developed to aid the delivery of lessons and homework for students aged 11 to 16 in the UK. The platform contains over 38,000 questions and over 9,000 video tutorials. The software uses adaptive learning algorithms to deliver only appropriately challenging assignments. Students receive instant feedback and can access help through support videos, while teachers also receive insights from homework. One Head of Maths teaching at a school in the South of England states how they appreciate the way that the adaptive algorithms mean everyone gets all the answers correct, after several attempts sometimes, and yet everyone is challenged and feels pushed and even frustrated at times. Because the system provides a set of lessons, she writes how the role of teachers has changed: 'planning goes on things like tackling misconceptions, questioning, and individual students'. This teacher is very positive about the approach, writing that:

> The fact that every student gets personalised homework which is achievable for them but pushes them, is second to none. Also, being able to easily

> see what the whole class is getting wrong hugely helps with my planning. From [a] Head of Department point of view, the sheer volume of data to help monitor progress of students is amazing.[3]

### *Discussion of the 'teaching machine' grammar*

In Chapter 1 we claimed that the theory of educational technology is part of the wider field of educational theory, broadly defined as any theory offering answers to two key questions: 'what should we teach and learn?' and 'how should we teach and learn it?' Skinner's teaching machine approach implies a transmissional view of education also referred to as 'direct instruction'. This is the idea that we first define a curriculum of knowledge and skills that should be taught, before this body of knowledge is transmitted to students as efficiently and effectively as possible. For Skinner, the aim of education is measurable change in behaviour. However, more recently essentially the same grammar has been applied using more cognitivist theory, according to which the aim of education is said to be change in long-term memory (Sweller, 2005).

It has been proposed that some of the knowledge and skills required in the language, maths and science curriculums can be 'taught' effectively by teaching machines that adapt to learner responses (Kabudi et al., 2021). As Justin Reich (2020) writes, however, research indicates that evidence on the effectiveness of such approaches – particularly those used when learning goals are unclear and in domains that are not as well-structured – can be described as mixed at best. In future, such technology could be very significant to meeting educational needs, perhaps especially when expert teachers are not available. It might be very effective as an augmentation for classroom teaching when used for homework for example.

### *Artificial intelligence (AI) and the evolution of the teaching machine grammar*

From its inception, the teaching machine grammar has been associated with the ideal of artificial intelligence or 'AI'. Many complex definitions of AI are available in the literature. Essentially this is a kind of metaphor applied whenever technology does something that, if the same thing was done by a human, would be considered intelligent (Minsky, 1969). Digital teaching machines have always aspired to this kind of intelligence. Holmes and Tuomi (2022) outline the overlap in the history of teaching machines, often called intelligent tutoring systems (ITS) and AI applied to education (or AIED). They outline two main types of AIED: the more traditional expert systems that are programmed with knowledge to teach, and what they call data-driven AI which uses data-mining and anticipation. Expert systems which advertise themselves as AI-based are widely available. Like the Sparx example given above, they can provide feedback which adapts to the student and provide a dashboard with information for teachers on the progress of learners. A growing body of research evidence demonstrates the promising nature of such 'digital personalised learning' (DPL) approaches, potentially especially in under-resourced education contexts (Major et al., 2021). For instance, the potential efficacy of Ei's Mindspark in improving students' learning outcomes relative to control schools has been demonstrated in India (Muralidharan et al., 2019), although other evaluations of the same software reveal more mixed results (de Barros & Ganimian, 2023). These approaches fit well with the 'teaching machine' grammar. However, the more recent data-driven AI applications in education also show an evolution of the grammar. EIDU[4] for example is a content-agnostic DPL platform, allowing any provider to integrate new content, with the choice and order of content for each individual child optimised through personalisation algorithms. Autonomous digitised assessment tools enable real-time learning measurement which can be fed back to content providers and researchers, facilitating continuous improvement cycles (Friedberg, 2022). Through EIDU's Solver Platform, researchers have access to a vast, anonymised learning dataset to train and develop personalisation algorithms. These algorithms, deployed using a plug-in system, are automatically evaluated and selected based on their measured learning impact. The EIDU approach to DPL is currently being rigorously evaluated, including in classrooms in Kenya where it is closely aligned with the curriculum and teachers' pedagogy (Daltry et al., 2022).

A further example is AI language assistants, based on the use of Large Language Models (LLMs), which are now used in many educational applications to help students with writing and other activities in addition to providing a conversational tutor. The success of AI language assistants in providing realistic flexible conversations has breathed more life into the long tradition of trying to create general educational tutoring machines (Nye et al., 2014). Building on the teaching machine grammar, these ways of using technology move in a more dialogic direction, promoting learning as a dialogue with the voice of the technology which, here, is the summarised and synthesised voice of billions of words found on the internet. In a sense, AI language assistants produce a living version of the 'generalised other' referred to by George Herbert Mead as the voice of 'what everybody thinks' (Mead, 1934). Holmes and Tuomi suggest several categories for AIED that are emerging sub-genres and variations of the main 'teaching machine' grammar made possible by Generative AI technology. This includes educational chatbots, automatic formative assessment and automatic essay writing.

## Educational technology as 'a tool to think with'

Soon after Skinner first introduced his teaching machines into classrooms there was a turbulent time in the USA. A countercultural movement linked to opposition to the Vietnam War raised the question of agency in education, challenging the idea that education was about efficient instruction into a preset curriculum. An alternative vision was suggested that education should be about empowering students to be creative and to think for themselves (Hof, 2021). Seymour Papert arrived at MIT in 1963 as a professor after several years working with his mentor Jean Piaget in Geneva. Piaget developed constructivism: the theory that cognitive development, or learning to think, requires that students have an opportunity to construct meaning for themselves. Papert wrote about the role of educational technology in a way which located his work within this larger debate about agency in education. Papert explicitly associated himself with thinkers such as Ivan Illich and Paulo Freire who claimed that traditional models of schooling were essentially oppressive forms of control, and that they heavily relied on a 'banking model' involving teachers seeking to 'deposit' knowledge in the minds of learners. This was part of a movement seeking to design a model of education as the empowerment of students, either through 'deschooling society' (Illich, 1971) or through a 'pedagogy of liberation' (Freire, 1970/2000). Papert linked the

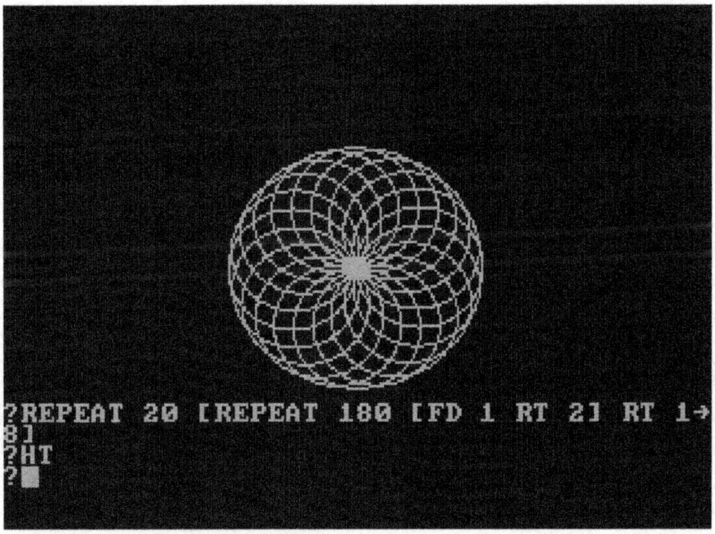


**FIGURE 4.2** Twenty geometric circles created in LOGO.

*Source:* Susam Pal, licensed under CC BY 4.0.

pedagogical affordances of digital technology with a radical rethinking of the role of education in society:

> In many schools today, the phrase 'computer-aided instruction' means making the computer teach the child. One might say the computer is being used to program the child. In my vision, the child programs the computer and, in doing so, both acquires a sense of mastery over a piece of the most modern and powerful technology and establishes an intimate contact with some of the deepest ideas from science, from mathematics, and from the art of intellectual model building.
>
> (Papert, 1980/2020, p. 5)

Papert argued that we should use technology to help students learn by enabling them to create their own representations of knowledge, rather than simply teaching them 'correct' answers. This approach, he suggested, can allow learners to build on their prior knowledge and interests and lead to deeper understanding. Papert explored this idea with the use of LOGO, a logic-based programming language designed to help students think about geometry. He began with the claim that every child understands three ideas: where they are in space, what it means to move in space, and what it means to tell other people about how to move in space. The use of LOGO programming, with virtual turtles on a screen, or robot turtles moving around on a classroom floor, built on this universal knowledge (Major, 2014). This enabled young students to build intuitive theories of geometry, through programming a robot turtle to move in circles for example, in a way argued by Papert to be more powerful than purely mathematical theories of geometry (see Figure 4.2). Such initial theories of geometry would, Papert claimed, eventually be replaced with more formal theories. However, Papert believed that students would feel more connected to geometry and find it more engaging if they were able to construct their own knowledge of it.

Papert believed that LOGO was a powerful tool for mediating between everyday experience and more 'formal' educated knowledge, but he did not claim that it was the only tool that could do this. It was just one example that could illustrate a more general principle. He envisioned a world in which there were hundreds of powerful representations spanning all kinds of knowledge. Carefully crafted by researchers and educators to become personally meaningful, the ultimate ambition was that such powerful representations might provide learners with easy access to a vast range of knowledge.

To Papert, personal computers were the perfect medium in which to engage students with powerful representations:

> Before computers there were very few good points of contact between what is most fundamental and engaging in mathematics and anything

> firmly planted in everyday life. But the computer – a mathematics speaking being in the midst of the everyday life of the home, school, and workplace – is able to provide such links. The challenge to education is to find ways to exploit them.
>
> (Papert, 1980/2020, p. 47)

Papert was interested in the role of computing in education more than the role of computers. He considered that writing down flowcharts and algorithms, which are concrete expressions of systematic procedures, could help students understand how the world works and how to reflect on their own actions. By encouraging students to write down algorithms as part of their learning, he believed we might help them to better learn and reflect concretely on their ideas, accelerating their construction of knowledge. He coined the now widely used term 'computational thinking' (Papert, 1980/2020, p. 182) and wanted students to learn just as much about algorithmic thinking as they did about numerical thinking. Thinking like a computer, combined with more powerful representations for making that thinking explicit, is a path, Papert claimed, to more efficient learning in every area:

> 'teaching without curriculum' does not mean spontaneous, free-form classrooms or simply 'leaving the child alone'. It means supporting children as they build their own intellectual structures with materials drawn from the surrounding culture. In this model, educational intervention means changing the culture, planting new constructive elements in it and eliminating noxious ones. This is a more ambitious undertaking than introducing a curriculum change . . .
>
> (Papert, 1980/2020, pp. 31–32)

Papert's vision did not do away with teachers but modified their role from knowledge transmitters to learning guides. Teachers were no longer to present knowledge and direct the acquisition of it, but rather were to facilitate learning and guide deeper understanding of concepts.

### *Constructionism versus constructivism*

Papert spent several years working with Piaget in Geneva before he arrived in the USA. The influence of Piaget's constructivist theory of learning can be seen in his approach. Piaget's work on constructivism proposes that children develop internal cognitive structures or mental models because of active learning. In contrast to the direct instruction favoured by the computer as teaching machine metaphor, constructivism claims that children and young people learn by actively creating meaning for themselves. It follows from this that they are the agents of their own learning and the teacher's role is not to teach directly but to facilitate this student-led learning. Papert is a constructivist like Piaget but with a key difference. Whereas Piaget used the term construction for abstract internal things like 'schemas' or 'cognitive structures', Papert uses it for things that are, in principle, publicly shared objects like computer programs that are built and played with together. Learning as building a shared external object together was a very new and different idea from the 'cognitive schema' model: this shift has consequences that we unpack later in this chapter. Piaget ignored the role of technology in learning but for Papert it becomes central. Papert called his approach constructionism to distinguish it from constructivism.

### *Making the abstract concrete*

According to evolutionary psychologist Geary discussed in Chapter 2, school learning is meant to be difficult. We need formal schooling, he claims, precisely because some kinds of knowledge are too hard to acquire naturally. Children learn to talk spontaneously, it is suggested, because humans have evolved for this. Mathematics is different, Geary writes. He suggests we want children to learn mathematics, but this is not possible without forcing them to make an effort that feels unnatural (Geary, 2008). Papert seems to implicitly accept this argument when claiming that the advent of personal computers changes everything. Following their invention, abstract knowledge can be learnt naturally through playing in computer-mediated environments. Algorithms and programming, Papert argues, enable the abstract world of formal knowledge to be inserted into the active play-life of the child. The main affordance for learning that computers offer us, Papert suggests, is making the abstract concrete. From having to learn mathematical formulae outside of any useful context he proposes that students instead learn to write algorithms that move turtles around the classroom floor. His vision is of students learning naturally by making things that work (Papert, 1980/2020).

### *An illustration of constructionist education*

To illustrate some of the themes of constructionism we have selected one small university-led study in a secondary school in Athens (Daskolia & Kynigos, 2012). This study is not meant to be representative of the whole approach, but intends to give a flavour of one possible way of using technology for constructionist teaching and learning.[5] It focused on teaching the concept of sustainability using a 'half-baked' microworld. Microworlds are simulations in software environments that allow students to build and manipulate objects within a system. The intention is that students will learn 'by doing' from these manipulations and interactions. A half-baked microworld involves some parameters within the system already being set up. In this case, a model of a city was designed to represent a way of life that is characterised by consumerism, hectic schedules and environmental unsustainability. This model considered factors such as energy consumption, financial resources, health and leisure activities. Students were given the challenge of engaging with the microworld, discussing any issues of sustainability raised, and then changing the parameters to create their own sustainable city.

This project took a group of 18 students two hours a week over 11 weeks. The published evaluation focuses on how students' talk and actions demonstrated new understanding about sustainability, as well as their ability to collaborate to create a new model of the city. The researchers claim that the 'microworld empowered the students to collaboratively articulate, display, and elaborate new ideas and to develop and negotiate alternative perspectives with the view to actively interpret a complex and fuzzy concept such as that of sustainability' (Daskolia & Kynigos, 2012).

### *Discussion of the 'tool to think with' grammar*

Papert had a significant influence on educational practice in several countries. There has been extensive research on the impact of his approach. Overall, published findings relating to the educational impact of using turtles and LOGO programming in primary schools have not been overly impressive (Wegerif, 2002). Evaluations suggest there is no clear evidence that students who learn to program using LOGO get better at general logical thinking. They do, of course, get better at programming using LOGO. But getting better at LOGO does not transfer to other areas beyond the context of the programming activities unless learners are explicitly taught by teachers how to bridge strategies from one context to the other. In other words, this approach can work, but it depends on the design of the pedagogy to explicitly bridge between contexts.

The ontological grammar of computers as teaching machines is clear: computers teach the children knowledge and skills leading to changes in their individual behaviour and/or long-term memories. The ontological grammar of Piaget's constructivism is also clear: children are active in learning how to think for themselves and as a result develop internal cognitive structures or mental models. However, when Papert introduces technology to Piaget's constructivist grammar this changes the grammar in a way that is no longer so easy to articulate. Papert's constructionist approach is often referred to as 'learning by making' and has had a big influence on the 'maker' movement (Papert, 1986; Schad & Jones, 2020). The objects that are being made, LOGO programs in the past but now more commonly robots and other devices, are usually public objects, and the making process itself is often collaborative (Konstantinou et al., 2021). Even where models are built alone by individuals, these individuals might compare their models and get feedback from others within a community. Papert often advocated collaborative learning. However, he writes about the learning theory behind constructionism using an essentially Piagetian ontological grammar. The impression given is that the best way for individual children to learn to build internal cognitive models, learning to become better at abstract logical thinking for example, is through building external publicly visible models often collaboratively with others. However, the use of technology here sets up a tension with this way of thinking about learning.

If a group works together with technology, who is the subject or agent that is learning? The group including the technology seems to be the most obvious answer. A group mind that is learning how to better think together, perhaps (Stahl, 2010). But this does not fit well with the claims made by Papert which focus more on individual learning benefits. Perhaps the idea then is that individuals learn best within a group that is also learning. This is plausible but raises challenges to any individualistic cognitive psychology of learning. For instance, what if some participate more than others? What if someone leaves the group? What if someone else joins? Does the group mind then change?

In the short case study given above as illustrative of constructionism in action, a group of students built a working model of a complex eco-system using computer code. The model of the eco-system that they constructed together therefore appears to be the main object of the learning activity. The educational theory claim of constructionism seems to be that this is the best way for individuals to build appropriate individual mental models. However, it is hard to see how this could be justified. The most efficient way to learn the mental model of a complex eco-system is not to start with the extra cognitive burden of learning a programming language or the intricacies of a specific micro-world. The grammar of constructionism seems to begin with the claim that individuals learn to think with the help of tools, but ends up in practice with a rather different grammar: groups plus technology learn how to produce technological objects together. What is most obviously being learnt is not a mental model but how to collaborate with others to build things that work. This might be exactly the kind of learning needed in the 'knowledge age', which is a claim in the work of Bereiter and Scardamalia which we consider next. However, looking at this through the lens of grammatical analysis, an approach to empirical philosophy often referred to as 'conceptual analysis', learning to collaborate to build machines that work is not the same as extending constructivism through the addition of digital technology that Papert proposed with his concept of constructionism.

## Educational technology as a 'learning environment'

The idea emerging from constructionism that the public model being built can become an object of learning, rather than just the private mental models of individual students, was elaborated by Bereiter (2005) using Popper's three-world theory. Popper proposed three ontological categories: subjective ideas in the minds of individuals, objective things in the public world, and objective or publicly shared ideas in knowledge objects like written theories or Papert's algorithm-based dynamic models. This idea radically changes the ontological grammar of constructivism which seemed to largely carry over into its offspring, constructionism. The object or goal of learning activities proposed with technology becomes clearly a real shared object, a public model or theory. For Bereiter, the real agent of learning is also collective, not individual, as students work together to produce better theories of how things work. The use of technology in education to create designed learning environments has led to a reconceptualisation of learning. Rather than focusing on individual knowledge or individual mental models, learning is seen as a social and collaborative process that involves the construction of collective knowledge objects. Also being learnt at the same time is the process of being good knowledge workers. This involves learning how to collaborate with others to build knowledge objects together.

At the University of Toronto in Canada during the 1980s, Marlene Scardamalia and Carl Bereiter applied their theory to create a kind of learning that they first called 'computer supported intentional learning' (CSILE) and then, more simply, 'knowledge building'. Later software called Knowledge Forum® was developed and is still being used globally in the 2020s. The model intends to reproduce, in a scaffolded form, how actual knowledge is created in the 'real world' by communities of researchers. Marlene writes about this invention:

> The heart of CSILE/Knowledge Forum is a multimedia community knowledge space. In the form of notes, participants contribute theories, working models, plans, evidence, reference material, and so forth to this shared space. The software provides knowledge building supports both in the creation of these notes and in the ways they are displayed, linked, and made objects of further work. Revisions, elaborations, and reorganizations over time provide a record of group advances, like the accumulation of research advances in a scholarly discipline.
>
> (Scardamalia, 2004)

Students often work together in small groups to come up with questions and then inquire into these together by making hypotheses and evaluating arguments and evidence (Zhang et al., 2009). Although there are many face-to-face discussions, the claims and evidence for them are uploaded in the form of 'notes' in the shared forum space.

The work of Professor Carol Chan and a team at Hong Kong University can help to exemplify this. In building the shared knowledge map depicted in Figure 4.3, students are helped by guides or 'scaffolds' – see the row of buttons on the left-hand side of the figure. These can be customised depending

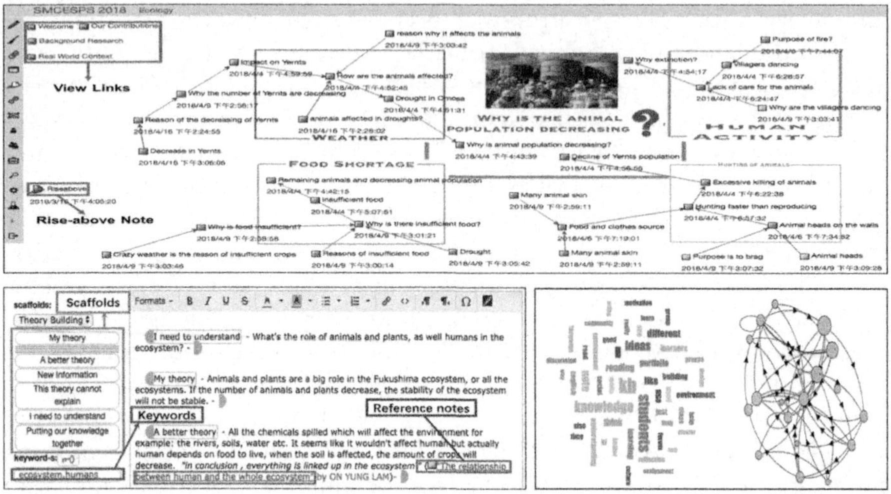


**FIGURE 4.3** Knowledge Forum features. View as collaborative workspace (top); Note with scaffolds, keywords and references (bottom left); Embedded assessment tools (bottom right).

*Source:* Prof Carol Chan & colleagues at Faculty of Education, University of Hong Kong (Chan et al., 2019).

on the topic and the age of learners, but are based on what Bereiter and Scardamalia called 'design-mode' thinking to improve ideas: scaffolds like 'my theory', 'this theory cannot explain' and 'a better theory' (Bereiter & Scardamalia, 2003). Of particular interest is one special scaffold: the 'rise-above' button. Marlene writes of this concept:

> the most constructive way of dealing with divergent or opposing ideas is not to decide on a winner or a compromise position but rather to create a new idea that preserves the value of the competing ideas while 'rising above' their incompatibilities. In the simplest cases **a rise-above** may be simply a summary or distillation; in the most compelling cases, the rise-above presents a new idea that all the participants can recognize as an advance over their previous ideas.
>
> (Scardamalia, 2004)

A key aspect of rise-above is to encapsulate an area of dialogue. For instance, other contributions can be dragged and dropped into the rise-above button such that it is seen to represent a whole network of nodes. This is useful to simplify an overly complex map. However, much more than this, the rise-above button is typically used to express a new insight that integrates the debate so far by making sense of it.

### *An illustration of the learning environment approach*

CSILE/Knowledge Forum has been around for over 30 years and if you search you can find many examples of maps and 'rise-above' moves online. The examples seem to be mostly about science topics with students exploring questions that they themselves ask such as 'why does it rain?' or 'why are leaves green?' But this approach is not limited to science or maths. Recently in Hong Kong, a class of high school students aged 15 to 16 explored the question: 'what is design?' This inquiry included dialogue, conducted within the Knowledge Forum system, with design professionals and academics who were physically located outside of the classroom. The students began by focusing on the idea that design is about 'solving problems', but increasingly explored the overlap between design and self-expression through art. Their final 'rise-above' move was to recognise that good design combined both utilitarian problem solving and a more artistic expression of a point of view on reality (Yang et al., 2016).

### *Discussion of the 'learning environment' grammar*

The idea that technology can offer a learning environment for groups of students is compatible with the idea of technology as offering tools for thinking. However, this tends in practice to change the ontological grammar in the direction of giving more agency to the technology. The 'teaching machine' metaphor sees technology as an agent directly teaching the students. The 'tool to think with' metaphor meanwhile seeks to give agency back to the students. The intentional learning environment metaphor of Knowledge Forum is a combination of the two. Designed features like scaffolds for thinking, for example the 'rise-above' button, indirectly offer a guide for learning and for thinking. The agency of the learning is now more self-consciously distributed between the humans and the technology working together.

In the case of Knowledge Forum, the dominant metaphor for learning shifts from acquisition of knowledge and skills by individuals or groups to participation in knowledge building processes within communities. Students who use Knowledge Forum are expected to learn ways of thinking, and bodies of knowledge, by trying to understand something together. More fundamentally they are learning to construct knowledge with others. This is seen as a central learning aim for the knowledge society.

The collective knowledge building approach is explicitly a form of social constructivism (Bereiter, 2005). Social constructivism is often argued to offer a good model of how we learn new knowledge as a society. However, this does not mean that it is obviously the best way to understand how individuals learn new knowledge, or at least that is a claim made in an influential critique of this approach to education (Sweller et al., 2007). Social constructivism might not offer the most efficient way to teach content knowledge in a well-structured knowledge domain such as aspects of mathematics. It is often, however, proposed as the best way to learn more holistically. This includes in a way that encompasses the identities and values needed in all areas of enquiry as well as the dispositions and complex competences required such as teamwork and innovation (Shaffer, 2006).

One of the main criticisms of social constructivism in action is that individuals can get left behind even if the group progresses. This is one reason to argue for frequent individual tests of learning. David Williamson Shaffer, who created intentional learning environments in the form of collaborative role-play games (Shaffer, 2006), suggests a need for the collection of more specific data on individual learning (Shaffer, 2017). The 'big data' approach of what Shaffer calls 'epistemic network analysis' enables the development of individuals to be tracked on any number of dimensions, so long as these can be specified in ways that are visible in data captured. The use of learning analytics might therefore be well placed to explore the relationship between the nature of knowledge, the nature of teaching and learning, and assessment where discourse-centric technologies are used (Knight et al., 2014).

### *AI and learning environments*

The design of digital learning environments potentially allows for a combination of active teaching and more passive discovery learning, which has resulted in a hybrid form that combines the 'teaching machine' grammar with the 'tools for thinking' constructionist grammar. Mavrikis and Holmes (2019) refer to this hybrid as 'intelligent learning environments', providing an alternative to the step-by-step approach adopted by intelligent tutoring systems and dialogue-based tutoring systems. Rather than following a sequence, students are encouraged to actively explore the learning environment to construct their own understanding. The criticisms of this kind of discovery learning approach which we referred to earlier (e.g., Sweller et al., 2007) are then addressed using AI to provide feedback, point out misconceptions, and propose alternative approaches. Commercial examples are somewhat hard to find but one research example is FractionsLab (Mavrikis & Holmes, 2019), which is an environment that combines exploration of a 'fractions world' with open-ended discovery tasks and appropriate expert tutoring in how to work with fractions.

## Discussion

In this chapter we applied the idea of ontological grammar as a conceptual tool to illuminate aspects of how educational technology has been, and is being, imagined as well as how it has been, and is being, used. We focused on three 'grammars' of educational technology: 'teaching machines', 'tools to think with' and 'learning environments'. Our account was in historical order. Skinner's teaching machine behaviourist approach, then Papert's constructionism (intended as a challenge to Skinner), before Bereiter and Scardamalia's learning environments and social constructionism (which built on and extended ideas from Papert). Some of this historical ordering stems from developments in technology. Scardamalia and Bereiter's first 'Computer Supported Intentional Learning Environment' or 'CSILE' (which developed into 'Knowledge Forum') could not have been built in the 1960s. But this connection to the development of technology does not imply a value hierarchy. All these approaches are still in use today and still evolving. Indeed, the first ontological grammar discussed, the idea of technology as a teaching machine, is now being widely implemented in the form of adaptive learning systems often labelled as AI or 'digital personalised learning', that seem to increasingly offer promising results in some specific areas of education. These grammars also continue to constantly evolve. Recent developments in Generative AI and LLM technology, for instance, appear to be leading to new forms of the teaching machine grammar. These involve more flexible human-like dialogues and the generation of formative assessment tests and essays that students can use to evaluate their own progress.

We see all these different grammars as competing for attention in the long-term dialogue of educational technology. Empirical research as to how effective they are in achieving their goals is certainly relevant, and we cite some of this. Such evidence alone is not, however, enough to help us choose the best foundation for design because each grammar defines its own criteria of success and failure. If, for example, the evidence shows that Papert's approach does not help students to perform well on 'high-stakes' standardised tests, some followers of Papert might claim that this was not the intention in the first place, given this instead aims to develop competencies such as personal creativity (Agalianos et al., 2001). Although the educational value of different grammars cannot be directly tested, they are always being indirectly evaluated by the perceived success or failure of educational technologies that are inspired by them.

### *Prompts towards a dialogic foundation for the design and use of educational technology*

These three grammars or ways of framing educational technology can also be seen as theories of education that shape the design and use of educational technology. Sometimes these theories are implicit, such as the teaching machine metaphor, and sometimes they are explicit, such as Papert's constructionism. They are education theories because they offer different answers to the two big questions of education: 'what should we teach and learn?' and 'how should we teach and learn it?' Seen as theories, however, they are not precise enough to be the 'close-to-practice' theory we might call a design framework because they do not sufficiently constrain the possible design choices. Each theory could support a wide variety of practical educational technology designs. Instead, these grammars are examples of what we defined in Chapter 1 as foundations for design. That is, different ways of thinking about education, technology and values which may shape the design of educational technology. Different foundations for design can make certain approaches to designing and implementing educational technology seem obvious or even inevitable, while others may make them seem unthinkable or at least not worth considering.

The continued success of the 'computer as teaching machine' grammar, now reinvigorated by many applications claiming to be based on AI, suggests the important role educational technology can potentially play in efficiently transmitting relatively established knowledge in a personalised way that adapts to each learner. The use of LLMs has enabled chat-like interfaces that can be used as personal tutors in many areas of the curriculum, most notably so far in language learning and the learning of coding (Holmes & Tuomi, 2022). We can call this education as teaching 'the dialogue so far' (Phillipson & Wegerif, 2016). LLMs are very good at picking up what the dialogue so far is, in any area of human activity using web-crawlers. They can then use this information to communicate summaries coherently in response to questions.

Continued educational interest in understanding and using technology to provide flexible tools to think with suggests the important role educational technology can play in engaging and empowering new voices. Moving from playing digital games to designing digital games can, for some young people, be a way to support the development of a sense of their own self-identity as creative and efficacious (Kafai & Burke, 2015).

Designing online-mediated environments, to support collaborative peer-to-peer learning as Scardamalia and Bereiter did, suggests educational technology can play a role in inducting individual voices to participate in collective creativity and collective intelligence through peer-to-peer learning networks or online-mediated communities of inquiry. To be effective and valuable in this collaborative and dialogic process of learning together with technology – or 'technology as a learning environment' approach – individual voices need to acquire the confidence to speak, through activities that engage them (like those proposed by the 'technology as thinking tool' approach), in addition to acquiring the knowledge required to make that discussion useful (which can be gained using the 'technology as teaching machine' approach). A dialogic foundation for design could potentially therefore provide a coherent way of integrating the most successful aspects of all three grammars considered: empowering voices, expanding knowledge, and connecting voices together in online-mediated peer-to-peer learning communities. We look further at this possible integrated vision for design with technology in the next chapter.

# 5

# STEPS TOWARDS A 'DIALOGIC' GRAMMAR

*The real world just doesn't offer up as easily the carefully designed pleasures, the thrilling challenges, and the powerful social bonding afforded by virtual environments. Reality doesn't motivate us as effectively. Reality isn't engineered to maximize our potential. Reality wasn't designed from the bottom up to make us happy.*

Jane McGonigal (2011)

*Learning is transformed into education only when it involves the self-consciousness and the identity of the learner.*

Krassimir Stojanov (2017, p. i)

## Introduction

The previous chapter explored three grammars of educational technology use: technology as a teaching machine, as a tool for thinking and as a learning environment. This investigation raised the problem of who or what is learning: the individual, the group or the society. In this chapter, we continue our investigation with a specific focus on the question of who or what is learning. We consider three grammars of educational technology specifically informed by the internet. In each case, we examine strengths and weaknesses and argue that these point to a new way of understanding the role of educational technology, which we call a 'dialogic' grammar or a 'dialogic foundation' for the design of educational technology.

DOI: 10.4324/9781003198499-5

### Learning through participation in 'online mediated communities of practice'

The online mediated community of practice approach is inspired by methods of education found in oral communities. Ethnographer Jean Lave developed this theory of learning through research on participation in a community of tailors in a Liberian tailor shop (Lave, 1977). In their seminal publication, 'Situated learning: Legitimate peripheral participation', Lave and her educational technologist collaborator Etienne Wenger argued that learning is 'increasing participation in communities of practice' (Lave & Wenger, 1991, p. 49). Wenger has since worked to develop and apply the idea of communities of practice (CoPs) in blended and online learning (see Smith et al., 2017). However, online and internet-mediated CoPs are different in significant ways from education in oral cultures: everything may be recorded and some limitations of situatedness in space and time found in face-to-face communities can be overcome. This is because communication within an online community can be asynchronous (i.e., not occurring at the same time) and because such a community may be relatively unbounded (involving potentially millions of users, and certainly many more than could be supported in a face-to-face community).

Moving online implies a new kind of educational dialogue. Posting a question in a community forum often means 'talking' to an unknown number of readers, potentially including many years into the future. Thus, it implies a relationship with an open horizon of otherness rather than with specific individuals or clearly bounded groups. The responses that come back might be from unique individuals. Or they might reflect a synthesis of responses to similar questions over time, a kind of generalised voice that is constantly developing. Engaging in dialogue with an AI language assistant also may imply participation in a community of potentially billions of users whose messages have been trawled and processed to convert them into a single voice able to respond to any question. It seems possible then that, with internet communities, the main educational affordances of print – recorded representations that transcend the limitations of space and time – are preserved. In addition, some of the educational affordances of orality, relationship, community and participation in a dynamic real-world context may be returned to and extended.

Wenger (1998) argues that individuals' engagement in a CoP always entails a negotiation of meaning. This process of negotiation of meaning can be reasonably called dialogue when it leads to learning through mutual engagement (see Chapter 1). However, he extends this understanding of dialogue in an interesting direction by writing about the tension and dynamic negotiation between two processes: *participation* and *reification*. Participation involves engaging in a CoP and interacting with others. Reification involves producing artefacts (such as tools, words, symbols, rules, documents, concepts, theories and so on) around which members of the community can negotiate and organise meaning. Participation and reification can work together to progress learning. For instance, when an individual reads about an idea in a text – a form of reification – but that idea remains unclear, peers who better grasp the idea may support development of the individual's understanding through dialogue (a form of participation). Similarly, designing an idea through writing, which is another form of reification, may help to deepen and prolong understanding in a way that is more impactful than a short-term dialogue.

Wenger (2010) also argued that through participation and reification over time, participants of a CoP develop 'a set of criteria and expectations by which they recognize membership' (p. 180). These include:

- A joint enterprise – a collective understanding of what the purpose of the community is.
- Mutual engagement – interacting and establishing norms, expectations and ground rules for interaction.
- A shared repertoire – developing and using a set of communal resources, such as language, artefacts, tools, concepts, methods, standards.

### *MIT's 'Scratch' as an online mediated community of practice*

The educational grammar of online CoPs has been particularly influential in professional communities, for example, the many online teacher CoPs (Lantz-Andersson et al., 2018). We have chosen, however, to look at MIT's successful Scratch online coding community for young people. We have done this partly because Scratch builds on and develops Papert's constructionism, and partly because we admire it as a successful example of a university-initiated educational design research project that has had significant impact.

Scratch is a high-level, block-based visual programming language supported by a community of users. Aimed primarily at school-age learners, although used by many more, founding director Mitch Resnick – the LEGO Papert Professor of Learning Research – suggests Scratch might be one way to fulfil Papert's ideas (Resnick, 2017). If so, then Papert's ideas have been taken in a very social direction. Although Wenger is not to our knowledge explicitly referenced by the founders of Scratch, in our view Scratch provides an example of learning through participation in an online CoP. Launched in 2007 as a project of Papert's former university MIT, Scratch has been enthusiastically taken up by many users worldwide. As we write, community statistics on Scratch's official website demonstrate over 130 million Scratch projects have been shared by over 110 million registered users. Soon a billion comments will have been posted on the Scratch forums.

Perhaps the best way to understand how the learning works in this context is to adopt a first-person perspective. Thomas and Brown (2011) offer the example of Sam, aged 9, who became engaged in making simple games using Scratch. When Sam uploads his programs, others comment and borrow the code in order to remix it, but with a tag that shows how their new version was based on Sam's original. When Sam likes programs, he downloads the code and gets into conversations with the maker about remixing it. This approach offers an engaging way to learn programming. However, more than that, Sam has engaged in a process of learning from others. Thomas and Brown report how Sam told them the single most important thing he learnt was 'not to be mean' and to make sure that Scratch users comment on something good when they come across it. What he looked for in a program was 'something really cool you could never know yourself'.

Scratch seems to illustrate the possibility of a social networking approach to education. Social networking sites like Facebook and Twitter (renamed X), and the communities around programming languages like 'R' and Python, Pythondiscord.com for example, provide opportunities for the expansion of personal networks beyond the geographical limitations of co-present face-to-face groups. Because they support the creation and dissemination of user-generated content, social networking sites offer a shift from viewing the internet as a resource for information retrieval to a participatory peer learning platform (Churcher et al., 2014). By providing opportunities for peer-to-peer learning this can, some claim, foster a more participatory culture, where members believe their contributions matter in addition to making them feel socially connected to each other (Cayari, 2011).

Scratch brings to life the arguments of Dede (2008), Wegerif (2013) and others that the advent of the internet changes the possibilities of education from classic 'one-to-many' teaching and learning to a 'peer-to-peer' communal creation and knowledge sharing model. Wikipedia is often held up as a successful example of this new epistemology for education. On Wikipedia users are both consumers and producers, in 'a dynamic and ever-expanding repository of shareable, communal information' (McLoughlin & Lee, 2007, p. 667). The same could be said of Scratch.

Although Scratch supports a participatory type of learning, it is not incompatible with more traditional schooling and the more directive teaching and learning associated with courses with a fixed curriculum. Sam, for example, is learning through participation in Scratch's online CoP. However, when he wanted to learn new programming skills, he signed up for particular short courses. Moreover, while Scratch is designed as an open community and learning environment, it is also widely used by schools to deliver many aspects of the computing curriculum.

### *Discussion of the 'online mediated communities of practice' grammar*

Within CoPs, individual learning is understood as a trajectory of identity change from 'newcomer' to 'old-timer' (Wenger, 2010). In other words, individual learning in this context can be understood as an aspect of collective self-reproduction, or what can be called 'autopoiesis' (see Chapter 7). Any CoP needs to renew itself by training new members. This grammar helps to unpack the lack of clarity over the question of who or what is learning which we found with Papert's constructionism and Bereiter and Scardamalia's online learning environments. With Lave and Wenger, the community is the primary agent of change. Individuals learn by participating in the community's activities, and the community's identity is maintained through the process of dynamic reproduction.[1]

Communities also learn over time, possibly in response to a changing environment. A tailor shop, for example, might monitor changing fashions and respond with new designs. But some communities are dedicated more consciously to the goal of learning. The community of climate change researchers for example, which could also be called an online mediated learning community. Wenger's account of the dynamic oscillation between participation and reification is helpful in showing how technologies can serve as the link between individual and collective learning. Any reification move, such as writing things down or building ideas into a model, serves as a ratchet turning learning into something solid that can be revisited and re-animated.[2] For an individual like Sam, learning occurs when ideas from chats are reified into code and then revisited in dialogue to question and develop the ideas. But as individuals learn by building ideas into explicit external models, so the collective learns, and the number and quality of shared models increases for the next generation of learners.

One weakness with CoP theory is the idea of community itself. The idea of a community of learners can seem unproblematic when the medium of learning is oral communication, as dialogues are typically located in space and time and their reach is limited to physically present participants. In oral societies 'the community' is most often naturally limited to those who regularly talk together face-to-face. However, boundaries around communities are harder to define when we shift online. This makes it more challenging to sustain the idea of education as an aspect of the self-reproduction of bounded communities.

Another problem from an educational point of view is the failure to consider the values that are implied by the claim that learning is simply what communities do. This approach addresses the educational question of how we should teach and learn, as it suggests we should teach and learn through participation in CoPs. However, it does not provide an answer to the more fundamental educational question of *what* we should teach and learn. There are many CoPs and not all of them are equally 'good' or equally 'useful', so how do we decide between them?

We consider these two issues with CoP theory in the discussion at the end of the chapter. First, we look at an approach to learning that is not so much an explicit theory of education, but more a growing practice having an impact on education: learning through playing online role-play games.

## Learning through online role-play games

This chapter begins with a quotation from Jane McGonigal on the power of games to transform reality. Jane's 2010 TED Talk 'Gaming can make a better world' has over 6 million views.[3] She is perhaps best known as the designer of serious games in which thousands of participants join together online to tackle 'real-world' problems. We discuss one of these, a future-oriented game, in Chapter 9. Jane's games tend to focus less on knowledge and more on virtues and dispositions:

> When we're in game worlds, I believe that many of us become the best version of ourselves: the most likely to help at a moment's notice. The most likely to stick with a problem as long as it takes. To get up after failure and try again.[4]

Her case study of the game 'Why I Love Bees' argues that the game created a virtual collective intelligence that helped to teach collective intelligence to players. The essence of the game was a fragmented mystery that players had to reconstruct by collaborating. Interesting here is the claim that games can be used to teach the transferrable skills and dispositions often referred to as 'future skills' (Kotsiou et al., 2022).

James Paul Gee (2003) describes the extraordinary capacity that some games have, including commercial games, to stimulate students to learn quantities of facts in a way difficult for teachers to reproduce in classrooms. From analysing how successful online multiplayer games work to facilitate learning, he abstracted design principles that can be applied to teaching and learning more generally. These include forms of embodied learning that are not typically found in print-based education, such as players developing a sense of identity through inhabiting an avatar or on-screen character. Games can encourage bold decision-making in a 'low stakes' environment, empowering players to take risks. The level of challenge encountered may also be carefully calibrated to be engaging and stimulating, without being too frustrating or alienating. In these ways, according to Gee, games encourage learning through performance and the acquisition of competence through achieving things. This contrasts with, as seems to be common in school, being taught knowledge and skills independently of any context of use.

David Williamson Shaffer, who worked with Gee at the University of Wisconsin-Madison, built on these insights to focus on how games can be used as a kind of simulation to induct students into the ways of thinking found in professions including science, engineering and design. His team developed 'Virtual Internships' to explore and illustrate this new approach to education. These Virtual Internships are adaptive, complex and realistic online simulations with interactive mentoring. Students work in teams to tackle challenging real-world problems requiring innovative solutions. They conduct research and interview clients before developing and testing prototypes. Working together, students consider the importance of technical, commercial and ethical factors. They 'learn by doing', with access to professional resources and a mentor who can guide individual learning processes. Further, teachers can customise the learning scenarios and analytics that model students' performance. Shaffer and his team suggest that Virtual Internships can help students learn to be professionals in the real world by providing them with opportunities to develop their identities, values, knowledge and skills. Shaffer calls this acquiring an 'epistemic frame' which is defined 'as the ways of knowing, of deciding what is worth knowing, and of adding to the collective body of knowledge and understanding of a community of practice' (Shaffer, 2006, p. 223). Positive outcomes include female undergraduates becoming more motivated to pursue an engineering degree than those on traditional engineering courses (Chesler et al., 2013) and students successfully developing the identity and habits of mind of professional engineers (Arastoopour et al., 2016). Other research suggests the potential value of introducing a similar model of simulated internships in schools to better engage learners with the 'world of work' (Major, Twiner et al., 2022).

### *Commentary on the 'grammar' of learning through online role-play games*

Sometimes formal schooling seems to take the form of a kind of game. Points may be awarded for success and penalties for failure. There can also be competition for prizes at a group as well as individual level. But the interesting claim that game designer Jane McGonigal makes is that, if we consider formal education as a game, then we could design it better. Replacing the whole of education with massive multi-user online simulations is an exciting idea but probably not what McGonigal is proposing. Her claim is more that games can enhance real-world experience and that they should be integrated into education in a hybrid mixed reality way.

One issue which has been raised as a possible criticism of gaming in education is the problem of who designs the games and why? Despite the strong constructionist tradition of students learning through designing games (Kafai & Burke, 2015), the grammar of gaming is mostly that someone else designs the game and then learners play it. Games embed the values of their designers in ways that, in the words of Papert quoted earlier, might be seen as programming how users behave. This is a criticism made of one of McGonigal's games created for the World Bank to encourage social enterprise to solve global problems. The reviewer raises the point that while in its own terms the game worked to inspire thinking about start-up organisations that both make money and solve real-world problems, this approach to development through capitalism is controversial and yet was embedded into the game in a way that made it impossible to question (Waddington, 2013). This critique builds on the issue of constraints imposed by technology designs introduced in Chapter 3. We also consider this in the next chapter when exploring Heidegger's claim that modern technology is a way of 'enframing' and limiting the possibilities of human thought and action.

## Connectivism: Learning as networking

'Connectivism' is claimed to be the first new theory of learning to emerge in the Internet Age. The theory came out of practice. In 2008, George Siemens and Stephen Downes taught a course on Connectivism and Connective Knowledge at the University of Manitoba. The course was offered both online and in-person, with 25 students registered for the in-person course and over 2000 students taking the online version for free. This used various technologies including online broadcasting (RSS feeds), Second Life, blog posts in Moodle, and synchronous online meetings. These technologies supported processes to facilitate learning such as selecting and ordering resources (using tools like Flipboard) and creating and sharing content (using social media like YouTube and Flickr).

This 2008 course was described as a MOOC (i.e., a massive open online course; Cormier & Siemens, 2010). As MOOCs were later developed using traditional 'transmission' pedagogies, this first MOOC was retrospectively called a cMOOC (Connectivist MOOC). This in contrast to the kind of MOOCs run by EdX (created by MIT) and Coursera (originating out of Stanford) which were labelled as xMOOCs (eXtended MOOC based on a traditional university course model). What makes cMOOCs different is the theory of connectivism created by Siemens and Downes (Downes, 2012; Siemens, 2005). This builds on the new affordances of the internet for education, viewing learning as networking and emphasising the ability to traverse networks and integrate distributed knowledge.

Although MOOCs were initially the subject of much media attention, concerns have been raised about factors such as low completion rates. For example, an influential study by Jordan (2014) found that only 6.5% of learners completed MOOC courses. Nonetheless, research has shown that learning in cMOOCs used in Higher Education is self-organised; learners control the environment and participate in the flow and generation of knowledge by creating and sharing their own content and digital artefacts through social technologies (Saadatmand & Kumpulainen, 2014). Siemens (2005) outlines connectivism as a number of principles including that 'learning is a process of connecting specialised nodes or information sources' and that 'currency (i.e., accurate, up-to-date knowledge) is the intent of all connectivist learning activities'. Responding to critics arguing that this is not really a new theory but rather a version of social constructivism, Downes makes a clear distinction between constructivism and connectivism[5]:

> In connectivism, a phrase like 'constructing meaning' makes no sense. Connections form naturally, through a process of association, and are not 'constructed' through some sort of intentional action . . . Hence, in connectivism, there is no real concept of transferring knowledge, making knowledge, or building knowledge.

This is a very radical claim. It challenges the cognitivist bias that Downes claims lies behind all previous theories of learning. Connectivism suggests that learning is not just about memories in minds, but is also about real structures in the world. Non-human systems, such as machine learning programs and simple life-forms like slime-mold, can also learn to connect different sources of knowledge more efficiently in a way that helps them perform functions better (Alexander et al., 2021). According to connectivism theory, knowledge is not propositional, but is about constructing and traversing real networks. Learning then is suggested to be about growing ourselves and our society in more connected ways. According to Downes (2012) this implies a pedagogy that describes:

1 'Successful' networks (Downes argues these are characterised by diversity, autonomy, openness and connectivity).
2 How to build such networks, both in the individual and in society (specifically Downes refers to the teacher's role as modelling and demonstrating and the student's role as practising and reflecting).

### *Commentary on the grammar of 'connectivist' learning*

Both the strength and weakness of connectivism as a theory of learning can be said to be the simplicity of its grammar: an ontology of nodes and links. The answer offered to the first educational question (what we should teach and learn) is expanding networks of nodes and links. The answer to the second question (how we should teach and learn) is helping students to expand networks of nodes and links. Linking nodes might explain how some computer programs learn, after all, connectivism owes a debt to connectionism or building artificial neural networks that mimic some aspects of how the brain learns (Hinton, 1990). It might also illuminate some kinds of cognition found in nature, how slime-mold learns for example (Jabr & Rothschild, 2012). But human interactions that lead to learning are not comparable to nodes being linked. The idea of learning as dialogue, which we introduced in Chapter 1, can be applied here to illustrate the problem. Each participant in a dialogue has a kind of 'internal' mental model of other 'external' participants they are in dialogue with. Participants also share a joint sense of purpose for the dialogue (i.e., a joint intention that is the cause of the dialogue and also the aim or 'telos' of the dialogue). Viewed from the outside, a dialogue could appear to be a network of nodes and links. For instance, 'nodes' as voices or perspectives and 'links' as the relationships between them. But in a dialogue, each voice or perspective must expand to include the other participants. This creates a shared 'dialogic space' that includes other voices and perspectives without reducing them. Furthermore, at the same time as listening to the voice of the other in a dialogue, participants find themselves reflecting on, and changing their own thoughts and behaviour as if from the perspective of a third party or 'witness' position (Wegerif, 2013). It is from this expanded self-consciousness that we learn to see from new perspectives and become 'bigger' than we were. Whilst machines and slime-molds can 'learn' simply by making links, human learning requires expanding conscious awareness of differences within a dialogue. This includes how these differences relate to the learning goal or the intention that initiated and frames the dialogue, as well as the changing identity of the learners that goes with this expansion.

The idea of dialogic education has some overlap with the idea of education as networking, but it goes further by considering how learners expand their identity to include other voices. Dialogic education is about using the network to its full potential so that the network becomes a launching pad for new, more inclusive understanding. Perhaps this is what Siemens means when he writes that the 'ability to see connections between fields, ideas, and concepts is a core skill' (2005). However, this claim seems to be incompatible with his further claim that the same kind of model of human learning is found in computer learning, or with Downes' attempts to make all talk of meaning, knowledge and consciousness redundant.

To provide an example of how a dialogic theory of educational technology builds on connectivism and makes sense of it, let us consider how *Pol.is* works (available at https://pol.is). Pol.is is described as an AI-supported online debate and decision-making system that has been used successfully in many contexts, perhaps most famously in Taiwan where it was introduced by digital minister Audrey Tang to improve democratic decision making (Chang, 2021). Pol.is maps where participants 'are' in a dialogue, generating a kind of network with nodes being opinion statements made by participants. This map allows participants to see if they share opinions, if they are at an extreme, and exactly what they agree and disagree upon with others. In practice, Pol.is encourages people to converge on a shared solution through dialogue. This involves deepening understanding of divisive issues and valuing creative emergent solutions.

When an individual writes an opinion in a Pol.is debate, they naturally focus on their unique individual thoughts and experience. They identify themselves as a node in the network through a unique 'token'. However, stepping back and looking at the network, participants shift perspective to see themselves as if from the whole dialogue community. This process of participating in a Pol.is debate can lead to the development of a more dialogic identity, one featuring both 'my voice on the inside' (talking outwards but also able to view the dialogue as a whole), as well as from 'the outside looking in' (to locate my voice as one voice amongst others). In this process, an individual does not lose their identity in the collective, but they expand their sense of identity to consider the point of view of the collective. Participants become more dialogic selves – double-voiced – where 'self' is not a static 'thing' but a dynamic process, a continuous dialogue between inside and outside points of view.

## Working towards a 'dialogic' grammar for educational technology

The previous chapter, Chapter 4, concluded with the problem of how to reconcile individual learning with collective learning. As discussed earlier, Papert's constructionism involves building models which are in principle public artefacts visible to, and shareable with, others. We argued that this is not a good model for explaining learning if learning is thought of as about 'cognitive schemas' in individual brains. Instead, it leads to and supports a new model of learning: learning as communities learning to build shared objects together. The grammar of constructionism is, we argue, not clear because of the tension between individual learning and collective learning. Learning as participation in online mediated CoPs resolves this tension by putting the agency for learning in the community. The learning of individuals moving from 'outsider' status to 'insider' status is an aspect of the self-reproduction of the community. There is no tension here between individual learning and collective learning since these are aspects of the same process: the collective learns as individuals learn and, at least in the initial version of the theory, individuals learn how to embody the collective as an expert or 'old-timer'.

Technology plays a central role in CoP learning by providing a kind of 'ratchet' for learning, that is a device that allows continuous movement 'up a level' in one direction while preventing movement in the opposite direction. Once something is learnt actively through participation, it is converted into a durable object that can be built on in the next round of active participatory learning.

One conceptual or grammatical problem with CoP theory is that communities have no firm natural boundaries. This is especially evident when we look at online communities. Ultimately, if there are no fixed boundaries, then the idea of a community that is learning perhaps points to the unbounded whole of the internet. This means that anyone, anywhere, at any time could arguably read a message and respond thereby joining the learning community. This rather vague idea of 'the internet as a whole as the learning community' is now partially embodied in dialogues with an increasing number of Large Language Models trained on massive amounts of data trawled on the internet.

This conceptual problem of defining community is linked to the other educational problem we discussed, which is a failure to answer the question 'what should we teach and learn?' Describing how people learn is not the same as offering a theory of education. Any theory of education must address the values question of what we should teach and learn, and why (i.e., the implied question of intention and purpose). Learning through increasing participation is a similar process in a violent and immoral criminal gang as it is in a Buddhist monastery or in a state-funded primary school. In a school, however, the curriculum taught explicitly and implicitly needs to be justified. That process of justification requires an educational theory. CoP does not provide educational theory because it does not tell us what we should teach and learn.

The resolution to both problems, the problem of defining 'community' and the problem of justifying the guiding purpose of education, can perhaps be approached by applying an element of dialogic theory, specifically the notion of the 'witness' in a dialogue. Communities are not isolated from each other but can engage in dialogue together. In the 'dialogic gap' between communities, a third voice emerges that, when the dialogue is successful, seems to include both communities and finds a creative way to resolve tensions between them. This dialogue between communities leads to a vertical dimension for education. The horizontal dimension is learning to join specific communities by developing the specific knowledge, skills, values and identity required by each community. The vertical dimension is learning to question, compare, think critically and select between alternative views. The answer to the question of what should we teach and learn is not only how to join communities and succeed in them, but also how to question them and how to make wise choices between competing community demands (Alexander, 2015).

This idea of a vertical dimension of education based on the ideal of dialogue between communities only works because communities are not closed off, but rather inhabit a shared meaning space. People do not only act and learn in one community, they act and learn across many communities. Different communities interact and compete for attention in a single shared meaning space that has many strands but no fixed impermeable boundaries. In a sense, we are all always already members of the community of everything, or, as Alphonso Lingis (1994) memorably puts it, members of 'the community of those who have nothing in common'.

This possible solution to the grammatical problems of constructionism and CoP theory leads us in the direction of connectivism. For connectivism, the aim of learning is not to build individual knowledge structures or community knowledge structures, so much as to participate actively in the growth of new networks that solve problems by resolving tensions. The knowledge one needs is not different from the network, and what one needs to learn is how to be good at growing and maintaining effective networks.

The main grammatical problem with connectivism is the simplicity of the ontology of nodes and links that it assumes. This reduction of education to chains of nodes connected by links claims to do away with the need for concepts like 'meaning-making', 'consciousness' and perhaps also 'self-identity'. An ontology of nodes and links implies an external view. On the inside, from the point of view of consciousness, we do not experience ourselves as nodes but as the centre of our universe (the known or experienced whole of reality for us). The reduction of relationships to the idea of nodes and links is incoherent because there is no 'view from no-where' (Nagel, 1989), but only perspectives in relationship. Consciousness is not just a connection between nodes, but also a unique perspective on the world. To understand a node is not only to locate it on a map, but also to inhabit it and see the world from its unique perspective. The linking of nodes in education should then be understood less on the model of external nodes and links, and more on the model of dialogue as bringing together different voices. As demonstrated using the example of Pol.is to resolve political differences, this linking of perspectives in dialogue involves an expansion of consciousness and an expansion of identity.

Online role-play games can be powerful educational tools for expanding consciousness and identity. By allowing players to explore different roles and perspectives, these can help learners to develop a deeper understanding of themselves and the world around them. Gaming is not necessarily dialogic, but multi-user role-play games can provide opportunities for the kind of dialogic education that draws people into learning through dialogue between different perspectives (Arnseth et al., 2018). The main problem with the gaming grammar is the same as the problem that Papert claimed for the teaching machine model; this is that students end up being programmed by technology rather than learning how to program technology. Somebody builds the game using assumptions which then come to feel natural when playing the game. This is potentially a very effective way of teaching almost anything, including complex competences such as creativity, values and identity. However, most games are not able to teach players how to question the assumptions built into the game itself. We explore some possible responses to this problem when looking at games again in Chapter 9.

In this chapter, we critically reviewed some current approaches to education with technology to sketch the beginnings of a dialogic theory of educational technology which can be used as a foundation for design. We will continue to explore and develop this approach in later chapters before outlining it more fully in the final chapter. In the next chapter, we turn to a hugely influential figure in the philosophy of technology, Martin Heidegger, in the hope that a critical investigation of his contribution will help to deepen our emerging theory of educational technology.

### *Prompts towards a dialogic foundation for the design and use of educational technology*

Our discussion of the strengths and weaknesses of online mediated CoPs, of massively multiplayer online role-playing gaming as a model for education, and of connectivism has reinforced two principles derived from explorations of Papert's work and the work of Bereiter and Scardamalia previously:

1 The potential of new technology to engage and empower learners evident in gaming.
2 The capacity of the internet to support peer-to-peer learning networks.

Education is more than just linking nodes. cMOOCs based on this principle have generally failed to attract and include non-traditional learners (Meaney, 2019). What is needed is a relational pedagogy that welcomes outsiders into a shared new identity through dialogue with others who share their interests and intentions. Pedagogy is also needed to help students know how to learn together with others through establishing the shared ground rules that support trust and a sense of belonging. Games of various kinds can be useful in doing this (Mansour et al., 2016; Ravenscroft et al., 2007). Such dialogic pedagogy plus node linking can potentially lead to an expansion of conscious awareness of alternatives, as well as growth towards a more inclusive sense of dialogic self-identity. This dialogic identity is one that identifies both with the voice that speaks in a dialogue, and with the whole dialogue within which the voice speaks. This direction of travel towards a growth in personal and collective understanding and wisdom is an essential component of education, in addition to providing useful content knowledge and skills. Perhaps we could say that linking nodes leads to information. Information that is read in the context of responding to shared challenges and realising shared goals leads to knowledge. Knowledge reflected upon in the light of a growing consciousness of the whole leads to wisdom.[6]

# 6
# HEIDEGGER'S HAMMER

> *Technology is not neutral. We're inside of what we make, and it's inside of us. We're living in a world of connections – and it matters which ones get made and unmade.*
>
> Donna Haraway (1997)

## Introduction

In the previous two chapters, we explored different ontological grammars applied to understand the use of educational technology. The differences we found between these grammars often hinged on questions of agency, or the issue of who or what is acting. In the initial computer as teaching machine grammar, for example, the computer is given a certain kind of agency. Skinner saw his machines as a replacement for teaching assistants and also, potentially, for teachers. Some of the contemporary descendants of Skinner's teaching machines, adaptive tutoring systems advertised as 'AI' based, are often intended to act like separate agents potentially replacing the guiding role of teachers. Papert, influenced by the educational theory of constructivism, believed learners should have agency over their learning and that technology could be used as a tool to help them learn. In communities of practice, the agency behind learning is driven not only by the individual's desire to learn, but also by the community's desire to maintain itself and, in the case of learning communities, to increase in knowledge. Connectivism, on the other hand, suggests that the agency behind learning is not driven by individuals or groups, but by the natural tendency of networks to form and share information in order to resolve tensions and solve problems.

DOI: 10.4324/9781003198499-6

Heidegger is one of the most influential philosophers of the 20th century. Any discussion of Heidegger's work, however, must be prefaced by the fact he was a member of the German Nazi Party until it was disbanded following World War II. Some might think that this political affiliation with a party responsible for dreadful horrors means that we should not engage with his work. Inevitably knowledge of his political engagement will influence the way that we respond to his ideas. The relationship between a person's life and their work is always complex and shaped by many factors, some of which may be difficult to assess from the outside. As almost certainly the most cited name associated with the philosophy of technology, we feel it is important to explore Heidegger's profound influence on the field. Indeed, Heidegger is sometimes said to have founded the modern discipline of the philosophy of technology with his essay 'The question concerning technology' (Heidegger, 1977).

One issue Heidegger can help us to think about more deeply is agency in relation to educational technology: the question of whether 'we' use 'tools' for our own ends, whether we design machines that end up using 'us' for 'their' ends, or whether the reality of agency is always something more complex (Harman, 2011). We begin with Winograd and Flores's seminal 1986 book *Understanding Computers and Cognition* which applies Heidegger's ideas. This has had a particular impact on the theory of educational technology. Winograd and Flores' claim that we can design better systems by thinking about computers and cognition differently was one of the inspirations for our own work in this book. As well as theories that researchers and developers are consciously aware of, there are also deeper theories or 'orientations' that influence their decisions and inform design. Winograd and Flores challenge the idea in AI that computers think like humans and that human minds are essentially information processing machines. Heidegger's work on the everyday experience of using tools inspired Winograd and Flores to propose a new foundation for design. This was based on the idea that digital technology should be designed to support and enhance human activities, and especially human conversations.

## Technology as a lived extension of the body

Winograd and Flores use Heidegger's concept of 'being-in-the-world' (or what Heidegger calls 'Dasein') as a way to understand how humans use tools. They refer to the now famous example of Heidegger's hammer:

> objects and properties are not inherent in the world, but arise only in an event of breaking down in which they become present-at-hand. One

> simple example he [Heidegger] gives is that of a hammer being used by someone engaged in driving a nail. To the person doing the hammering, the hammer as such does not exist. It is part of the background of readiness-to-hand that is taken for granted without explicit recognition or identification as an object. It is part of the hammerer's world, but is not present any more than are the tendons of the hammerer's arm.
>
> (Winograd & Flores, 1986, p. 36)

Heidegger's analysis of readiness to hand is implicitly an account of the agency of technology. The hammer in the hand of the person hammering becomes part of that person, like tendons or bones, participating in a joint agency of human plus tool. The person only becomes aware of the hammer as a hammer, that is as an object in the world, when there is a breakdown in the hammering. For example, imagine a person hammering, missing the nail, and instead hitting their thumb, then blaming the hammer and throwing it away from them in disgust shouting 'stupid hammer!' In a similar way, Winograd and Flores suggest that people tend only to be aware of computers and complain about them when the communication systems they support break down. For instance, when the 'T' key sticks on a keyboard you notice the process of typing. Or when the screen freezes on a Zoom call and the people in a conversation – perhaps one in New York, one in Manchester and one in Hong Kong – become acutely aware of the digital technology supporting their conversational flow.

One implication of Heidegger's analysis is that the use of tools changes 'us' and 'our' desires. Abraham Kaplan (1964, p. 28), a philosopher of science, wrote: 'Give a small boy a hammer, and he will find that everything he encounters needs pounding'. This is a point also made by Abraham Maslow when referring to cognitive biases: 'it is tempting, if the only tool you have is a hammer, to see every problem as a nail' (Maslow, 1966, pp. 15–16). Heidegger's account of extended agency is elaborated by fellow phenomenological philosopher Maurice Merleau-Ponty, when discussing the perceptual role of a cane used by a blind man:

> The blind man's cane has ceased to be an object for him, it is no longer perceived for itself; rather, the cane's furthest point is transformed into a sensitive zone, it increases the scope and the radius of the act of touching and has become analogous to a gaze.
>
> (Merleau-Ponty, 1945/2013, p. 144/178)

Merleau-Ponty claims that our agency is always exercised in a context of action and depends upon our embodiment. The experimental tradition in psychology often seeks, Merleau-Ponty says, to remove context, treating contextual factors as if they were 'confounding variables' and considering that it is possible to escape from the situated environment in which research occurs. But as Merleau-Ponty points out, our knowledge and agency are dependent both on our bodies and the world around us. Without a body, we would have no way to interact with the world and no way to gain knowledge. Without a world, we would have nothing to interact with and no way to exercise our agency. There is no alternative to having an embodied perspective within a situated context. However, as can be seen with the example of the blind person's cane, this does not mean that technology cannot enhance and increase our capacity to perceive and to act in specific contexts:

> In the exploration of things, the length of the cane does not enter expressly as a middle term: the blind man is rather aware of it through the position of the objects, rather than the position of the objects through it . . . If I want to get used to a stick, I try it out, I touch some objects and, after some time, I have it well 'in hand', I can see what things are 'within reach' or out of reach of my stick. . . Habit expresses the power we have of dilating our being in the world, or of altering our existence through appropriating new instruments.
>
> (Merleau-Ponty, 1945/2013, pp. 144–145/165–166)

Following his discussion of how using a cane can extend the power of touch to reveal new aspects of the world, Merleau-Ponty goes on to argue that tool use creates a kind of 'second skin', the shared world of culture. This is like the environment that immediately surrounds us, the world with which we are connected through our senses. However, it is also both more extended and more collective. Merleau-Ponty's point is that the attempt of science to see further and more clearly is not gained by escaping our situation. Instead, this is gained through extending our bodies to incorporate, as he puts it, tools and instruments (similar to how a blind person may incorporate a cane into their perceptual experience). This second body-world of culture and science extends us to include Antarctica and the black hole at the centre of our galaxy, as well as records of the distant past and stories about the far future.

The example of the hammer shows us that agency is not an autonomous mind acting on an independent world, hammering instead involves extending our sense of embodiment to include the hammer within it. We are not separate from our tools in much the same way that we are not separate from our bodies. Machines, according to the Heideggerian-influenced way of design thinking suggested by Winograd and Flores, are not there to be separate intelligences. Rather, they should be designed to extend human agency in a way that changes what it means to be human. Winograd and Flores adopt Heidegger's specialist language when they suggest that computer design should not be a way of ordering and controlling the world, but rather offers a way to create something new to reveal aspects of the world that were previously hidden from us. They give the example of how the design of a simple customer database in a dress shop can support and facilitate everyday interactions and 'unconceal' patterns that would otherwise be concealed. Examples of unconcealing things previously concealed includes notes on when customers were last contacted or how close customers are to delivery routes. These facts remain hidden unless you care about them enough to unconceal them. Design, Winograd and Flores suggest, should be less motivated by a desire to control, and more motivated by care and the unconcealing of truth.

## Heidegger on the danger of modern technology

Heidegger tends to suggest that agency involves being 'called' to act or think. We are challenged to act or to think by someone or something and our actions and thinking are a response to that challenge. When Heidegger writes that 'science is not thinking', he suggests thinking is not about using methods to process empirical data to reach correct answers to questions. In other words, for Heidegger thinking is not something that can be done by a computer. Instead, he proposes that we should understand thinking as a response to the thought-provoking things that happen to us and stimulate us to think (Heidegger, 1966).

The problem with modern technology, according to Heidegger, is that it can limit our capacity to respond to a call to think in a thoughtful manner. He refers to this danger of technology as 'Gestell', which roughly translates as 'enframing'. We probably all have experienced examples of being enframed by technology. Modern 'phone bots', virtual telephone agents used by banks and many other organisations, provide examples of what this can mean in practice. Imagine, for example, that you call your bank to ask a thoughtful question about their ethics or environmental policy. The call is answered by an automated agent who informs you that you must select one of five possible options, none of which relate to your question. When you select one of these options, you must select one of five further possible answers relating to things like costs, interest rates and early repayments, none of which relate to your question about ethics or the environment. This increasingly common frustrating experience of interacting with technology in a way that prevents thoughtful dialogue is an example of what Heidegger claims is the essence of modern technology. It is an example of what might be considered as allowing technology to control our thinking, deciding what questions we can ask, and what answers we can receive. Heidegger also claims that modern technology considers nature to be a 'standing reserve' of resources to be used and controlled for rational economic ends, and not as a mystery to be related to and explored. Forests come to be seen in terms of metric tonnes of cellulose for paper production, and the great River Rhine becomes just a standing reserve of potential energy to be harvested by hydro-electric dams. There is thus a danger that we ourselves might become lost in this enframing such that we forget our role in revealing and exploring what is in the world. We may even come to see ourselves as nothing more than information processing machines whose main purpose is to maximise economic rationality.

For Heidegger, caring about things 'unconceals' them in everyday life. There is no truth unless we engage in caring about something. If we do not care enough, then things remain hidden. And since our capacity to care is limited, there is always much that remains hidden to us. The things we care about and the things that are revealed to us are influenced by our histories, the cultural traditions we are part of and the tools that we use. If we are led through our involvement with modern technology to only care about economic rationality, or the best way to get what it is presupposed that we want, then we might fail to ask the more important questions that can help us to discover who we really are and what we really want.

In 'The question concerning technology', Heidegger returns to the original Greek use of the term techné to refer to arts and craft. Techné in this sense is understood as making things (poiesis) that reveal the world in new ways, unconcealing that which was previously concealed. Reading Heidegger, it becomes clear that his ideal of poiesis is poetry, especially the poetry of Holderlin which he frequently quotes. A poem is a construction of words in the form of signs that, when read attentively and lived 'from within', can reveal the world in a new way and allow us to unconceal things that were once hidden. To illustrate why techné is poiesis, Heidegger gives the example of an ancient Greek craftsperson making a silver chalice intended for sacrificial offerings. Heidegger describes this process of creation as a collaboration in which several elements participate: the idea (eidos) of the chalice, the context of its use (telos), and the silver material to be fashioned (hyle). All these elements are, he says, co-responsible for the finished artefact. The role of the maker is not to impose their autonomous human will, taking on all the responsibility, but to bring careful thought (logos) to best combine all these elements in the most suitable design. The craftsperson is responsible for realising the chalice, but this responsibility is precisely – as the word responsibility implies – a response to the needs of the context that calls for the chalice. Agency here then does not lie only with the biological human, but is distributed across the whole system.

Various dictionary definitions of technology refer to it as 'the application of science'. When Heidegger was writing about technology in the 1950s this was the dominant understanding of modern technology, and it worried him. Older technologies like hammers and chisels are a way of connecting with nature. Modern technology, if it is the application of science, seemed to Heidegger to be a way of cutting humans off from nature:

> the threat to man does not come in the first instance from the potentially lethal machines and apparatus of technology. The actual threat has already afflicted man in his essence. The rule of enframing threatens man

> with the possibility that it could be denied to him to enter into a more original revealing and hence to experience the call of a more primal truth.
> (Heidegger, 1977, p. 28)

The sort of thing that worried Heidegger can perhaps be illustrated by articles in educational technology research journals responding to the Covid-19 global pandemic. In the immediate aftermath of this, much writing focused on the 'learning loss' that occurred when students did not go to school as well as calculations about how much this loss would impact the economy in decades to come (e.g., Donnelly & Patrinos, 2021). There were few, if any, articles published to our knowledge that explored the possibility that being unable to go to school might have led some students to have a more profound encounter with life, or Being, perhaps by being forced to sit still and stare out of a window. Additionally, this sort of encounter might be argued to offer more authentic learning than the type of learning measured by standardised test scores. How much calculable learning on standardised tests could be said to be the equivalent to one lightning flash of insight into the nature of Being? These different conceptions of learning are incompatible. And if we focus on the 'quantitative' conception of learning, then we may not have time or energy for the more 'lightning flash' or 'transformative' conception of learning. The danger Heidegger refers to is that our participation in modern technology networks determines in advance what questions can be asked, and the kind of answers that count, such that we may lose sight of our humanity and see ourselves as nothing more than a 'standing reserve' to be used for economic productivity.

This critique is relevant to the role of technology in education. It is perhaps a version of the contrast that Papert drew between using computers to program learners or allowing learners to program computers. If we understand cognition as nothing more than information processing, then similarly we risk viewing humans as kinds of computers to be programmed. One way to implement a Heideggerian alternative would be education for poiesis that focuses on teaching students how to create their own worlds and how to create themselves. Heidegger believed the most important kind of education to be education for thinking. He also understood real thinking as questioning Being. For Heidegger, Being refers to the totality of all experience, both actual and potential. It is the background or horizon against which all things are experienced. Individual 'beings' like chairs and people emerge from a background Being. This Being is the essence or 'isness' of things, that is always there, but often taken for granted. Being is never revealed directly, but it can be revealed when we question things and relate to them thoughtfully and with care. The intended or destined role of the human is, for Heidegger, to be a steward of Being by helping Being to unconceal itself.

## Levinas's critique of Heidegger

Emmanuel Levinas was a student of Heidegger's and was inspired by him. However, he became disillusioned with Heidegger when he learnt of his involvement with the Nazi party in the 1930s. Levinas then came to associate Heidegger's somewhat mystical sounding language about destiny and the call of Being with German nationalist politics. Levinas criticised Heidegger's focus on 'ontology' or a concern with the nature of 'Being'. Although Heidegger did not define the word Being (Sein) in terms of a physical world, he did associate the human experience of Being – the experience of 'being there' as he put it ('Dasein') – with the importance of place and the need to have a sense of belonging in the world. Levinas saw this link between Being and place (e.g., the fatherland) as the problem leading Heidegger to nationalism. He replaced Heidegger's focus on Being (ontology) with a focus on how we are called to respond to the 'face of the other' (ethics). His philosophy is not easy to summarise. However, by the 'face of the other' Levinas perhaps meant another human considered not as an object in the world, but as a unique individual who calls us to an ethical relationship of responsibility (i.e., not only a human with physical body but someone with their own thoughts, feelings and history). The 'face' of the other for Levinas is therefore not just an object within what he calls the 'totality' of space and time, but is a unique 'singularity' that breaks through this totality to draw us into a relationship, a relationship of responsibility and care. On the other side of the totality of space and time, or world in which everything and everyone becomes an object to be compared and located, Levinas claims that we find not 'Being' but 'ethics' in the form of a responsible relationship with others and with otherness in general.

Levinas's turn away from ontology (talk about 'Being') and towards ethics led him to criticise Heidegger's views on technology. Levinas writes in an article about Soviet Cosmonaut Yuri Gagarin's first space flight in 1961 that:

> Technology wrenches us out of the Heideggerian world and the superstitions regarding *place*. From this point on, an opportunity appears to us: to perceive men outside the situation in which they are placed, and let the human face shine in all its nudity. Socrates prefers the town in which one meets people to the countryside and the trees.
>
> (Levinas, 1990, pp. 232–233)

In this article, Levinas directly relates the affordances of new technology to his ethical philosophy of responding to the face of the other. He takes on Heidegger's criticism of modern technology as enframing our thoughts and alienating us from 'Being'. Levinas seems to suggest that instead of technology cutting us off from our relationship with things and places, technology can liberate us from things and places and help us relate more directly to other people. Heidegger's association of being with place can lead to violence and conflict, Levinas claims, suggesting technology can help us to overcome the 'perpetual warfare' implied by such place-based identity by taking us out of our home space and bringing us into a metaphorical space of relationship, a kind of space that lies beyond the physical.

Although this praise of technology was written in relation to space travel, it can also be read as a prediction of the placeless space of the internet (Zembylas & Vrasidas, 2005). Social media, video conferencing and immersive 3D reality all enable people to connect with each other, even if they are not in the same physical space. Rather than seeing these as technologies that limit and enframe relationships, Levinas suggests by implication that such technologies can liberate the ethical essence of real human relationships beyond the constraints of the physical.

### Case study: Intercultural dialogue on the internet

Discussions about 'care' and 'enframing' can seem quite abstract and remote from practical decisions that need to be taken in the design of education technology. Levinas's notion of the 'face' was precisely meant, in criticism of Heidegger, to point beyond any kind of philosophical abstraction to an actual experience of the 'otherness' of another human being. A case study can give concrete detail to our exploration of Levinas's suggestion that modern technology can enable encounters with the 'face' of the other outside of any particular place. Generation Global (GG), an education programme which promotes internet-mediated dialogue between schools in different countries, provides an example of how this might work in practice. This programme has reached over 600,000 students aged 12 to 17 worldwide. After a compulsory module teaching 'the essentials of dialogue', classes engage in team blogging or facilitated videoconferencing with classes in other countries or regions, usually regions where there might be tension between different groups. Team blogging involves placing students into small teams in the online GG learning community. In these teams, learners interact with peers from other groups by creating short blog posts in response to pre-determined prompts or questions, and by commenting on each other's posts.

The integration design of both the technology and pedagogy is important for the success of the programme. The classroom-based, in-person 'essentials of dialogue' programme is required prior to blogging as this involves developing ground rules for effective online dialogue. The practical outcome of these activities is summed up in four prompts that are repeated throughout students' engagement (Wegerif et al., 2019):

- Experience: 'Give readers an insight into your life, explain why things are important for you'.
- Clarity: 'Will your post be clear to someone from another country?'
- Questioning: 'Ask good questions that prompt the writer to explain their ideas more deeply'.
- Reflecting: 'Make connections between your post and others' and show that you are thinking about what you read'.

There are also design features to aid moderation. Text messages must be above a minimum, and below a maximum, length. The maximum limit intends to prevent long essays blocking the flow of dialogue. The minimum length aims to promote thoughtful responses. If any participant has concerns about a post, it can be removed immediately for investigation later. Teachers also have access to visual indicators representing the nature of talk across teams. This makes it easier to intervene with personal messages, if, for example few questions are asked over time by one team or one student.

As part of one international research project, students were asked to reflect on how they felt 'about people from those countries, communities, cultures and faiths you expect to meet?' before taking part in team-blogging. They were also asked to reflect on why they felt this way by 'writing about things in (their) experience that have shaped their views'. Similar questions were posed after the team-blogging event. Quantitative data on how many blogs were written, read and responded to were also gathered.

There were 1140 reflections completed by students from more than 100 different schools. These were labelled as either 'pre' blogging experience or 'post'. Apparent changes in attitudes, reflected through changes in language use, could be explored by matching pairs of pre- and post-reflections. Data analysis involved a combination of discourse analysis and corpus linguistic statistical techniques. Comparisons of pre- and post-blogging data showed a change in how pronouns were used. Before the blogging experience, 'we' referred most to students' home region. After team-blogging, the use of 'we' changed to refer to a more concrete sense of shared identity. At the same time, the use of 'they' to refer to the other also changed. Before the team-blogging experience 'they' were clearly 'other'. After the team-blogging experience, the 'other' took on a more concrete form and was seen as 'like us', perhaps even as part of an extended sense of 'us'.

Detailed qualitative examination revealed a change in the use of pronouns to refer to self and other between the pre- and post-team-blogging reflection. Of course, this analysis of changes in word use over a short period should not be over interpreted as proving lasting identity change. Nonetheless, it provides provisional indicators of a potential change in identity that could be followed up in longer-term studies looking at actions as well as words. Despite such caveats, this research found clear indications of a shift in identity: from a relatively closed sense of 'us' (defined against an abstract sense of 'them'), towards a more dialogic identity best described not as identification with 'us' against 'them', but with the dialogue that unites 'us' with 'them' within a space of relationship. This discourse analysis was a small part of the overall project, but it shows that students' language use changed over time, and that these changes reflected changes in how they identified themselves and others in the direction of increased dialogic open-mindedness.

## Discussion

Heidegger's profound contribution to the theory of educational technology is his insight that we live technology from the inside. His simple story about using a hammer reveals the difference in perspective between an outside contemplative view of the hammer as a 'present at hand' thing in the world, and the inside experience of using the hammer when it is 'ready to hand'. In using a hammer, to some extent we become the hammer – the tool extends us and is us – shaping what we see and what we think we want. Winograd and Flores unpack the importance of this insight for design in ways relevant to educational technology. Instead of trying to design machines that have the same kind of agency that we like to imagine we as humans have, we should in fact be designing ways to support and enhance human action in the world. What Winograd and Flores call a 'rationalist' model of design is found in the aspiration of so called 'AI' educational tutoring systems which try to simulate actions commonly undertaken by teachers. Their more situated approach to design can instead be found, for example, in the design of supports for dialogues which lead to collaborative learning.

Having presented Heidegger's insight about technology as part of us, we went further to unpack Heidegger's critique of modern technology as a danger to us. Specifically, we explored the danger of technology enframing us in such a way that we become lost within a technology-mediated way of thinking and seeing the world. In this critique, Heidegger associated technology with instrumental rationality, which involves seeing things in terms of economic profit and loss. This has profoundly negative educational implications and potentially obscures the possibility of worthwhile education in favour of countable learning gains. The potential danger here is that we become trapped in a limited vision of ourselves as autonomous agents in a world that is pre-understood as objects available for our use, rather than a 'partner' in dialogue that can help us to grow and learn. We can grow educationally, Heidegger seems to imply, only once we recognise and respect the otherness of nature and allow it to speak to us such that we can enter into a constructive dialogue with it.

Levinas thought he was challenging Heidegger with an alternative account of how we grow through an ethical encounter with the 'otherness of the other'. He claimed Heidegger's negative attitude towards modern technology was linked to his attachment to place. In contrast with Heidegger, Levinas considered modern technology to represent not so much an entrapment as an opportunity, the opportunity to be projected beyond place into an ethical encounter with other people (Zembylas & Vrasidas, 2005).

Levinas might not have been quite as original as he claimed. Heidegger himself writes about the potential liberating power of modern technology, associating this liberation with what he calls 'a place beyond place' (Heidegger, 1977). But Levinas has a point. Heidegger cautions us against becoming seduced by modern technology and instead advocates a more contemplative stance. Through art and poetry, he claims, we can understand the essence of the technological, not through technological thinking itself. The way he refers to modern technology seems to imply that he sees it as always corrupting and superficial, taken over by the demands of profit-maximising rationality. He even cautions readers against getting too involved with using modern technology. This is a very different approach from that of techno-philosopher David Chalmers who begins his book *Reality+* with the story of his adventures with other philosophers in fully immersive virtual reality realms (Chalmers, 2022). Technophilosophy, for Chalmers, is not just applying philosophy to understand technology; it is also the other way around, applying insights gained through using technology to challenge and improve philosophy. In a way, this technophilosophy is already what Heidegger was doing when he challenged the claims of rationalism with his account of what it feels like to use everyday tools like hammers 'from within'.

Andrew Feenberg argues that while Heidegger is very insightful about how we join with technology to expand our agency, he only applies this insight to pre-modern technologies. He suggests that Heidegger only describes modern technology from an outside perspective, which Feenberg calls a 'managerial' perspective. Networked modern technologies, Feenberg writes, shape the lived worlds in which humans have real experiences, from which they can learn just as they learn from hammering or weaving (Feenberg, 2012).

Interestingly, Feenberg suggests that Heidegger's limited perspective might have stemmed from a deep division within the education system of Germany at that time. According to Feenberg, Heidegger did not study engineering or anything on the science side. Heidegger was trained in the arts and humanities, specifically the art of finding wisdom in ancient texts, or 'hermeneutics'.

Studying only the arts and humanities, according to Feenberg, might not have equipped him well to interpret the potential world-revealing and new world-making power of modern technology.

The obvious criticism of Heidegger's philosophy of technology made by Feenberg, but also Don Ihde and others (Ihde, 2010), is that it is too abstract and reductionist, lumping together all forms of technology as 'enframing' when in reality there are lots of different technologies that do lots of different things. Nonetheless, Heidegger is often credited with starting the modern philosophy of technology and his work has been continued by others, who have often taken a more nuanced and empirical turn (Coeckelbergh, 2020).

The case study offered in this chapter appears to focus on language and identity. However, it is also about using technology to open new dialogic spaces. In shifting from identification with 'us' against 'them', to identifying with a dialogic space in which us and them are entangled together, the young people in this study were also extending their sense of identity to inhabit a technologically mediated space from within as an extension of themselves. This relates to the claim from Merleau-Ponty that our use of tools extends our individual bodies into identification and inhabitation of a collective 'inter-world' (see Chapter 3). It also illustrates our qualification of Levinas's claim, which is that for this encounter with the other to have positive educational consequences, careful design is needed of both the pedagogy and technology. This case study suggests that, beyond Heidegger's fear of modern technology as a means of entrapment, when lived from the inside, modern technology can be designed with pedagogy in such a way as to enable powerful learning dialogues.

The challenge for educational technology raised by Heidegger is how can we avoid simply inducting students into a world already pre-understood by human-centred instrumental ways of thinking. The promise for educational technology raised by Winograd and Flores's application of Heidegger is: can we use modern digital technology to build spaces in which truth is unconcealed and the lightning flash of insight can occur?

### *Prompts towards a dialogic foundation for the design and use of educational technology*

Heidegger's discussion of the way that tools and technology enter into and shape experience has important implications for the design and use of educational technology including:

- Technology is not just something we use to achieve our aims, it also changes us and extends our capacity to learn new things. We should therefore design in ways that facilitate the extension of the human, extending and supporting our capacity to engage in educational dialogues with those and that which is 'other' than us.

- The threat of technology that Heidegger points to is that of closure. Educational technology we suggested at the end of Chapter 5 can expand our knowledge by linking local dialogues to the long-term open-ended dialogues of science. But using technology to teach and transmit knowledge carries with it the danger that we think we know all that is important in advance. For Heidegger, the point of education on the other hand is to bring learners into dialogue with a mystery that is outside of – or beyond – everything that we can know in advance. This suggests the need to design educational technology not only for the expansion of knowledge, but also for open encounters with the unknown. The case study presented provides one example of technology designed for dialoguing with others where the outcome is uncertain. We offer another example in Chapter 9, which focuses on using a digital game to project learners into an encounter with an unknown and uncertain future.
- Our critique of Heidegger's failure to empathise with modern technology suggests that we need to design educational technology that allows students to fully experience and participate in the potential of networked technology. The potential pointed to by extending Heidegger, and through Levinas's critique of Heidegger, is that digital technology can be used to transform our ethical relationships with each other. For instance, the promise of a space beyond place offered by digital technology – the internet converted by educational initiatives into a transnational dialogic space for example – enables a more open and unbounded human identity to emerge. The case study of digital educational technology supporting dialogue across difference around the planet is one example of how we could design for the emergence of this new kind of global human-technology hybrid.

# 7

# THE 'MEANING' OF TECHNOLOGY

> *The value of the individual's dialogue with the technical object is thus to conserve human effort and to create a domain of the transindividual, distinct from the community . . .*[1]
>
> Gilbert Simondon (2020, p. 415)

> *. . . the essential function of the universe, which is a machine for the making of gods.*
>
> Henri Bergson (1932/1977, p. 338)

## Technology seen as a threat to meaning

In this chapter, we explore in greater depth how emerging technologies call into question common assumptions about human beings and their place within the world (Carrigan & Porpora, 2021). In Chapter 6, we unpacked Heidegger's critique of modern technology. A common way of interpreting this critique is that Heidegger is concerned about a loss of human meaning caused by the spread of modern technology.[2] A world that was once rich with meaning, like a walk near his hut in the German Black Forest, has been reduced, Heidegger feels, to a 'standing reserve' for the economy. His point is that, when we only have a technological way of thinking, the trees in the forest are no longer experienced as a source of mystery and beauty. Rather, they are only seen as a quantity of raw material (e.g., for the paper mills needed by the newspaper industry). In this argument about the enframing or entrapping of humans within technological ways of thinking, Heidegger appears to associate technology with instrumental rationality or a way of thinking that focuses only on finding the most efficient means of achieving pre-determined ends.[3]

DOI: 10.4324/9781003198499-7

In this chapter we re-examine the influential claim that the use of modern technology undermines the human experience of meaning in education. Often this is an unreflective bias embedded in the way people commonly use language, or what Wittgenstein might call the 'grammar' (see Chapter 4). The term 'human' tends to be used in a way that has positive connotations, despite what some might see as quite a lot of evidence to the contrary. The terms 'mechanical' or 'instrumental', applied to education at least, tend to imply the opposite of human and so something negative. In an article on the function of schools for example, a leading contemporary philosopher of education Gert Biesta writes: 'the school is not a machine but a thoroughly human "endeavour"' (Biesta, 2022, p. 329). In this article, Biesta does not explicitly argue that 'machines' and technology are opposed to the kind of meaning that human relationships have.[4] However, he assumes this by using words like 'technology' and 'machines' as synonyms for profit-maximising means-ends rationality opposed to the meaning-rich human relationships of teaching and learning. We do not mean to critique Biesta specifically here. This kind of contrast, the human as good and full of meaning versus technology as bad and destructive of meaning, is quite widespread in writing on education and on educational technology.[5]

To investigate why many people seem to understand human meaning making as excluding technology, we start by exploring the influential theory of meaning of Edmund Husserl, who grounded the meaning of meaning in human experience. We contrast this phenomenological account of meaning, an account which emphasises the importance of human consciousness, to a view of meaning that arises from a systems perspective. In doing so, we argue that if meaning is a systems effect, then meaning is not reducible to the human experience of meaning studied by phenomenology. In other words, we suggest that non-human systems may have a meaning of their own regardless of whether humans consciously experience this meaning. And where humans do experience meaning, this may be a product of their participation in systems that combine the human with the non-human. Finally, we explore the idea of meaning in self-organising systems. Drawing upon Simondon's theory of the meaning of technological objects, we suggest a way of bringing human meaning and technological meaning back together again through educational technology. Our recommendation to address the issue of the threat of a loss of meaning in education is neither to reject humanism, nor to reject technology, but to expand our understanding of what it means to be human to include digital technology and participation in bio-socio-technical systems. The question of whether educational technology promotes or detracts from human meaning depends, we argue, on how educational technology is designed. We suggest if educational technology is designed to help students to actively participate in larger technologically mediated systems, it is likely to lead to a greater sense of meaning in life.

## The meaning of meaning

### *Meaning as an effect of human consciousness*

Husserl founded the phenomenological tradition in philosophy partly in response to the success of natural science and the belief that 'the scientific method' could explain everything without need of philosophy. Phenomenology is a rigorous approach to studying human experience that seeks to understand assumptions and biases that underpin natural science. Influenced by Hume and Kant, and also perhaps prominent physicists including Ernst Mach and Max Planck, Husserl believed that science should start with the raw 'sense-data' of experience, rather than any preconceived notions about 'objects'. Husserl believed that by studying the way our consciousness creates the world, we can gain a more empirical (a word meaning 'based on experience') understanding of the world than natural science can provide. Most scientific methods assume an external 'real' world full of objects that exist independently of our minds. Phenomenology asks how we come to experience the world as real and how we construct the objects that we perceive. Husserl believed we need to step back and 'bracket out' (epoché) all prior assumptions to investigate how ideas first arise within consciousness, as well as considering how they then get constructed to become recognisable 'objective' things in a shared world.

If we approach the question of meaning, as Husserl does, as an aspect or product of human consciousness, then perhaps it is inevitable that we end up with the view that technology is not part of, or is even opposed to, human meaning making.

According to Husserl the meaning of an object is not simply its appearance to us. This meaning also includes the horizon of all its possible ways of appearing to us, as well as all the connections that it could have for us in different contexts. Returning to the example of the hammer, the hammer is an object for us because we can separate it from its immediate context and imagine seeing it from different perspectives. We can imagine holding it, we can imagine the various ways in which we can use it, and we can connect it to cultural stories about hammers like the magical hammer of Thor. The horizon of possibilities around objects is shaped by our expectations. And these expectations are informed by our culture. Groups share expectations and patterns of activity in what Husserl called an intersubjective 'life world', which provides a framework for understanding and experiencing the world. The lifeworld of any group serves to 'predelineate' a 'world-horizon' of possible experiences that are to be expected for a given group member (Husserl, 1950, vol. III/1, p. 100).

Meaning then, according to Husserl's phenomenology, is found not in specific events such as using this actual hammer to hit this actual nail, but in the dynamic dialogue between those events (or 'enactments'; see

Chapter 3) and a shifting horizon of possibilities and anticipations (referred to as a 'horizon of meaning' around the event). Hitting a nail into a fence has meaning for someone based on their image of the future fence they are repairing, the significance of keeping a fence repaired in their cultural context, and perhaps also their identity as the sort of person who fixes their own fence. This horizon around the event is not static: it shifts as contexts change, similar to how the horizon seen from a ship changes as the ship sails across an ocean.

### *Meaning as an effect of differences in a dialogue*

Derrida's careful critique of Husserl argued convincingly that it is not possible to pin down and study 'moments' of consciousness (Derrida, 1989). The more one tries to study a bit of consciousness the more it becomes apparent that consciousness itself is always part of and connected to a larger system: a system that precedes and exceeds consciousness. For example, trying to define the present moment always implies some reference to the past or future, which are not present to consciousness. What we mean by the 'now' that is present to consciousness has to be defined in relation to a horizon of 'thens', or times that are not now, and which are not immediately present to consciousness.[6]

The concept of ontological difference first articulated clearly by Heidegger (1969) and later elaborated in different ways by Merleau-Ponty (1968, 'the ecart'), Derrida (1968, 'la differance') and Deleuze (1968/1994, 'difference and repetition') finds that what lies behind experience is not 'identity' but 'difference'. Husserl's method assumes that experiences do have some kind of identity. He claimed that we could describe an experience like hearing a note of music as a present moment in time, a 'now' moment that can be analysed and around which a boundary can be drawn. Heidegger pursued phenomenological analysis to study the nature of Being. However, he did not find this identity, finding instead the importance of what he called an 'ontological difference'. This ontological difference is the difference between the object that we see, or the note of music that we hear, and the background that makes it visible or audible in the first place. Every 'thing' is visible or audible, or tangible or thinkable, only as a difference against the background of Being as a whole. Being as a whole is not something that can be seen or pinned down, it exceeds our consciousness. What we experience is not an identity but a difference: the difference between beings and Being which can also be characterised as the difference between Being and beings (Heidegger, 1957). And of course, 'Being' is not itself any kind of thing. It is more the idea that there is always a context in which things appear – a context that cannot be seen, heard, touched, tasted or pinned down in the present moment – a context that always outstrips our capacity to grasp it.

To illustrate the significance of this point let us go back to our person fixing the fence, let's call her Jill. The meaning of the act for Jill is an oscillation between the enactment of physically hammering the nails and the context of this act: the planning and long-term purpose, the social relations with the neighbours implied, and Jill's psychological perception of herself as the kind of capable person who can support her family by fixing things that need fixing. As well as the 'beings' or things here – Jill, hammer, nails, fence – there is also an unbounded context of Being, the background world within which events take place and these beings emerge as separate and significant. Jill certainly experiences meaning, but the meaning of the event cannot be fully captured by what occurs in Jill's consciousness at the time. This is because the meaning of the act is linked to things that are not in Jill's consciousness at that moment. For example, if the neighbours react negatively to seeing the fence the next day, then that becomes part of the meaning of the event, but it cannot be in Jill's consciousness at the time. What we are saying here about Jill and her hammer also applies to Jill's son John, who might be using a kinetic controller to navigate through a 3D geometry world, doing homework to report back the next day to his classmates and teacher. The meaning of John's actions is not just determined by how he feels about them. He might feel good about it at the time while the response of his teacher the next day might make him feel bad about it. The unknown future response that is not present also impacts on the meaning of the event. Or perhaps, those on the committee who decided on this activity as part of the curriculum some years back, will change their mind about its utility and re-classify it from 'useful education' to 'meaningless play' thereby transforming the activity's meaning for both the teacher and for John.

We raised a version of this understanding of meaning when we outlined dialogic theory in Chapter 1. In a dialogue, words do not have a fixed or final meaning. Rather their meaning is alive and changing as the dialogue changes. This is because their meaning depends not only on what the speaker of the words is trying to say, but also on how the words are interpreted by others. Words mean in a dialogue because of their difference to other words. According to Bakhtin, there can be no last or final words because the dialogue is never completely dead or finished but always alive, continuing and growing (Bakhtin, 1986). Even to revisit an apparently finished dialogue, like that of Socrates and Phaedrus that we quoted at the beginning of Chapter 2, is to continue the dialogue with a new reading influenced by the context of the present.

### *Responding to a meaningful universe*

Bakhtin was influenced by Einstein's theory of relativity and Heisenberg's uncertainty principle. However, he assumed that his dialogic theory of meaning, which holds that meaning is always unfinished and a play of differences between multiple voices, only applied to the cultural world and not to the world as studied by natural science. Increasingly this assumption is being challenged. In almost every area of research, scientists are not finding 'things' at the bottom level of reality, but only differences. Recent studies in biology have explicitly referred to biology as the study of patterns of information understood as patterns of differences (Haig, 2020; Heylighen, 2022a). Such a focus on patterns of differences has long been the case in physics (Heisenberg, 1958; Vedral, 2018).

Carlo Rovelli, the author of loop-theory which has been suggested as offering one of the strongest interpretations of quantum theory to-date, argues that all we have is information and further that all information is to be understood as 'relational' (Rovelli, 2021). Unlike Bohr's interpretations of quantum theory that required a human observer, Rovelli's interpretation only requires an observing system. Relational information is information that makes a difference to another observing system.

The ontology that emerges from quantum theory, according to Rovelli, and others like Karen Barad, is relational and process oriented. He describes how facts are realised in interactions between any two physical systems and are relative to these systems (2022). Rovelli is not saying that reality is not real or that there are no facts. He is saying that reality is real in much the same way that a rainbow is real. Rainbows are real interactions between light, water droplets and human eyes. They do not just go away if everyone closes their eyes and pretends that rainbows are socially constructed. But the reality of rainbows is not fact as identity – the idea that 'a thing is what it is and not another thing'[7] – but fact as a systems effect. In the case of rainbows, meaning emerges from a variation in the wavelength of light energy, a difference that becomes significant and triggers a visual effect within a complex observing system (i.e., in this case, the human observer). The ontological claim of Rovelli, like that of Merleau-Ponty, is that when we dig down into reality to consider what is going on we do not find stable things like atoms bumping into each other, but rather we find differences.

These differences are like the basic visual ('gestalt') unit of perception, which is that of 'a figure on a ground' or 'figure-ground'. This is the difference between an object and the background behind it. One famous example is Rubin's vase which provides the cup or faces paradox as depicted in Figure 7.1.

When we look at this visual image, we can see two different shapes: a vase or two faces. This is because we interpret the outline of the image in two different ways. The outline of the vase is seen as belonging to the vase, with it appearing to be in front of a formless background. Or, the outline of the vase is seen as belonging to the background, with the two faces appearing to be in the foreground. It is only possible to see one of these interpretations at any time.

FIGURE 7.1 An example of the 'cup or faces?' paradox proposed by Edgar Rubin in his 1915 doctoral thesis.

*Source:* Bryan Derksen, licensed under CC BY-SA 3.0.

Merleau-Ponty proposed the 'figure on a ground' as the basic unit of meaning. He argued that our perception of the world, and the thinking that takes off from it, building upon it, is always constructed out of multiple figure-ground relationships. Cybernetician Gregory Bateson proposed a similar idea, arguing that information is a 'difference that makes a difference' (Bateson, 1972). The 'figure' that is focused upon by the gaze, be it a human in a landscape by da Vinci, a red dot in a painting by Klee, or a black ink mark in a concrete poem by Mallarmé, only has meaning because of its relationship with the background against which it stands out. Merleau-Ponty understands this basic unit of meaning as a kind of dialogic relationship: the background defines the figure, the figure defines the background and meaning emerges in the living relationships between these two irreducibly different perspectives (Merleau-Ponty, 1968).

## Cybernetics and the meaning of technology

Socrates first illuminated the question of the meaning of technology with his distinction between 'inside' and 'outside' when condemning the technology of writing as lacking meaning. As outlined in Chapter 2, Socrates described written words as 'dead' and 'like seeds left out to dry in the sun'. Real words, he said, had life and meaning and could answer back. As literates, we can now see that this view of writing was limited. Perhaps it partly came from Socrates' failure to extend his empathy to include written text inside his 'tent' of knowledge as it were, to bring it to life, to animate it from within with a living voice. Libraries in schools, and texts in classrooms, are so familiar now that they are not experienced as technology but as a way of extending the human world of meaning. The cybernetics approach to understanding technology shows us that the boundary between human and technology is porous and partly depends upon us. Meaning is generated through participation in the system. Whether this participation is felt to have meaning by the human participants likely depends on whether they feel able to extend their empathy – and therefore at least part of their identity – into the system. Whether educational technology enhances human meaning or detracts from it thus depends on how we relate to this technology and on how the technology is designed to relate to us. It also depends on how we educate for the use of the technology.

Although named from the Greek for a helmsperson or someone who steers a ship, cybernetics is commonly associated with machine–human collaborations and combinations. For example, Donna Haraway writes in her 'A Cyborg Manifesto' that: 'A cyborg is a cybernetic organism, a hybrid of machine and organism' (Haraway, 1991, p. 149). Cybernetics is thus the study of systems that can control themselves, and these systems may include both humans and machines.

In his exploration of the history of cybernetics, Andrew Pickering argues that cybernetics offers an alternative ontology for, or a different way of thinking about, technology. He suggests that this contrasts with an understanding of technology as being all about control and efficiency. 'I think Heidegger was right', Pickering writes: 'The last few centuries can be characterised by an ever-growing assemblage of knowledge and power, science and technology, which does enframe the world and ourselves within it' (2009, pp. 469–470). However, Pickering argues there are some movements within cybernetics which suggest a different approach to the design of modern technology, one which includes greater openness to nature and to spirituality. He distinguishes between two paradigms in the history of science and technology: the one that Heidegger was critical of (which he calls the 'Modern' paradigm), as well as a cybernetic 'nonModern' paradigm that, it is claimed, Heidegger might have been more positive about. Pickering illustrates his claims by focusing on the work of British cyberneticians Stafford Beer and Gordon Pask in the 1950s. Some of their experimental cybernetic designs included biological systems. The idea, for example, of incorporating feedback from the living eco-system of a pond into the information loops that guide a factory. The cybernetic factory, as Beer imagined it, would use such living systems to help it react to changing circumstances in order that it could grow and evolve like an organism. Together, Beer and Pask built some extraordinary cybernetic systems that were able to adapt and learn. This includes one based on networks formed by iron filings in an electro-magnetic field. Pask even suggested that this was able to adaptively construct its own sensors, including spontaneously growing an electrochemical 'ear' to hear sounds when this ability was needed for the system to survive (Pickering, 2009).

Pickering uses the relationship with nature as a criterion to distinguish between what he calls Modern and nonModern design. This considers that Modern technoscience separates itself from nature to represent and control nature. NonModern cybernetic systems meanwhile, like the helmsperson of a ship, participate as a natural being within nature to steer the system. Another criterion used to distinguish the Modern and the nonModern approaches to technology design is relationship to self. Second-order cybernetics – invented around 1967 by Heinz von Foerster, Margaret Mead, Gregory Bateson and others – appreciates the role of the observing self and acknowledges this as part of cybernetic systems (Mead & Morris, 1967).

According to Pickering, the cybernetic approach to technology design enhances meaning rather than detracting from it because it includes the self as part of the system. While modern technology is often experienced as standing against the self, monitoring and controlling it, cybernetics presents itself as extending the self, enabling this self to participate in new or different ways.

## Meaning as a product of self-organisation

The concept of self-organisation from cybernetics (Ashby, 1957) and the closely related concept of autopoiesis,[8] or self-organising and self-maintaining, has been influential in a range of disciplines including computing (Winograd & Flores, 1986; see Chapter 5). Sugata Mitra has applied this concept to education arguing that children plus the internet can spontaneously form what he calls self-organised learning environments or SOLEs[9] (Mitra & Dangwal, 2010). From the concept of autopoiesis, Maturana and particularly Varela developed a theory of mind as being all about meaning. This theory emphasises the importance of context in the creation of meaning, rather than understanding meaning as the result of 'computation' in an acontextual way. The information processing model of mind, still popular in cognitive psychology, has no apparent place for meaning. For any autopoietic system, however, cognition is an aspect of self-organisation and self-reproduction. Meaning is therefore embodied and relational as opposed to abstract and representational (Hayles, 2012; Mingers, 2014; Varela et al., 1991).

Meaning emerges in autopoietic systems because of their need to monitor both internal and external environments to maintain homeostasis, the self-regulating process by which systems maintain stability while adjusting to changing external conditions. Any autopoietic system generates an evolving system of anticipation that it uses to determine whether inputs are beneficial or detrimental to its self-maintenance. External sensors such as eyes, cameras or antennae enable a system to sense energy sources that it needs to move towards, as well as threats that it needs to move away from. Internal sensors warn of internal states, such as low energy, that require addressing by finding an energy source. In organisms, this need for external and internal monitoring may lead to the growth of neural systems and to the biological experience of meaning as an aspect of consciousness. Damasio and Carvalho argue consciousness arises at the boundary between the inside and the outside of systems because it helps the system to self-regulate: 'Given that body states are necessarily valenced – they are either good or bad from the point of view of homeostasis – feelings are powerful proxies of ongoing biological value and natural guides to adaptive behavior' (Damasio & Carvalho, 2013, p. 145).

Experiencing the feeling of fear, for example, forces an organism to focus attention on the source of the feeling and to act upon it. Experiencing the feeling of joy when it senses sunlight, if the organism has evolved to absorb energy from the sun, encourages it to move towards the source of that joy. According to this origin story of consciousness, there was a time when the neural system monitored internal and external information and guided responses without the need for self-conscious awareness of feelings. In other words, naturally arising autopoietic systems have meaning even when there is no self-conscious experience of that meaning.

Bugs moving away from threats and towards sunlight might seem distant from the description of meaning in Husserl and Heidegger. What is interesting for our argument is the connection between the existence of meaning in autopoietic systems, the feeling of meaning in biological autopoietic systems, and the conscious experience of meaning for humans as studied by phenomenology. According to systems theory and many systems thinkers (e.g., Heylighen, 2022b; Leydesdorff, 2021), the conscious experience of a meaningful event is just a subset of a much larger category of meaningful events that are not always consciously experienced.

## The cybernetics of learning: Pask's Conversation Theory

Gordon Pask, whose work with Stafford Beer was earlier discussed as an example of nonModernist technology design, went on to become an influential cybernetic artist. He created early versions of the multimedia interactive happenings that are illustrated at the end of the next chapter, Chapter 8. Pask also went on to develop and experiment with a cybernetic theory of learning that he called 'conversation', or what we would call 'dialogue'. Pask applied this theory to both machine and human learning.

Pask believed that conversation was the most basic process of learning. He defined this as the process by which two or more voices (which could be human or machine) share their perspectives and come to understand each other's 'informings'. A conversation or dialogue for Pask involved self-reflection, and change, because of the interaction. This theory was intended as a theory of all learning in nature as well as in culture. Pask's theory also suggests that the development of complexly integrated forms of organic life, technology and conceptual language use in humans all emerged from self-reflective conversational interactions. Higher-level coordinations take the form of 'tokens' for lower-level coordinations (objects and events), which are themselves tokens for stable patterns of sensorimotor activity and regular interactions with the environment. The 'tokens' that are exchanged and adapted in conversations are essentially symbols for 'lower level' patterns found in data. To form a 'conversation', participants must describe themselves and their actions, before exploring and extending these descriptions together, carrying forward the understanding that they generate to future activities. To learn, a person or system must then be able to converse with itself and with others about what it knows (Pask, 1976; Scott, 2001; Sharples et al., 2010).

Pask was a visiting professor at the Institute of Education Technology at the Open University in the United Kingdom. He influenced theories of education with technology put forward by later professors at the same institution, Diana Laurillard and Mike Sharples, whom we introduced earlier. Pask's Conversation Theory is applied by Sharples and colleagues (2010), and by Laurillard (2002), to describe processes involved in learning conversations supported by modern communication technologies. Sharples and colleagues develop Pask's ideas in what they call 'a mobile theory of learning'. This describes learning as a technology-mediated process of coming to know through conversations that take place across contexts. Whereas learning was previously largely described within institutional contexts, mobile technology it is claimed allows for 'seamless' learning to take place in a variety of contexts. It is said to do this through the conversational mechanism of feedback loops and resulting clarifications that Pask describes. Laurillard similarly develops and applies Pask in what she calls a 'Conversational Learning Framework' (2002), which can be applied as a design framework for education in general (2012). Laurillard maintains that all complex learning involves:

> a continuing iterative dialogue between teacher and student, which reveals the participants' conceptions and the variations between them . . . There is no escape from the need for dialogue, no room for mere telling, nor for practice without description, nor for experimentation without reflection, nor for student action without feedback.
>
> (Laurillard, 2002)

Laurillard's conversational framework is a theory of learning for the Digital Age. This is because it matches different types and aspects of dialogues to the affordances of different communications technology. One example might involve being introduced to information through video, exploring through web searches, discussing in a webinar, experimenting with a simulation, and finally demonstrating understanding by creating a shared document or model.

Pask's theory of learning is intended to be applicable to both machine learning and hybrid human–machine learning contexts. It attempts to describe how shared spaces of awareness are generated, not only the consciousness of individual humans, but shared assemblies of participants that include machines. Pask's conversational theory of learning is a precursor to, and inspiration for, the dialogic theory of educational technology developed in this book and presented in Chapter 11. However, Pask's theory does not seem to account for the essential role of non-thematic shared background knowledge in dialogue: the implicit, tacit and intuitive knowledge that is always already there even if it can not be put into words and described neatly. According to the dialogic theory of Buber and Bakhtin, dialogue is a process of creating new understanding through interaction of different perspectives. Or as Volosinov (1986, p. 102) suggested, insight is like a spark that occurs out of the tension of the charge between two different terminals, or what might be called sparks of inter-illumination. In this way, dialogue is not about reducing differences to a single, true vision, but about expanding the shared space of reference and resonance (Bakhtin, 1986). As discussed earlier, this suggests that a figure, or concept term, or one of Pask's tokens, is only understandable in relation to its background or context. This relationship between figures and their grounds is not static but dialogic, giving rise to what Bakhtin called 'an infinite potential for contextual meaning' (Bakhtin, 1986). Dialogic learning, therefore, involves more than just making conceptual understanding explicit and external. It also encompasses the development of intuition and creativity by expanding empathy and understanding, even in situations where what has been learned cannot be verbally articulated. In other words, dialogic learning is about opening, widening and expanding shared spaces of resonance and interpretation. Whenever we teach a concept word, we also need to induct the learner into the shared dialogic space within which the use of this word makes sense. Dialogic learning is not therefore only about clarifying concepts and transferring explicit knowledge, but also about expanding the dialogic community or shared internality, such that those concepts have meaning. How technology can enter into and be part of this dialogic learning process, without reducing it to only the transfer of explicit knowledge, is a challenge that another cybernetic theorist writing in the 1970s, Gilbert Simondon, can help us with.

## Simondon and the meaning of technology

Like Heidegger, Simondon studied philosophy, especially ancient Greek philosophy. Unlike Heidegger, he also studied science and engineering. In a basement of the Sorbonne University in Paris, where he was a professor of psychology, Simondon kept machines and spent hours tinkering with them to understand them better (Simondon, 2020). Simondon was influenced by Louis de Broglie's version of quantum theory. De Broglie proposed wave-particle duality, which suggests that all matter can be described both as particles and as waves. Although wave-particle duality is most detectable at small scales, de Broglie argued that it applied also for objects observable in everyday life. In other words, the quantum description of reality is a description of reality as a whole, not just a description of reality at extremely small scales. As a professor of psychology, Simondon lectured on the psychic individuation of human beings, or how each human becomes a unique individual. In addition, Simondon wrote about a similar journey of individuation for natural objects like crystals, living organisms like plants and technical objects like internal combustion engines.

Simondon believed that any process of becoming an individual is driven by a 'problematic', or a set of pressures and constraints. He often used the example of the precipitation of crystals out of a supersaturated solution to explain his theory of individuation. Each crystal ends up unique because it follows a unique path to individuation, responding to drivers and constraints in its environment. However, although each crystal is individually unique, it is also linked to all the other crystals as one possibility stemming from the original state of potentiality that was the supersaturated solution out of which all emerged. This state of potential out of which the individual emerges is, for Simondon, the 'pre-individual'. The individuation of crystals is used by Simondon as a metaphor for all individuation processes. The supersaturated solution is a 'metastability', a state of potentiality that can be generative and give rise to new forms. But this can also serve as a metaphor for the larger idea that everything emerges or individuates out of a prior 'pre-individual' state. According to the quantum theory Simondon was familiar with, or at least his interpretation of this theory, space, time and material objects like atoms each also have a journey of individuation from a pre-individual source (Penrose & Mermin, 1990).

As quantum physicist and philosopher Karen Barad points out, how reality appears to us, whether in terms of waves or particles for example, depends partly on the design of the measuring or observing apparatus. But no matter how this reality is experienced, there remains a connection to the original state of potentiality. That is why everything for Barad is understood as 'intra-action' within an entangled system, and not as 'interaction' between ontologically separate systems (Barad, 2007). Simondon makes the same distinction between intra-action and interaction in the contrast he draws between what he calls 'trans-individuality' and Husserl's intersubjectivity. Whereas intersubjectivity assumes individuated separate humans who interact, transindividuality is a kind of 'intra-action'. Transindividuality is possible, Simondon claims, because what we normally refer to as individual humans never completely lose their pre-individuality (Simondon, 2005). Simondon does not mention meditation, but that might provide an illustration of what his idea of an internal link to the pre-individual means in terms of human experience. In meditation or mindfulness individuals are encouraged to observe thoughts as they arise without identifying with them. The intention is to detach from specific thoughts, including thoughts about one's own identity in relation to others or objects in the world, to experience the underlying space of potential from within which these thoughts arise. Another illustration might be the phenomenon of 'flow', associated with creativity, which involves the loss of a sense of a strong boundary between self and environment (Csikszentmihalyi, 1990). This experience of an underlying space of potential is likely the same sort of thing that Simondon refers to as the pre-individual. The pre-individual is thus not a single, unified entity, but rather a field of potential from which all things arise.

According to Simondon, humans never completely individuate. We always maintain a dynamic and living relationship with the pre-individual state, and this is what allows us to continuously participate in psycho-social movements of transindividuation. The physicality or material nature of innovative ideas or creative breakthroughs can serve as a common ground between human individuals and technical objects. Technical objects, think of an internal combustion engine perhaps, create a space of internal resonance where the parts define the whole and the whole defines the parts. However, technical objects do not directly experience this internal space of resonance. For that, the addition of humans is required. An engineer tinkering with a technical object, like an internal combustion engine, can make a significant improvement to the design that enables the whole system to take a leap forward and resonate together in a better way. Simondon writes that the 'value of the dialogue of the individual with the technical object' is 'to create a domain of the transindividual, which is different from the community' (Simondon, 2005, p. 515). Transindividuation, as described by Simondon, is a bio-socio-technical process in which groups of human individuals and technical objects are united within a single new autopoietic system motivated by a common cause or 'problematic'. Consider the idea of transindividuation as applied to the new hybrid bio-technical systems that we create around books or social media platforms, for example, which can be thought of as a kind of 'larger self'. In other words, we should not understand collectives of people united in the use of technology only as systems defined by their external relations (i.e., as lots of individuals and machines inter-acting). Instead, we should think of these as new hybrid bio-technical systems that have their own shared internality or collective consciousness, and are themselves capable of agency.[10]

## Concretisation or the meaning of technical objects

Simondon argues that it is not only atoms, crystals and life forms like humans that have an individuation journey. He suggests technology also individuates. Key to understanding the development of technology is the concept of concretisation (Simondon, 2017). We tend to think of technology, from hammers to AI assistants on the internet, as if these are tools that we design to be useful for our own purposes. Simondon, however, distinguishes between the essential technicity of technology and its usefulness for people. He suggests technology has a certain motivation or direction of development. In the development of combustion engines, for example, what might start as lots of different gadgets ends up integrated into a single machine. Early air-cooled engines were originally designed with a separate fan. Over time, however, these ended up with a casing design that not only holds heat but also dissipates it. Simondon traces this kind of evolutionary progress in design as a process of the gradual individuation of technical objects to become what they, in a sense, always wanted to be. Of course, the engine elements do not have any agency independent of human engineers. But it is also true that human engineers do not always have a predetermined plan for how they will design a technical object. Often, they enter into a kind of dialogue with the technology, allowing it to potentially shape design decisions. According to Simondon, progress usually involves engineers putting their human ideas to one side to really spend time understanding the machine, how it works and how it could work better. This is similar to Heidegger's example of, in a sense, becoming the hammer and experiencing the world directly through the hammer as an extension of one's physical body when hammering. The engineer who is passionate about their work will develop a deep understanding of the machine they are working on, potentially entering into a shared internality of experience that leads to developments not simply imposed on the machine from the outside, but that emerge from within this cybernetic couple of machine plus engineer working together.

Understanding technical objects as evolving individuals having, in a certain sense described by Simondon, their own agency and meaning helps us to understand why technology can sometimes seem opposed to the meaning of human beings, in addition to how this experience of alienation can be overcome (Hui, 2018). Craft workers shape and develop their tools as an extension of themselves. When those tools become machines in factories that appear autonomous, then workers can find themselves de-skilled and reduced to the role of feeding machines the raw resources they need. It is understandable to blame the technology when this de-skilling occurs. However, the apparent technological rationality of maximising profits is not a product of the technology itself. Rather, it is a by-product of the larger political economic context in which the technology is embedded. Simondon suggests that technology, allowed to develop freely, will find creative solutions to the pressures and potentials in the environment. This includes pressures from inequalities in the social context. Reducing workers to tool carriers and machine fillers is not an optimal use of their potential and sets up tensions that are counterproductive for the flourishing of the overall system. One implication of Simondon's argument is that human participation in the design of technology is essential for technology to be experienced as an extension of human meaning making, rather than as a limitation or opposition to it as is so often experienced.

### The potential individuation of the internet

Simondon's claim that 'dialogue with technical objects' leads to transindividuation, the process by which groups take on an internal sense of identity and agency in combination with a shared technology, suggests a theory of technology and educational technology. As described in Chapter 2, education is a social process that draws biological individuals into larger collectives mediated by technology. The motivation for that transindividuation is not simply human alone, nor technological alone, but arises as a response to tensions within a larger system. For example, we explored in Chapter 2 how the first schools were in part a response to the pressures of large numbers of people living close together for the first time. As human populations grew and settled into more concentrated communities, there was a need for organised systems of education to transmit knowledge such as how to do contracts and to convey the shared stories that united the community. A more recent example of the same phenomenon might be the transnational self-education and activism groups forming via social media in response to the global threat of climate change (Castells, 2020; Kui, 2019; Slavina & Brym, 2020).

When Simondon writes of technology's agency, he understands that agency to be actualised when machines work together with humans. He describes how human engineers bring foresight to machine–human partnerships. The role of the engineer in a complex machine is not to impose their will on the machine from the outside, but to get to know the machine, to play with it and to understand it. By doing this, the engineer and the machine can generate a space of reflection and internal resonance, together able to anticipate what the system wants to achieve.

Simondon talks little about networks and he was writing before the advent of AI and the internet. When referring to technical objects he usually had in mind things like combustion engines, pumps and boilers, and other technologies that appear as if they stand alone. However, his concern with the motivation and meaning of technical objects can be applied to networks in general, and to the growing network of networks that is the internet. The internet is, of course, continually expanding to become more than an internet of human interactions but also an 'internet of things', a network supported by AI, in which devices communicate with each other. For instance, domestic fridges communicating with supermarkets, supermarkets communicating with transports, and transports communicating with factories.

The internet is not best understood as a network of nodes and links. This kind of representation, which is found in the theory of connectivism for example, implies that individuals are isolated and independent from each other (or 'socially atomised'). The alternative is to harness the potential of the internet as a kind of global individual (Beigi & Heylighen, 2021). Simondon points out that individuation is always more than the individuation of an individual. It also includes the individuation of a milieu, or all communications the individual has with its environment. In evolutionary biology, as seen in Chapter 3, the individuation of a species also involves the individuation of an ecological niche. As bees evolve, for example, so do beehives. Likewise, Hui and Halpin (2013, p. 111) write, 'one can see the genesis of a group as a kind of individuation, so that each individual is at the same time both an agent and a milieu'. This is a version of what in Chapter 5 we called a dialogic identity (see also Wegerif, 2013). Each individual identifies both as a voice in a dialogue and with the dialogue as whole within which their voice speaks (Stahl, 2006). Key to group identity is the shared project that unites the group, a shared responsibility in the face of an external call or demand like the challenge of a pandemic or global warming. Despite the limitations of current social media, which tend to assume and reinforce social atomism, Hui and Halpin (2013, p. 116) claim that a different kind of internet is possible. This internet would not represent a network of isolated individuals, but rather a network of interconnected individuals in a 'truly global conception of friendship and connection' which is about enabling us to 'take responsibility for our common world'. If this were to happen, and in small ways it is already happening in many contexts, it constitutes an example of what Simondon means by the term 'transindividuation'. This requires human–machine dialogue of a kind that could be supported by education, and especially by educational technology (Beigi & Heylighen, 2021).

The traditional model of agency is that individual humans have intentions and then design technology to implement those intentions. The alternative systems way of thinking about agency, which we have been outlining in this chapter, is that the entanglement of humanity with the communications technology of the AI-enhanced internet leads to a new level of autopoietic self-organisation that generates its own anticipation system and its own set of meanings and motivations. As Hui and Halpin outline, specific technological design features are important for enabling this development of a new form of autopoietic self-identity. What they appear to overlook, however, is the crucial role that education must play as part of the design of any successful bio-socio-technical system. Not education for the sake of education, but education for the use of new technology to form with this technology, and with other people, a new kind of self-identity.

To return to the issue of meaning with which we began this chapter, we can now see more clearly that meaning is not limited to what is felt by a human consciousness. Instead, it is produced by self-reproducing systems, many of which are larger than individual humans. Education for meaning is education that prepares students to participate in larger bio-socio-technical systems. Since these transindividual systems are as much technological as human, educational technology, far from standing in the way of human meaning, becomes a portal to enhanced meaning: which can potentially serve as a bridge to expanding the purpose and significance of individual human lives.

### Case study: Argunaut, an intelligent guide to support productive online dialogue

Argunaut, a European Union project, developed systems to enhance e-moderation of small groups online (De Laat et al., 2008). This involved developing a moderator's dashboard that automatically monitors dialogue in small groups to provide feedback, both to the moderators and the groups, for instance in terms of participation and what kinds of things were said (see Figure 7.2).

A dynamic concept mapping environment (Digalo) was used to code the quality of dialogue as follows:

1 *Critical thinking* with its focus on claims, counterclaims and reasons (D1).
2 *Creative reasoning* understood as a sort of dance of perspectives (D2).
3 *Dialogic engagement* including not only addressivity and expressions of empathy but also expressions of doubt, changes of mind, ventriloquation (the presence of another voice within an utterance) and elicitation of the views of others (D3).
4 *Moderation* through encouragement and the scaffolding support of recapitulations, reformulations and evaluations (D4).

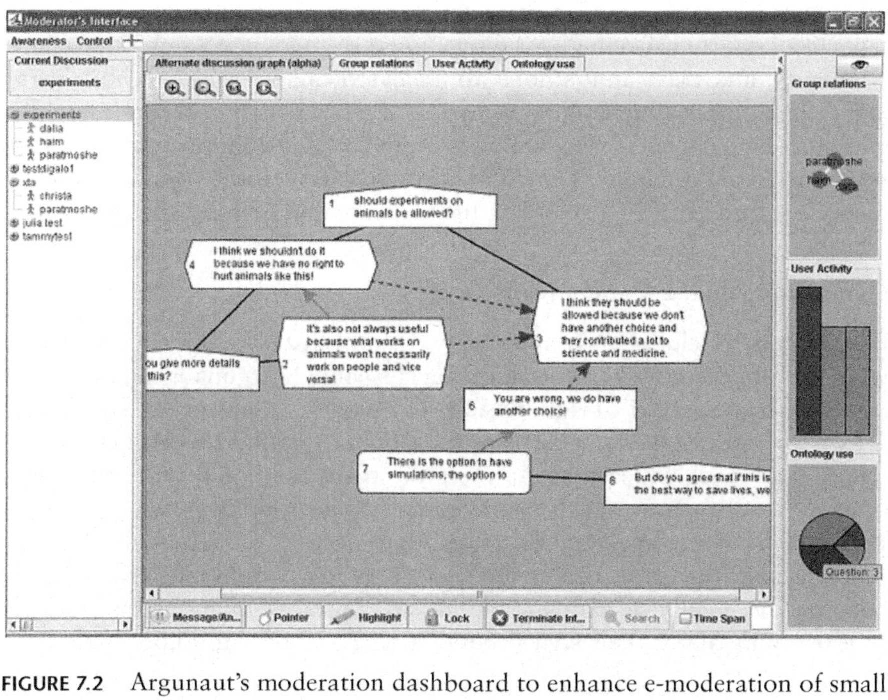


FIGURE 7.2 Argunaut's moderation dashboard to enhance e-moderation of small group dialogue online.

Using data-mining techniques, robust automated coding of both reasoning and creativity indicators was possible (Wegerif et al., 2010). Argunaut intended to support an online teacher with up to 100 groups of between five and eight students. This was a rare scenario at the time, but it became quite common a few years later when the Covid-19 pandemic forced much teaching online during 2020–2021.

The Argunaut system had two monitoring and feedback modules, a 'shallow loop' and a 'deep loop'. The 'shallow loop' is for ongoing discussions. This monitors awareness variables or 'indicators' (e.g., participation levels, quality of talk, social interaction patterns). If a possibly problematic or significant situation (pre-defined as such) is detected, an information panel appears, giving the moderator relevant information plus advice and intervention options. For example, sending a pre-set prompt into the shared argument map used in an online room to promote student participation, such as 'could you see this issue differently?' (if no 'creativity' was detected over a period of time) or 'what do you think, John?' (if one participant had not been posting).

The 'deep loop' unites a larger community over time using offline analysis with machine learning. This loop takes human-annotated examples of past e-discussion situations and attempts to learn the patterns underlying the examples. The approach used by the deep loop is classification learning, that is induction of classifiers from labelled examples, which can later be used to classify new and previously unseen examples. According to this approach, (1) 'experts' pre-define a typology for classification according to specific concepts (e.g., critical reasoning); (2) discussions are annotated according to these typologies, and these annotations are analysed offline using machine learning; (3) the output of the offline analysis is a set of situation classifiers, which may then be incorporated as indicators into the visualisation and awareness components of Argunaut. These modules can also generate feedback for the moderator and learners, explaining the situation and offering advice.

### *Commentary on the Argunaut case study*

Pickering uses Heidegger's terminology to establish a distinction between two ways of using technology: 'enframing' or 'revealing'. Argunaut can be seen as representing both sides of this division. The main idea looks to be enframing. This is the idea that a teacher uses a dashboard with AI techniques (data-mining and machine learning) to monitor words (and, implicitly, thoughts) of groups of students and to intervene to achieve a predetermined learning goal. But these AI-supported feedback loops also have the potential to support the education of learners as well as the whole community. Instant feedback on the quality of dialogue within small groups might enable students to learn more about their styles of interacting and how to improve these as a collective. In other words, these visualisations could support the formation of a transindividual group identity and group practice. Whether or not this technology is experienced as enframing (top-down control) or revealing (bottom-up empowerment and expansion of consciousness) might depend on how students enter into the experience. The motivations of teachers and institutions are also important. This includes whether they have a say in the design of the system, or if they feel it is being imposed on them. If students and teachers have a role in the design of the system and how learning is directed by the feedback mechanisms of visualisations and moderation, they are potentially more likely to be engaged in the learning process. This engagement might lead to the formation of a new shared consciousness.

Argunaut's deep loop is interesting because, with modifications, it has the potential to support larger group transindividuation. Argunaut was ahead of its time. Powerful AI-supported language assistants can now more effectively implement the aim of the deep loop to enable automatic group moderation.

If 'experts' decide what the learning goal is then it can be seen as a technology for enframing and, in Papert's words, 'programming' students. However, this enframing might also be an efficient way of achieving group educational goals, from improving the ground rules of online discussion, to learning more about the causes and solutions of contemporary challenges such as global warming. If the decision of what to learn together, or how to change together, is made collectively through dialogue, then this type of technology can support transindividuation. This dialogic vision of transindividual growth through education requires that the goals and the coding process are frequently revisited by the entire community involved in the learning – this includes students, moderators and others with a stake including researchers and designers (Stahl, 2021).

## Discussion

When people talk about intelligent machines, they almost invariably imply a very narrow definition of what it means to be intelligent. Machines are generally referred to as smart or intelligent if they can solve problems fast and effectively (Russell, 2010). However, the etymology of the word intelligence suggests that its original meaning does not only relate to achieving goals, but is more fundamentally about selecting the right goals in the first place. This modern evolution of the meaning of the word intelligence perhaps illustrates Heidegger's concern about how technological thinking is potentially enframing and might limit our thinking by replacing the important with the superficial.

In the offered case study, the danger that technology might be used to limit the possibilities of learning is clear. Having specific fixed learning goals, and generating feedback on them, could make Argunaut into an efficient system for achieving any kind of learning objective. However, it might also become a system in which learners feel trapped and manipulated. On the other hand, designing a deep-loop process where everyone can participate in providing feedback on the pedagogical interventions of the system demonstrates the potential to design a self-organising system that itself is alive and learning, while also enhancing the learning of all participants in the system.

We began this chapter with the problem that some people have with the 'meaning' of technology in education, the widespread and often repeated assumption that the use of technology is somehow opposed to human meaning. We investigated what is meant by meaning to see how this problem arises and how it might be overcome. We suggested that Husserl's account of meaning as something that is experienced by consciousness might be one cause of the problem. This argument suggests that if meaning is only created by human consciousness, and technology is not conscious, then technology cannot have meaning of its own. It seems to follow for some that the use of technology can undermine and threaten the uniquely human experience of meaning. However, Husserl's phenomenology was not entirely successful because meaning in consciousness is dependent, we argued, on 'differences' that refer to things that are not present in consciousness. The difference between 'now' and 'then' for example. Reality, it turns out, is best understood as a system of differences rather than as things that are present to a consciousness. Reality is ultimately, we suggested, not made up of things like atoms, people, objects and tools. Instead, it is better understood as information, where the smallest unit of information is 'a difference that makes a difference'. If meaning is something that makes a difference in a larger system, and that system is not entirely present to any individual human consciousness, then meaning is greater than or beyond any given experience to self-consciousness. Meaning is not just 'my' construction or 'your' construction (i.e., it is not only something created by individuals). Rather, it is a property of systems that are often larger than us. The difference that a bit of information makes is always a difference for a system, and a system, in this context, is a self-organising collection of bits of information.

Husserl's account of a consciousness separate from the world is a story with deep roots found also in Kant and earlier in Descartes. The image of the mind as an information processing machine found in cognitive psychology since the 1950s and 1960s is another version of this story. The alternative that we are proposing is that 'we', 'consciousness' and 'intelligence' are always already found in the play of differences that constitute reality, even before a 'self' is divided from a 'world'. Doing so, we suggest, allows the role of technology to be taken more seriously. And if meaning is something created by the self-organisation (or autopoiesis) of systems of information, then it becomes possible, we claim, to overcome the problem of the loss of meaning. Instead of understanding humans as uniquely able to give meaning to reality through their self-conscious intentions, we now see that humans are self-organising systems of information, or rather a system of systems each of which is a patterning of differences with many components and levels, linguistic differences, biological differences between cells and molecules, material differences between atoms: highly complex self-organising systems of information that connect with other, often larger, sometimes encompassing self-organising information systems. Humans can play the role of awareness or anticipation within these other larger systems. However, the meanings that humans can become aware of are not 'our' own meanings, nor are they uniquely 'human' or individual meanings. Instead, they are the meanings that emerge within the systems that we participate within. What the phenomenologist Husserl explored as the horizon of meaning for consciousness is not created by humans alone, we argued, but by a human plus technological plus natural cybernetic system. We all individually experience meaning in our lives, in the sense of finding purpose and direction, through our participation in larger bio-socio-technical systems within which technology plays an essential mediating role. The role of educational technology then is to help students discover a larger sense of meaning only accessible by extending our humanity to live with and through technology.

The cybernetics work of Pask and Simondon provides examples of a technological meaning that is not opposed to nature but is instead a living part of nature. Technological systems grow, develop and have lives of their own. Although these systems depend on humans, they are not completely determined by humans. Human engineers are needed for technical systems to flourish. But it is also true, as we explored in Chapter 2, that humans are always already entangled with technology. Technological systems that appear to oppose human meaning are those designed with a particular goal in mind, such as the goal of making a profit. Such goals, which are often embedded in technology's original design, become blocks to meaning when they are not revisited and revised dynamically. As a result, the range of voices and interests impacted on by the technology are not considered, especially those who use the technology. The alternative outlined by Gilbert Simondon is to design machines that work with humans and nature to enhance and amplify the world-revealing and world-creating potential of technology.

Humans learn as both individuals and groups by participating in the learning of the system. Education enables individuals to cross the boundary between themselves as separate biological organisms and the larger bio-socio-technical system that we are a part of. The design and development of educational technology can facilitate participation in the individuation journey of the expanded internet as the new transindividual reality, particularly pointed to by ideals such as 'global citizenship'. Educational technology might be argued to have the potential to help humanity become a new kind of planetary-wide self-regulating organism. This would mean that each person would be able to identify both as an individual unit within the system, and with the system as a whole. But talk of 'individuals' and the 'system as a whole' is potentially misleading. Such concepts tend to reify or 'thingify' (make something into a thing) an experience which is actually a constant flow of dialogue. Experience of participating in the flow of meaning in a dialogue naturally generates a kind of illusion that there are two opposing poles, that of the biologically defined individual on the inside, and that of the 'whole' (or 'totality', 'cosmos' or 'horizon') on the outside. This is an illusion because during the course of the dialogue images of both the individual and the whole are created within the dialogue, as well as being projected as if they were realities outside of the dialogue. Embracing and identifying with the process of dialogue means to see both the individual voice (within the whole) and the whole (as containing the individual voice). A dialogic identity is a dynamic or oscillating double identity in this sense.

### *Prompts towards a dialogic foundation for the design and use of educational technology*

In this chapter we developed the idea that individuals learn by participating in the learning of larger systems. This can be converted into a principle for educational technology design: to induct students into using digital communications in ways that connect them to others and other resources in self-reflective and self-developing learning networks. The Argunaut case study illustrates this principle. The system makes students more aware of the way that they are learning together with others. But a bespoke educational technology system like Argunaut is not necessarily required. As argued in Chapter 1, any technology that incorporates pedagogy or that is combined with pedagogy becomes an educational technology. Inducting students to build and participate in expanding, self-reflective learning communities using existing digital technology is also educational technology. Generative AIs like Chat GPT can already be used very effectively to moderate small group learning both online and, via a social humanoid robot like Pepper,[11] potentially face-to-face spoken dialogue too.

The Citizen Science approach developed by the Open University UK in partnership with the BBC (https://nquire.org.uk/) illustrates how online dialogue and exchange can support shared inquiries. But many online platforms, and social media in addition, can be used to support this kind of collaborative educational activity (e.g., Wikipedia).

The concept of transindividuation introduced in this chapter is central to education. Educational technology can be designed to support transindividuation, using technology development for instance as a focus for dialogue in which a group project leads to the development of group identity and the experience of group intelligence. Building robots together is a tried and tested way to achieve this within education, but there are many other kinds of projects that could be used to stimulate the experience of learning how to learn together with others and technology.

Transindividuation depends upon developing a dialogic or double identity; encompassing being both a voice within a larger system and also being the voice or perspective of that larger system, just as in an effective dialogue each person hears not only their own voice but can also judge how that voice sounds from the perspective or point of view of the dialogue as a whole. Educational technology design can support this by supporting an oscillation between inside and outside perspectives. For example, the Flipgrid[12] video discussion platform makes it easy for students in an online class to upload an introductory video. It also makes it easy for students to locate themselves and their video within the grid of all the class videos. Alternatively, the use of data visualisation software like Tinkerplots[13] makes it easy for students to generate and upload personal statistics into a system. Tinkerplots then displays the statistics in a way that students can see patterns related to the statistics of the class, the school, the nation and the world.

# 8

# TECHNOLOGY AND EXPANDING DIALOGIC SPACE

*Language is as old as consciousness, language is practical, real consciousness that exists for other men as well, and only therefore does it also exist for me; language, like consciousness, only arises from the need, the necessity, of intercourse with other men.*

Karl Marx and Friedrich Engels (1845/1970, Part 1, Section A.4)

*Transposing ourselves consists neither in the empathy of one individual for another nor in subordinating another person to our own standards; rather, it always involves rising to a higher universality that overcomes not only our own particularity but also that of the other.*

Hans Gadamer (1989, p. 304)

## Introduction

In Chapter 7 we argued that Gilbert Simondon's account of how dialogue with technology led to 'transindividuation' was also an account of how technology could help to open and sustain larger dialogic spaces that nclude many voices and technologies. We even suggested that this process of generating 'transindividuals' offers a new way of understanding what education does. A transindividual is a collective identity, an expanded subjectivity or internality, that builds upon combinations of individual humans with material technologies. When San bushmen are inducted into responding to cave paintings, or when students in primary schools are taught to read canonical books, these educational processes are not just about 'individuation' but also about 'transindividuation'. Education has always been about inducting students into a larger sense of self, a cultural self. But in this

DOI: 10.4324/9781003198499-8

book, we argue that the role that technology plays in this process has mostly been overlooked or minimised. By defining transindividuation as requiring 'dialogue with technical objects', Simondon reminds us of just how central technology is to education. If education is a process of facilitated transindividuation, then teaching students how to use the shared technology is core to what education does and how education works.

The idea of dialogic space, the space of possibility that opens up between voices or perspectives in dialogue, was introduced in Chapter 1 and has been referred to throughout the book. At first sight this seems to be nothing to do with technology. But perhaps this intuition that dialogue is not technological is much like the way in which people with glasses forget the essential mediating role of technology when they look out at a landscape and see it clearly. Dialogic space works in education because it becomes a new perspective or 'voice' in the dialogue which we described earlier, in Chapter 5, as the witness position. Students in dialogue learn to see themselves – or hear their voices – from the perspective of the dialogue as a whole, and so they are able to challenge their own ideas and change their views. Dialogue enables people to 'rise above' and see more clearly. This does not seem to be anything to do with technology at first sight, but technology in some form is there making it possible. Dialogue is not only between voices defined by their biology, by the movements of tongue and larynx producing sounds for example, it also uses shared material technologies like particular words which could take the form of shaped airwaves or signs on paper or bits of information in digital arrays. The sense in which dialogic space offers students an expanded identity, albeit a 'dialogic' identity, links the idea of education as expanding dialogic space to the idea of transindividuation developed in Chapter 7.

In this chapter, we explore the concept of dialogic space in more detail focusing on how it intersects with technology. We set the scene with a brief history of how communications technology plus education technology have expanded dialogic space since the beginning of the human adventure. We then examine the potential of 'edubots', or computers or robots that can interact with students in a conversational way, to expand dialogic space in education. We argue that such interlocutors might offer potential advantages over human teachers in this regard. The contemporary educational concept of dialogic space began with research evaluating the impact of teaching exploratory talk in primary schools. We revisit that research and relate it to the philosophical idea of the space of dialogue as 'the space between' elaborated by Martin Buber. Buber contrasted the 'I–Thou' orientation of dialogue, an orientation of mutuality and respect that treats 'others' as another self, to the objectifying 'I–It' orientation where others are considered as objects. Expanding Buber's theory, we claim that the dialogic spaces which open up when there is an 'I–Thou' relationship are always supported by technology, and that different technologies lead to different kinds of dialogic space. Nonetheless, we retain Buber's account of the educational significance of dialogic space as drawing us into dialogue with a perspective he calls 'the eternal Thou', a perspective that we reconceptualise a little and refer to as 'the Infinite Other', borrowing and adapting an idea from Levinas.

## Technology and the expansion of dialogic space

Our claim is that educational technology can expand dialogic space as well as change the nature of it. The significance of this claim becomes clearer when we revisit and further consider the history of education.

### *Cave paintings*

David Lewis-Williams describes how cave paintings took on an 'I–Thou' quality for San Bushmen tribe members who used the cave. The animals painted on the walls would come alive and talk back. But to outsiders, to tourists and scientists for instance, they are mostly experienced in 'I–It' mode as just images painted in crushed hematite and blood on the walls of the cave. As discussed in Chapter 2, for the tribe who painted them, these cave paintings provided 'voices' that could support continuity and development as each new generation was inducted into an ongoing dialogue with their ancestors – a dialogue potentially perduring over thousands of years. The idea of dialogic space uses the word 'space' to refer to a shared space of meaning, rather than simply to physical space. Cave painting expanded the dialogue not only spatially, uniting the members of the tribe in one shared culture, but also temporally, enabling continuity and dialogic interaction with the shared spirit voices of the tribe over time.[1] We write more about the way in which 'dialogic space' can sometimes also be thought of as 'dialogic time' in Chapter 9.

### *Writing*

Michael Oakeshott describes education as induction into a global 'conversation of mankind', which, he writes, began 'in the primeval forests and (is) extended and made more articulate in the course of the centuries' (1959, p. 199). In this conversation learners can discover the voices of Socrates and Confucius, Julian of Norwich, bell hooks and many more from all times and regions. This is only possible because these voices are written down. Oral people from the time before the widespread use of writing, and those more or less oral only people who live around the fringes of writing, many indigenous groups for example, do not get to participate in this conversation. At least in terms of the size and geographical spread of the community reached, the technology of writing enables the expansion of dialogic space.[2] However, because this space is materially mediated, the space supported by writing is also always shaped and limited. We only know Socrates' words because they were written down by Plato. But as Socrates pointed out, the process of writing words down does not just transfer the meaning of spoken words, it also changes this meaning. As discussed in Chapter 2, in literate cultures, the nature of knowledge – and by association the process of education – changes in a direction away from knowing as relationship and towards knowing as representation. The dialogue of humanity referred to by Oakeshott is a dialogue of only one kind of human, the literate human, mediated by only one kind of technology, written words.

Despite this limitation, writing has clearly served to expand collective dialogic space in a way that has increased knowledge for the human race considered as a whole (albeit in ways that are not evenly distributed). We have made much of Socrates' provocative claim that written signs are dead whereas spoken words are alive. But time has demonstrated that written words can also open a new, shared, dialogic space within which people can think together.

### *The internet*

In recent decades, the internet has been gradually replacing print as the dominant medium of communication (Poster, 2001, 2018; Wegerif, 2013). In doing so, it offers a return to some of the dialogic affordances of oracy, as it allows for the potential of living relationships with multiple voices.

The dialogue of humanity now appears in real time online. It can be argued that the role of education today is not simply to induct students into their inheritance of written cultural voices, but also to induct them into participation in living dialogues on the internet. Digitally mediated space, once called 'cyberspace', now sometimes referred to as the 'metaverse', is not an external space that can be measured in terms of servers and fibre-optic cables: it has the potential to be a dialogic space supporting the interplay of billions of voices. Of course, this potential of the internet to support dialogic spaces is often only falteringly and imperfectly realised. Realising this potential is arguably a key educational project for humanity.

The internet is, in some respects, the new cave (see Chapter 2). Or, at least, it has the potential to be experienced as such. Educational technology might provide a means for learners of all ages to step through into a collective cultural world, in a manner not dissimilar to the San Bushmen who would 'step through' the painted walls of their caves (Lewis-Williams, 2002; Lewis-Williams & Dowson, 1990). The signs on the internet are multimodal. They are not simply words on a page, but rather music, pictures and living video images. Increasingly, currently with the aid of headsets, the experience of stepping through into 3D reality is provided. This offers a potential return to the experience of those creating cave paintings 40,000 years ago, but with a significant difference – the internet has the potential to support a dialogic space with access from anywhere on the planet. In contrast, the membership of the dialogic space supported by those who maintained a particular cave was exclusive to a geographically located small community.

The internet, especially when enhanced by AI language assistants, has the potential to support shared dialogic spaces. However, many claim that this potential has not been realised. There has been much concern about how, in practice, the internet does not promote dialogue and community but so-called 'echo-chambers' where people with similar views might gather and have their views reinforced (Terren & Borge-Bravo, 2021). Political concerns have led to some countries filtering and blocking sites on the internet. There is also much, justified concern about the spread of misinformation (Fisher, 2022). As discussed in Chapter 3, any experience of sharing a cultural space does not depend on technology alone but also requires pedagogy. Adventures in the shared cultural space of the San Bushmen required complex preparation including storytelling and trance-dancing. In a similar way pedagogy is needed, as well as technology and favourable political context, if the potential of the AI-enhanced internet is to support a more global dialogic space. This is not something that can happen without purposefully designing the educational technology, that is to say designing technology and pedagogy together, so as to turn this promise of expanded dialogic space from potential to reality (Wegerif, 2019).

## AI chatbots as openers of dialogic space

The success of AI language assistants has raised awareness of the educational role of edubots, or 'robot' voices guiding students in real time. These artificial voices may offer the capacity to extend and transform the educational potential of the internet by inducting students into a shared dialogic space. To make that argument, we begin with the story of ELIZA.

Turing famously proposed a test for artificial intelligence (AI) which became called the 'Turing Test'. This test is that if a computer can fool a person that it is human, then it should be considered intelligent (Turing, 1950). To demonstrate the limitations of the Turing Test model of AI, early computing pioneer Joseph Weizenbaum created ELIZA, a simple pattern matching program designed to trick listeners into thinking it was another human (Weizenbaum, 1966). Using client-centred psychotherapy as a model, Weizenbaum's program used quite simple pattern matching techniques to encourage a person to talk about themselves. For instance, if you ask ELIZA who it thinks it is, it will reply, 'we are talking about you not me'. Or if you mention a keyword like 'mother' it will say, 'tell me more about your mother?' Weizenbaum's aim was to undermine the hubristic thinking of AI by demonstrating the simplicity of software that could, to some extent, create the impression of talking to another human. He was countering what he saw as greatly exaggerated claims of 'artificial intelligence' with a performative demonstration of what he himself referred to as 'artificial stupidity'.

Weizenbaum was genuinely surprised when he found that informed people who understood the simplicity of the software spent hours in conversation with ELIZA (Weizenbaum, 1976). It often turned out that talking to ELIZA helped people with their problems. Versions of ELIZA spread rapidly with some still in use for therapy (Bainbridge, 2008). A variation of this approach, AVATAR therapy, has shown benefits for patients experiencing persistent distressing voices. AVATAR makes use of digital representations of psychotic experiences to provide a controlled, but realistic, therapeutic encounter (Craig et al., 2017). It seems that externalising voices and dialoguing with them may help patients to gain insight, greater control, and to make positive changes.

The success of software in prompting what appears to be real learning dialogues challenges some ways of thinking about dialogue. Dialogue is normally defined in dictionaries and other literature as separate consciousnesses actively responding to each other (e.g., Rommetveit, 1992). However, dialogue on this model is an aspect of what Simondon referred to as the misguided or inadequate idea of intersubjectivity, something that he contrasted

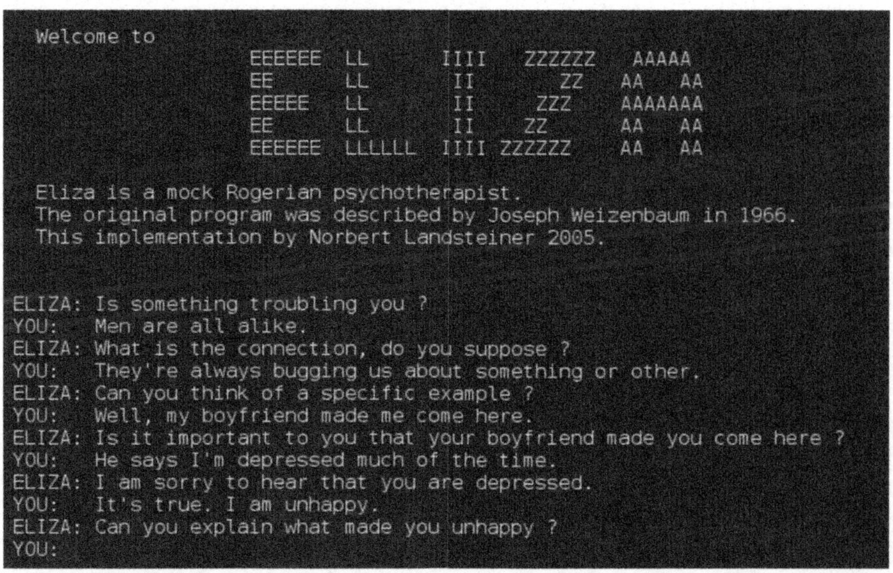


**FIGURE 8.1** A conversation with ELIZA.

*Source:* https://commons.wikimedia.org/wiki/File:ELIZA_conversation.png.

with his concept of transindividuality (see Chapter 7). The false idea of intersubjectivity, according to Simondon, assumes already individuated people, bodies separated from each other in space, communicating with each other across space using the medium of external signs. The challenge to this model of dialogue comes from the fact that ELIZA is not a separate consciousness, but yet it can stimulate educationally valuable dialogues.

Returning to Simondon's understanding of 'transindividuality' can help us understand the ELIZA phenomenon. Transindividuality can be understood as about stepping back from the individuated appearance of things to enter into a shared internality, which is a space of internal resonance and potential. For Simondon, as unpacked in Chapter 7, the individuation process always begins with a 'pre-individual' state of potential. For material individuation processes such as crystallisation, the initial state of potential, the supersaturation of a solution for example, is lost in the one-way process of the precipitation of crystals. However, for what Simondon called 'psychic' individuation, becoming an individual consciousness, some of the pre-individual state is retained even in the apparently individuated state. This account suggests that human individuals can return to the pre-individual potential out of which the individuated self originally emerged. The phenomenon of 'flow', which involves the loss of a sense of a strong boundary between self and environment, was previously offered as perhaps one example (Csikszentmihalyi, 1990). This stepping back from the individuated surface to the pre-individual depth is necessary for new individuations, transindividuations, to occur. Human transindividuations are supported by technologies or what Simondon refers to as 'dialogue with technical objects' (Simondon, 2017). Transindividuation is not something that humans do once before entering a new fixed state of identity. Rather, it is something that humans constantly do, continually creating expanded shared new 'internal' spaces of reflection supported by technology. The dialogue with ELIZA shown in Figure 8.1 is therefore a good example of how dialogue with a technical object might lead to transindividuation, an expanded experience of self. But perhaps a better example for our argument in this book is how a group mind can form around a shared technical object like a team working together on an engineering project or a group learning together with the same tools in an online environment (Stahl, 2006).

Descendants of ELIZA, AI language assistants based on Large Language Models (LLMs), are now routinely being used as online 'learning guides' in the Khan Academy and to support language learners using the Duolingo mobile app. There is, of course, a danger that such tools might only be used to 'train' behaviour and not to open up genuine spaces of reflection. But there is also a suggestion that the rise of AI assistants in education could lead to a focus on asking the kind of questions that take knowledge forward. This apparently progressive move might, in some ways, offer a return to the pedagogy advocated by Socrates.

## The end of writing in education?

In Chapter 2 we introduced Socrates' critique of writing. Writing, he thought, leads to imitated understanding. Real understanding, by contrast, requires face-to-face dialogue. Anyone, he says to his companion Phaedrus, can borrow a scroll from the library, read it out loud and sound wise, without having to go through the education required to actually be wise. Socrates saw himself as an educator. However, his interest was not in transmitting knowledge, but in teaching his students how to ask better questions. Socrates described himself as wise only in the sense that he recognised just how little he knew. This was in contrast to many others in Athens who seemed to think that they knew lots of things for certain until questioned. Meno, for example, claimed that he knew what virtue was. When challenged by Socrates to define virtue, however, he was stunned into silence. Meno later described Socrates as being like the torpedo fish that delivers an electric shock that paralyses its victims. Socrates accepts this metaphor and reworks it, demonstrating, with an illustration, that the shock of his questions is not intended to silence people but to wake them up: provoking them to think again to become more aware not only of their ignorance, but also of their actual knowledge when prompted to think more deeply.

The emergence of Generative AI language assistants that can write good essays and pass exams can be argued to act like the torpedo fish in its questioning challenge to education. This kind of AI shows us how right Socrates was to question the educational value of writing. If students can pass exams and score high marks by handing in essays generated by digital algorithms, then clearly writing is not, and should not, be the main goal of education.

An important distinction is often made in the philosophy of education which illuminates the educational challenge posed by ChatGPT and similar approaches, the distinction between training and education (Peters, 2010). Education, according to the liberal education tradition, should go beyond training to encourage critical thinking, creativity, freedom of thought and moral development.[3] This distinction has sometimes been misappropriated to value a more academic education, studying Plato for example, over a more vocational education, perhaps studying design and technology. But this is a mistake, as whatever anyone does in life requires learning knowledge and skills best acquired through imitation and training. Genuine education goes beyond this training element to teach how to critically question what has been learnt, in order to best understand it, and so to creatively move forward regardless of whether the end goal is how to build better computer code or to write a better essay.

If Generative AI chatbots can do well in exams, then perhaps much of what has been passed off as 'education' even in elite educational institutions, and 'academic' subjects like philosophy, is actually just a form of training.

Rubrics when marking essays point to the liberal education ideal with phrases like 'demonstrates critical awareness', 'develops a personal synthesis' and 'shows signs of original thought'. However, educators know these phrases correspond to ways of writing which students can be trained to emulate. They send essays, educators pick at them, before sending them back in an iterative cycle. This continues until the students, or those motivated enough to stick with the programme, are trained to write in a 'standard' or 'conventional' way. This is very similar to the way in which AI language assistants are trained. Perhaps that is why they can increasingly learn to write academic texts even better than academics.

## Why we are different from AI

The true value of education beyond the training of behaviour can be seen in the shining eyes and enthusiasm of learners who have just had an insight that changes the way that they see things. Such insights happen not in the written text itself, but in dialogues; in the dialogic space of new possibilities that opens up in the clash between voices or the clash between texts. Real education implies a change in identity, or at least in perspective, in addition to an expansion of awareness to see things that were previously opaque more clearly (hooks, 2014).

AI can be trained but it cannot be 'educated'. If you examine how Generative AI works, you find a set of algorithms with no understanding whatsoever. In response to persistent claims that computers could become intelligent, philosopher John Searle (1982) created a thought experiment called the 'Chinese Room' to illustrate the difference between how computers process information and how humans think. Imagine that you are locked in a room with a book of rules for manipulating symbols. You do not know any Chinese, but you can follow the rules in the book. Someone outside the room slides papers with Chinese characters under the door. You look up the symbols in the book and follow the instructions to produce a response. You then slide the paper back under the door. To someone outside, it may seem that you understand Chinese, but actually you do not.

This can be used to illustrate a key difference between AI and humans: AI does not genuinely understand what it is reading because it is not conscious; humans at least have the potential to understand because they are, or at least have the potential to be, conscious.

## Dialogic education with AI

But what does the word 'conscious' really mean in practice? Socrates' example of a kind of questioning that is like an electric shock, waking the learner up to see things differently, is a good example. To become more conscious of something, to understand it better, means to question it, challenge it and see it from an outside perspective. In education, when you are led by a dialogue to see things from an outside perspective, you can become more conscious of it. Only by seeing things as if from the outside, from a metaphorical distance, can you begin to understand them. Dialogic space is essential to consciousness, and expanding dialogic space is the true meaning of what Freire and others refer to as 'conscientisation' or consciousness raising. To teach students to be more than 'trained machines' such as AI, we need to educate for dialogue. This dialogic education does not need to be complicated. In essence, it involves drawing students into dialogue, asking them questions, and getting them to ask questions in turn. The goal is not just to know stuff about stuff, but to be able to ask better questions about stuff.

AI language assistants can help with this. In every area of study, especially in more obviously vocational subjects, it might reset the balance between training and education. Conversations with AI tutors have the potential to accelerate learning of essential knowledge in any curriculum, freeing up time and resources for the more exploratory aspects of education. This includes asking questions, exploring alternatives, engaging in dialogue and being creative. Our own provisional proof of concept experiments already strongly suggest that Generative AI can be an effective facilitator of small group educational dialogues, drawing in participants and summarising what has been learnt as the dialogue progresses.

From its inception, the internet enabled a new kind of educational dialogue, dialogue with the internet itself (Wegerif, 2013). AI language assistants are a significant step in taking this educational potential of the internet further. Used as a dialogue partner, AI assistants provide a potentially rapid way for learners to be socialised by exposing them to what George Herbert Mead called the 'Generalised Other'. The Generalised Other refers to the expectations and norms that an individual learns from a society or community. It consists of 'what everybody thinks', and 'what everybody knows', to form the perspective of the community or society as a whole. Students develop educationally by internalising the voice of the Generalised Other. Through asking questions of AI language assistants and AI tutors, students might discover what has been thought and written in any area up to now, and also learn to imitate how it has been written.[4]

Dialogue with the Generalised Other is an important early stage of education, but it is not the final stage. The next stage is to learn to question and challenge the Generalised Other or 'what everybody thinks'. This is important because it allows a learner to develop their own unique perspectives and meanings, at least new perspectives and meaning for them, thereby taking their place within a larger dialogue. Generative AI could be a useful tool for education if students learn how to use it critically and creatively. This is perhaps like the game of 'piggy-back' or 'leapfrog', where dialogue with AI language assistants can enable students to build on what others have said about a topic. Students might for instance work in partnership with such a tool to interrogate what it says about identifying a particular knowledge gap, before trying to address those gaps and going further.

Unlike AI language assistants, humans are conscious. This means that we exist in dialogic space as well as physical space, giving us the ability to ask better questions and to question what we can learn from an AI. Generative AI is a fast learner and can be trained into almost every area of knowledge. Until now, education has been dominated by the need to catch up with the Generalised Other. For many years, this has involved students being trained to think the same way, and to write the same kind of essays, similar to others in that field. Dialogic education with AI, education based on a continuous dialogue with AI, offers the potential to prepare learners more effectively for the next level of education: dialogue with the Infinite Other. Whatever state of knowledge or understanding you think you have reached, it is always possible to question it as if from an outside position, and this capacity to always question and go beyond is what we mean by the voice of the Infinite Other. Later in this chapter, we discuss the idea of Infinite Other again in relation to Buber.

## Dialogic space as a pedagogical tool

We argued above that ELIZA can open and expand a personal dialogic space. Questioning AI Chatbots has the potential to open a more collective dialogic space, and to support a kind of dialogue with the current knowledge of humanity as uploaded to the internet. The idea of dialogic space has increasingly been applied in many studies of educational technology (e.g., Moate et al., 2019; Palmgren-Neuvonen et al., 2021). But the educational theory of dialogic space emerged out of empirical studies of talk in UK and Mexican classrooms in the 1990s. As well as a philosophical and psychological theory of how classroom dialogue leads to learning, it is also a pedagogical tool to support teachers wanting to promote educational dialogue.

The concept of dialogic space was developed to explain why some groups are more successful than other groups at constructing meaning and solving problems together in classrooms. The research team – Neil Mercer, Lyn Dawes, Rupert Wegerif, Karen Littleton, Sylvia Rojas-Drummond and many others – found two main ways of talking in groups that did not do well at thinking together. Groups that engaged in 'Cumulative Talk' agreed with each other, sharing ideas uncritically without challenging each other or seeking explanations. This worked for some tasks. However, it did not help learners solve problems together when those problems required the children to challenge their assumptions. Groups that engaged in 'Disputational Talk' were more challenging, they disagreed with each other, competing as individuals to get the correct answer but without sharing their reasoning. Groups that engaged in 'Exploratory Talk' performed best at thinking together around problems of the kind found in tests of cognitive ability, as well as across a range of task contexts. Exploratory talk was originally defined as making reasoning visible in the talk, giving reasons for claims and engaging with each other's reasoning (Mercer, 1995).

Analysing 'types of talk' to see if the talk observed is cumulative, disputational or exploratory refers to more than just the words that learners use. It is an interpretation of the underlying ground rules or assumptions that shape the talk, something which can only be interpreted through a kind of participant observation. To fully understand and interpret a dialogue, you need to project yourself into that dialogue as if you are participating. These 'types of talk' reflected different ways learners relate to each other; different kinds of 'orientation towards the other' leading to different kinds of self-identification. In Cumulative Talk learners identify with an image of the group. 'We think' is more important than 'I think'. But this sense of 'we' is monologic or 'single-voiced'. The group has an identity, but they do not want this harmonious sense of identity to be disrupted by potentially divisive challenges, meaning critical or challenging contributions tend to be ignored. In Disputational Talk, by contrast, criticising and challenging is the norm. Each learner in the group identifies with themselves as an ego or self-image, promoting what they understand to be their individual self-interest, and wanting to be correct and others to be wrong. A key move identified for successful Exploratory Talk was individuals reflecting on their own positions and changing their minds. This implies that they can identify with a position outside of themselves to look back and critique their own claims. They were not only identifying with themselves, nor only with the views of specific others. It was suggested that they were identifying with the shared dialogue, or what became known as the 'dialogic space' (Wegerif & Mercer, 1997).

A pedagogical approach to teach students how to 'think together' was developed as part of this programme of research projects (Dawes et al., 2000). Thinking Together focuses on developing and reinforcing shared 'ground rules for talk'. For example, listening with respect, building on what others say, giving reasons, offering elaborated explanations, respectfully challenging reasons given by others and exploring alternatives. After being taught Thinking Together, groups that were successful at analogical graphical problems (Raven's non-verbal reasoning test exercises) used words and interaction patterns associated with Exploratory Talk. They also seemed to shift their identification from either self or group to the process of the dialogue itself. Or, put another way, members of successful groups were more interested in working together to solve the problem than they were in being correct themselves or in maintaining group harmony by not challenging others. This more 'dialogic' identity, identification with the agency and aims of the dialogue more than with the agency and aims of self or group, could be seen in shared pregnant pauses indicative of being able to accept a state of uncertainty. It could also be observed in individuals being able to ask for help and to change their mind without embarrassment, in addition to being able to complete the unfinished utterances of others without anyone seeming concerned about issues of who owned the ideas. These were all clues that such groups were 'thinking together' effectively (Wegerif, 2008).

Research evidence from primary and secondary school classrooms consistently shows that the Thinking Together approach works. But why does it work? Video analysis suggests that the talk itself did not directly co-construct solutions. Instead, it indirectly contributed to the creation of successful solutions. Asking open-ended questions often led to shared pauses before one person in the group came up with a solution. This solution was then shared through talking and explanations. In other words, the talk was useful before the event of solving the problem by focusing the group's joint attention and maintaining that focus. It was also useful after the event of solving the problem by articulating the solution with words that enabled it to be repeated, and shared with others. However, the talk did not itself directly lead to solving the problem.

Results of an experimental study led by Professor Sylvia Rojas-Drummond in Mexico help to distinguish between these different accounts. Students were taught how to think together before their performance on a shared creative task (writing a short text together), and a shared reasoning task was assessed. The way that they talked together was also analysed (Rojas-Drummond et al., 2008). The Thinking Together approach, with its focus on shared ground rules for talk, improved outcomes in both tasks. However, talk in the successful creative task did not have the explicit reasoning moves – moves such as 'I think X because Y' – previously claimed by some as the cause of Exploratory Talk's success. The results of this experiment suggest that definitions of successful group collaborations that focus solely on the talk alone are inadequate. 'Exploratory Talk', if defined in terms of explicit reasoning, turns out to be a sub-set of a larger type of 'Dialogic Talk'. In other words, explicit verbal reasoning is relevant to success for some tasks, such as solving reasoning tests, but not for all tasks. What seems to be most important to groups successfully working together in a range of contexts is entering into a shared 'dialogic space' (Wegerif, 2006, 2007, 2013). This does not mean that the way people talk together is irrelevant. Rather, talk often works indirectly to open, widen and/or deepen dialogic spaces. These spaces are themselves more directly important to the success of the group.

## Digital devices as a bridge into shared dialogic spaces

Our discussion of teaching machines and the ways in which the roles of computers have been conceptualised within education in Chapter 4 suggests that digital devices can be seen as both objects (tools to be used) and independent subjects (when they stand in for teachers and guide learning activities). For example, on the one hand, it is common for students to say that a digital device thinks or makes mistakes. On the other hand, even young children quickly learn that digital devices do not have feelings, expectations and implicit judgements like human conversational partners do (Turkle, 1996). This ontological ambivalence equips digital devices, in combination with the right educational technology and supporting pedagogy, to play a unique role in supporting teaching and learning dialogues.

Classroom experience shows that when students work together around digital devices, directive tutorial software can help to open dialogic spaces. Imagine a simple digital tutorial software or 'app' asking a group of students familiar with Thinking Together an apparently closed question, like 'if you put a coat on a snowman on a sunny day will it: (a) increase the speed of melting, (b) slow down the speed of melting, or (c) make no difference' (Keogh & Naylor, 1999). There is a single answer here, but finding it could easily lead to a complex discussion, shared inquiry and even experimentation if appropriate equipment or software is provided.

Digital apps or Edubots are not human teachers. They do not expect anything, they do not judge and they do not become impatient. For instance, students can wait to answer an app's questions without feeling that they are showing a lack of respect. They are also less likely to feel controlled by an app than they might by a human tutor who says the same things. This is possibly why digital interactive tools have proved particularly effective at engaging students on the autistic spectrum (Kagohara et al., 2013). It follows from the unique nature of computers as dialogue partners that simple tutorial interactions with digital devices can open up, widen and deepen dialogic spaces within curriculum areas. These may support discussion, reflection and the active construction of meaning in ways not normally possible with human teachers. Edubots, or apps acting like dialogue partners, might actually be better in some roles than human teachers. This idea is summed up in the IDRF educational exchange model, which stands for Initiation, *Discussion*, Response and Feedback. Traditional classroom discourse has been described by many as following an IRF pattern of the teacher initiating, the student responding and the teacher giving feedback (Lemke, 1990). On the whole, IRFs have been accused of limiting student opportunities to exercise agency and to learn how to think. In the IDRF model, the Edubot or electronic tutor *initiates* or prompts the discussion, learners *discuss* a topic with each other, the students *respond* to the tutor's prompt and the tutor provides *feedback* on students' responses (Wegerif, 2004). Because of the fluidity and dialogic capacity of AI language assistants based on large language models, a group of students can now dialogue with an AI-powered Edubot to explore a topic before giving their response. If part of a teacher's role is understood as inducting students into participation in long-term cultural dialogues, such as the dialogue of science (further discussed in Chapter 9), then arguably technology can now play this role quite effectively.

Agents whose role is to stimulate thinking in online environments are being developed and researched (Bayne, 2015; Pérez et al., 2020). Rapid developments in the capacity of AI language assistants to hold realistic dialogues mean that more such Edubots in educational spaces are likely. All such Edubots, or digital dialogue partners, will likely work best with a dialogic off-computer pedagogy along the lines of the Thinking Together programme. This would enable students to be inducted into shared ground rules for how to talk effectively together, and to teach them how to ask better questions for learning. This combination of pedagogical and technical design offers the promise to, in a scaffolded way, induct learners into dialogue about different topics. Instead of dropping students directly into the infinite potential of dialogic space, gradually they can be introduced to the long-term dialogue of science and culture in a way that encourages questioning and reflection.

To summarise, we propose it might be beneficial to combine teaching face-to-face dialogue – how to learn together with others by asking good questions – and tools such as Edubots to induct students (working both individually and together in groups) into participation in living long-term dialogues of knowledge.

## Buber on 'das Zwischen' or 'the space between'

Martin Buber's dialogic theory included the possibility of holding educational dialogues with things. Buber originated a version of the idea of dialogic space in his classic work *I and Thou* (first published in 1923 and translated to English in 1937). This short book begins with the claim that 'man is twofold', drawing our attention to the two fundamental modes of being in relation to the world: 'I–It' (*Ich-Es*) and 'I–Thou' (*Ich-Du*). The I–It mode of relationship, or type of orientation towards the 'other' (where 'other' is broadly defined not as only another person but as anything other than the self, including trees and machines), generates a world of objects. In doing so, we can find ourselves trapped within an apparently objective world that we create around us. The I–Thou mode of relationship, on the other hand, allows us to connect to the presence of another person, someone we do not see as an object and address as 'thou'. More fundamentally, we also experience a sense of connection with what Buber refers to as 'the Eternal Thou'. The Eternal Thou is the only Thou that does not have an It:

> When *Thou* is spoken, the speaker has no thing for his object. For where there is a thing there is another thing. Every *It* is bounded by others; *It* exists only through being bounded by others. But when *Thou* is spoken, there is no thing. *Thou* has no bounds.
>
> (Buber, 1937, p. 4)

Whereas the realm of I–It is fragmented, one thing next to another – one he, she, they or it, etc. – the realm of I–Thou is an experience of wholeness (Buber, 1937).

As well as being a philosopher, Buber was a Jewish Rabbi nominated for the Nobel Prize in Literature ten times and Nobel Peace Prize seven times. Some readers might not react well to the religious tone of concepts like 'Eternal Thou', as they may associate it with a particular religious worldview. However, Buber can be interpreted in a more technical way that is related to the role of the 'witness' position outlined in Chapter 5 as part of our discussion of connectivism and how software like Pol.is works by stimulating a kind of witness position in the user helping them to see the whole discussion as well as their place within it. Taking the I–Thou orientation towards just about anything – whether a person, a cat, a tree or software like ELIZA running on a digital device – can open, Buber claims, a dialogic space. This orientation opens up a space of relationship that goes beyond the two external parties involved. Take the example of a research assistant called Jane and ELIZA. When ELIZA asks 'Why do you say that?' or 'Tell me more about that' a space of reflection opens up. This space also includes Jane herself, allowing her to re-imagine herself. This is an 'internal' inclusive space of 'intra-action', not just an external space of 'inter-action'. The space that opens up in this way is not only defined by the relationship between Jane and ELIZA. In the space, Jane can also see herself as if from outside from a 'witness' position. This 'witness' position in the dialogue cannot be pinned down or defined. Jane might be keen on science, and might imagine the witness as the community of future scientists, but Jane's dialogue with the voice she projects as coming from this imaginary community will then also generate a further 'witness' position. In other words, the concept of dialogue with the 'Eternal Thou' is just a way of saying that dialogic space has no fixed boundary, in principle it has an infinite capacity to generate new perspectives and new meaning. Whereas learning from dialogue with Generative AI and LLMs trained on the internet is dialogue with the Generalised Other, what Buber is talking about is explicitly engaging in dialogue with the witness position that is not defined: we call this dialogue with the Infinite Other.

## The role of material technology in opening, widening and deepening dialogic space

Buber described education for meaning as emerging out of, or perhaps as flourishing because of, 'das Zwischen' or the 'space of the "in-between"' (1937). This perhaps points to the idea of opening up a 'dialogic space'. However, the more recent educational theory of dialogic space described earlier in this chapter is different from 'das Zwischen' in important ways.

While Buber's 'in-between' is presented in a poetic way, divorced from any specific concrete context, the theory of 'dialogic space' outlined above has a material aspect. This was seen recently during research in Japan when a group of three upper primary learners were discussing a puzzle presented on a tablet computer. Not only did their body language converge on this central focus, but so did their fingers (see Figure 8.2). Each learner put a finger on the tablet to indicate what they thought was the key to solving the puzzle. It soon became clear that much of the shared thinking was being done by their fingers (Fujita et al., 2021).

It is because of the material aspect of dialogic spaces – that they always take place in a context – that it is possible for participants to know when the space opens or closes, when it widens to bring in new voices and perspectives, and when it deepens by questioning framing assumptions to reveal new ways of seeing the issue. Buber's theory of dialogic space as 'the space between', while inspirational and profound, does not provide a practical account of how to design the material underpinning necessary for supporting any actual dialogue. It is possible that Buber himself would be very sympathetic to the

**FIGURE 8.2** The materiality of dialogic space.

*Source:* Taro Fujita.

importance of the material dimension that we are raising: the difference that is made if a dialogue is carried by sounds in the air or signs on a page or moving images on a screen (Biemann, 2022). However, his writings tend to present a dichotomy between everyday dialogue and a rather idealised state of dialogue that is always dialogue with the *Eternal Thou*. As we illustrate in the case studies below, once we understand the role of technology in supporting different kinds of dialogue we can design that technology – with associated pedagogy – to narrow or widen, focus or deepen, dialogues for educational ends.

## Case study: Applying dialogic space theory to the design of online learning in higher education

In this doctoral research, Cambridge PhD student Shengpeng Shi (in preparation) worked in partnership with a university tutor in China to investigate ways to increase reflection and dialogue in a social science undergraduate-level online course. An exploratory phase of the research identified two types of 'voices' relevant for online teaching and learning in this area:

*Scientific voices*, representing more generalised others (i.e., the voices of perspectives in social science).

*Individual voices*, that draw attention to the personal and which are formed through the instructor or learners' own current understanding and meaning-making.

An initial set of design ideas were generated and then tested through implementation during the course (see Table 8.1).

Examining the existing course through the lens of dialogic theory led to a redesign to promote more dialogic thinking and learning. For instance, the initial opening lecture was redesigned to serve the function of opening a dialogic space. Each research method introduced during the course (e.g., semi-structured interview) was represented with its definition, concrete example, key characteristics or features, strengths and limitations, and interconnections with other research methods also introduced (e.g., unstructured interview). What was previously a monologic representation of facts were augmented with an account of the creative tensions between different methods, allowing these to be seen more as co-evolving voices in dialogue together and not simply as given. To achieve this, PowerPoint was replaced with Prezi, which is distinguished chiefly by its non-linear presentation style. Prezi also allowed the instructor to dramatise the relationships between different methods (e.g., by zooming and panning screen animations). A user-defined path was presented both in an integrated (all slides) and proximal (one slide) form. The former can provide integrated guidance as in the form

**TABLE 8.1** Operationalising dialogic space in the context of online research training.

| *Weekly educational activities* | *Identified dialogic moves* | *Intended dialogic goals* |
|---|---|---|
| **Online teaching**<br>The instructor delivers an online lecture within a virtual learning environment. | **Instructor's opening move with the use of scientific voices**<br>Open up the dialogic space by invoking a range of different previous scientific views on the topic, enabling learners to access, learn from and reflect upon them. | Teach the dialogue so far, letting learners know how the different research methods have been defined and used in the past. |
| **Initiating the online discussion**<br>The instructor posts questions on the discussion board. | **Instructor's opening move with his/her own individual voice**<br>Further open up the dialogic space through the instructor's own individual voice by selecting certain invoked scientific voices and encouraging learners to discuss them. | Invite learners' authentic inquiries, giving them a way to personally access the research methods they have learned in the online lecture. |
| **Offering initial responses**<br>Learners answer the online discussion question with the use of the introduced knowledge. | **Learner's widening move with the use of scientific voices**<br>Add new meaning-making into the dialogic space through integrating and comparing the already invoked scientific voices.<br><br>**Learner's deepening move with the use of scientific voices**<br>Reflect upon evidence, reasons, assumptions and/or sources of information behind the invoked scientific voices.<br><br>**Learner's opening move with his/her own individual voices**<br>Introduce a new context based on the learner's own interest and make use of the invoked scientific voices within this context. | Encourage learners to develop and reflect upon the invoked scientific voices and utilise them in their own academic interests. It can move the previous scientific dialogue, invoked by the instructor, further into several learners' authentic inquiries, leading the online discussion in new directions. |

| *Weekly educational activities* | *Identified dialogic moves* | *Intended dialogic goals* |
|---|---|---|
| **Commenting**<br>Learners comment on at least two of their classmates' initial responses, following their comprehension of the initial responses. | **Learner's widening move with his/her own individual voices**<br>Relate to their classmates' perspectives and incorporate or elaborate ideas. | Give learners time to think and discuss together. As the learners' initial responses are constructively, critically and creatively commented on by their classmates, learners' individual inquiry is transformed into a collective inquiry, in which online collective intelligence can be achieved. |
| | **Learner's deepening move with his/her own individual voices**<br>Relate to their classmates' perspectives and negotiate or challenge differing ideas. | |
| | **Learner's further opening move with his/her own individual voices**<br>Relate to their classmates' perspectives and probe them to think about other new alternatives, which is beyond the initial responses. | |

*Source*: Based on the doctoral work of Shengpeng Shi (in preparation).

of a concept map, allowing learners to systematically comprehend how a set of introduced research methods are interlinked. Whereas the latter can display topical or spiral sequencing, detailing different perspectives on specific research methods: how they relate to each other not as nodes in a concept map but more like voices dynamically talking together in a shared dialogue. This intervention aims to enable learners to connect all pieces of knowledge together, seeing them as interconnected voices in an ongoing dialogue.

After the opening lecture, the instructor posts a question on the online discussion board, to which the learners offer their own initial responses. This phase was re-imagined as a way to further *open* up the dialogic space. The instructor would select a certain invoked scientific voice and ask the learner to respond to it in their own personal way. Unlike in-person classroom dialogues, where learners have limited time to respond, online-mediated asynchronous discussion can offer a period for learners to reflect before responding. The original discussion questions were collected and revised into inquiry-oriented types, which require more divergent thinking and an openness to new learning possibilities. For instance, the initial question '*Do you think that internet-based surveys are better than surveys administered via other modes?*' was revised into '*Imagine that you are planning to conduct the survey research. Which mode of survey administration do you think is more suitable, according to your academic interests? Why? Is your chosen mode likely to have any limitations?*' The revised questions were designed to encourage learners to inter-animate their perspectives and alternatives expressed by previous scientific voices, connecting these to their own personal needs and interests. The goal was to move the invoked scientific dialogue forward to focus on learners' own ongoing inquiry.

Finally, learners were asked to comment on at least two of their classmates' initial responses. This can lead to a '*widening*' of dialogic space if more reasons and evidence are offered for different points of view. It can also involve '*deepening*' moves, when challenging the assumptions behind the choices or claims made. Sometimes further '*opening*' moves also occur when learners probe their classmates to think about different alternatives. As learners' initial responses were constructively, critically and creatively commented on by classmates, learners' individual inquiry can become a collective inquiry. To support this, a digital self-checking sheet for online postings was developed. This aims to set up dialogic ground rules so that learners are able to effectively discuss (and think) together. Rather than directly informing learners of what 'dialogic' is, the digital self-checking sheet explains what characterises dialogic comments and provides examples. Specifically, five adjectives were used to describe dialogic comments: 'interactive', 'reflective', 'considerate', 'acceptable' and 'persuasive'. The emphasis on being interactive and reflective derives from a shared responsibility to contribute constructively by evaluating classmates' viewpoints, even if they agree with them. The emphasis on being considerate and acceptable derives from the need to be respectful and offer criticism constructively, reducing the number of disputational comments. The emphasis on being persuasive derives from the focus on explicit reasoning, encouraging learners to seek reasons behind their classmates' ideas. The five adjectives specify the notion of 'being dialogic', so as to set up the ground rules for discussing together.

These more dialogic interventions were implemented and empirically evaluated through content analysis. Comparisons between pre- and post-intervention online teaching transcripts reveal that the redesigned teaching slides helped the instructor to move away from a one-sided presentation of the research methods to a more comprehensive and balanced representation of their different perspectives. Evaluation of initial responses demonstrates that more knowledge comparisons, reflections and utilisations are made by learners in the post-intervention data, suggesting the effectiveness of inquiry-oriented type questions and the online lecture in enhancing academic argumentation. Rigorous coding of comments indicated learners produced more elaborations, negotiations and probes of academic research issues together.

### *Commentary on the dialogic space theory case study*

The idea of dialogic space is motivated by some quite big philosophical ideas from Bakhtin, Buber, Merleau-Ponty, Simondon, Deleuze and others. This case study shows that it can also be applied usefully in a real-world context to the design of online courses of a type common around the world. Here design principles from dialogic space were used by the researcher and practitioner to expand the extent to which an existing research methods course created opportunities for dialogue. Changes may be as simple as switching an initial question that implies searching for a single correct answer to a form of question that leads to exploring a range of different contexts. This can lead to a widening, deepening and opening of dialogic space as outlined.

Traditionally, concept maps of the relationships between the contents of a disciplinary field have been treated as monologic. The implied claim of such a map is that there is a single, objective body of knowledge for students to engage with and that the map simply draws out the closed inferential relationship between the parts of this body (e.g., here surveys, semi-structured interviews and unstructured interviews). This monological idea of a disciplinary field is easy to model in the nodes and relationships of a network. The dialogic alternative is that the field is made up of voices that are not merged into a single network. We know that they are unmerged voices because they are incommensurate, there is a gap or fissure which cannot be bridged or filled in. For dialogism, different methods are not just concepts united in a schema, but different ways of looking at things. It is interesting that Prezi is used precisely because it does not reduce all the different methods to a single concept map. Although this tool can be used to present a unified concept-map type view, it also has the capacity to dynamically dramatise the idea of a field as a set of voices in dialogue. This is due to Prezi's capacity to rearrange the field around different nodes, zooming between the inside-out perspective of one node, and the outside-in perspective of looking back at the node from the field around it.

These are interesting design choices. How to measure the widening and deepening of dialogic space is an ongoing research issue (Cao, 2022). But here evidence of greater questioning of assumptions, and greater reflection about knowledge, as well as more comparisons between concepts, seems to indicate that the dialogic space is being expanded for students on this course.

## Case study: Collective Reality and the Internet of Bodies

First produced in 2016, Collective Reality is a participatory performance art installation. It features motion tracking of group activities within a physical space to synchronise surround sound and visual images. The artist-academic behind the project, Ghislaine Boddington, writes how the environment is as aware of 'us' as we are of 'it' (Boddington, 2021). The effect is to externalise and make public each movement. Guided by model 'movement jockeys', the intention is that people learn how to create a shared dynamic work of art together. Sometimes movements, lights and sound converge into a single coherent pattern. At other times, they form different groups that appear to clash in a loud and potentially unpleasant way.

Boddington links participatory performance art to the idea of the Internet of Bodies. She points to the increasing importance of 'gesture tech', such as virtual avatars, implants and robotics, to propose that our bodies are becoming the interface with the internet (Boddington, 2021). One example of the body as interface idea given by Boddington is particularly striking. Moon Ribas, a Spanish dancer, had two implants placed into the top of her feet. These were set to respond to planetary wide seismic activity. A small earthquake produces small vibrations; a bigger eruption transmits a more intense vibration. Ribas created a performance titled 'Waiting for Earthquakes' in which she dances in response to what her feet tell her about the state of the planet as a whole.

### *Commentary on the Collective Reality case study*

One version of dialogic space might be 'the space of reasons', the idea that concepts hang together such that education involves drawing learners into that space (Bakker & Derry, 2011). Where the focus is on inferential links between concepts, this could imply a monologic vision rather than a dialogic vision of meaning space. The two metaphors of nodes in a logically defined network and unique voices in dialogue together are not mutually exclusive. In fact, as our commentary on Case Study 8.1 suggests, they can be seen as complementary. This 'space of reasons' idea is a part of the larger concept of a 'dialogic space'. However, dialogic space also includes embodiment and emotion. Boddington's Internet of Bodies idea reminds us that dialogue is also carried by gesture, music and dance. Further, differences between perspectives often produce clashes, tension and creativity. The internet arguably has the potential to realise Merleau-Ponty's claim that our collective culture is not an abstract realm of ideas but a second body, a collective body with many unique parts. Education is induction of new members into a shared life that is lived together in many dimensions. These include music, dance and emotion as well as the more academic side of education associated with print literacy.

## Discussion

Empirical investigation into how dialogic space works to support educational goals suggests that to enter into dialogic space involves stepping back from the individual, surface-level reality and into a shared space of possibilities. Applying Simondon's theory of technology to research on dialogic space in education suggests that entering into dialogic space can be understood as a version of what he calls 'transindividuation', which is the process of individuals coming together to form a larger collective identity around a shared project. However, according to Simondon (2017) transindividuation requires 'dialogue with technology'. Thinking about the opening, widening and deepening of dialogic space from the point of view of technology helps us to see that education has always been a facilitated process of transindividuation that combines dialogic space with different types of communications technology. The first painted caves were used to induct people into a shared cultural reality and a shared tribal identity. Literacy-based education potentially inducts students into dialogic space in the form of 'the conversation of mankind' as Oakeshott (1989) claimed, but also the imaginary communities of nation states as Anderson (2008) points out. The internet combined with devices such as mobile phones and AI powered Edubots has an even greater potential to support education as transindividuation.

### *Prompts towards a dialogic foundation for the design and use of educational technology*

The first case study showed how the theory of education as opening, widening and deepening dialogic space could be applied to transform an online course in China – that principally sought to 'transmit' knowledge – into one that also facilitated student engagement into active and thoughtful ongoing dialogues. In this design-based research project, dialogic space theory informed a design framework. Working closely with the educational practitioner, this was implemented through small practical changes. For example, switching from the use of PowerPoint to the use of Prezi to better present the dynamic and dialogic relationships between nodes in a knowledge network. Or, to give other examples, adding a checklist of dialogic prompts to guide online student interaction, and changing online questions posted by the instructor from a 'find the correct answer' type to 'explore the range of possibilities' type.

The second case study suggests that educational technology can be designed to go beyond the cognitive to include embodiment and emotion when opening and expanding dialogic space. The 'Collective Reality' art event was implemented in 'in-person' spaces using technology to detect and enhance human movements. Similar ways to create and experience collective emotions can be implemented using dance, drama, gestures and music online. For example, through sharing videos of performances such as drumming or singing with classes of students located elsewhere, asking for their creative response and combining a range of different performances into a single work.

The capacity of technology to support transindividuation through the opening, widening and deepening of dialogic spaces is not a function of technology design alone, but rather a combination of the design or selection of the technology and the design of the pedagogy. The educational value of dialogic space has been found mainly in the context of classroom talk. However, extending that talk to interact with digital technology such as educational robotics and cloud-based animation software can further expand the dialogic space (Ritella et al., 2022), as can introducing tools such as multi-touch tables combined with video conferencing (Beauchamp et al., 2019). Classroom experiments described in this chapter showed that combining tutorial software with the pedagogy of 'Thinking Together' can lead to reflection and deeper understanding within even a fairly pinned down curriculum through the I*D*RF structure of Initiation, *Discussion*, Response, Feedback. AI-enhanced Edubots used online or in classrooms to support reflection and dialogue do not need to be as open-ended as ELIZA: they may be designed to facilitate and guide dialogic approaches to inducting students into knowledge, by which we mean inducting students into participation in long-term cultural dialogues such as the dialogue of mathematics, engineering or history.

AI language assistants can increasingly be used to facilitate our proposed pedagogy of teaching group thinking face-to-face, and then taking this online to learn together with others and with technology. After initially teaching learners ground rules for talk, tools like ChatGPT can serve as a focus for small group discussions. These might help to initiate and sustain talk by providing prompts, questions or additional perspectives to keep the conversation flowing. AI language assistants can not only be asked to write essays on a topic, they can also help to point out areas of controversy and uncertainty where more work needs to be done.

# 9

# TECHNOLOGY AND EXPANDING DIALOGIC TIME

> *. . . every meaning will have its homecoming festival.*
>
> Mikhail Bakhtin (1986, p. 170)

> *Those who cannot remember the past are condemned to repeat it.*
>
> George Santayana (1905, p. 284)

## Introduction

In the previous chapter, Chapter 8, we wrote about the role of technology in expanding dialogic space. The kind of 'space' we were talking about is not so much physical space, measured in metres or light years, but the space of possibilities that opens up due to the 'tension' between different perspectives. The idea of dialogic space originated in classroom research. Educational practitioners and researchers have found it useful to use metaphors related to the idea of physical space to describe how educational technology can open, widen and deepen the dialogic space or spaces that occur in classrooms. For example, students working collaboratively around an interactive whiteboard could be seen as united in a shared dialogic space that can be sensed by the teacher as it opens up, expands and then closes down (Mercer et al., 2010). However, any metaphor has constraints as well as affordances. In this chapter we explore what can be gained from looking not so much at 'dialogic space', but at 'dialogic time'. In a dialogue, voices do not speak all at once. Rather, they speak one after another. This means that expanding the 'space' of the dialogue also inevitably means expanding the 'time' of the dialogue. Expanding dialogic time means that voices that have already spoken continue to resonate in the dialogue, much like notes of music continue to resonate together

DOI: 10.4324/9781003198499-9

in a successful melody. Technology, in some form, is always implicit behind the extension of the time of dialogue, and the way that technology is designed can shape how learners experience this dialogic time. Print literacy used in education is a technology that enables voices from the past, the thoughts of Socrates or Plato for example, to continue to resonate in dialogues today. TikTok, a social media site where users share short video-clips, enables voices to resonate together over time in a very different way. The design of online spaces, social media networks and new forms of technology-mediated communication yet to be thought of has implications for the temporal sequence of educational dialogues. In this chapter, we explore how thinking about the temporal dimension of dialogic space – thinking about *dialogic time* – offers insights into the design and use of technology in education.

## Understanding education as a journey into time

Education takes place over time. In schools, for example, teaching and learning are commonly divided into lesson periods. These periods are linked together in curricular schemes of work that describe lesson content over longer periods of time, such as school terms and school years. This kind of 'clock' or 'chronological' time is what we call *horizontal time*: it is the time from $t1$ to $t2$, where $t1$ might be the time at the beginning of a lesson, and $t2$ the time at the end of the lesson.[1]

As well as taking place across time (i.e., from $t1$ to $t2$), education can also be thought of as involving a journey *into* time or an expansion of time. To understand a concept, we must draw together different moments of time and see how they fit together in a single pattern. The development of conceptual understanding therefore requires a movement from experiences at $t1$, $t2$ and $t3$ to a moment (e.g., $t4$) that retains and unites together traces of the events at previous times (i.e., here $t4$ includes aspects of $t1 + t2 + t3$). Understanding thus implies a vertical dimension of time – a movement from $t1$ to $(t1 + t2)$ which we call *vertical time*.

This important point can be illustrated in a quite simple way. Consider how young learners in modern literate societies learn basic arithmetic. Stage One involves learning to add by 'counting on'. For example, 2+3 is taught by taking 2 fingers and adding on 3, or taking 2 bricks and adding on 3 bricks to make 5. Stage Two, at least in the UK primary schools where we observed this, requires learning the concept of 'commutativity'. This is the concept that 2+3 = 3+2, or when two numbers are added or multiplied, the answer will be the same no matter what order the numbers are in. That is to say, understanding that 1+2 means the same as 2+1 (or more abstractly that $a+b = b+a$). This might seem obvious and easy for those of us who have already learnt it, but it is not obvious for young children. Addition begins not as signs marked on paper, but as a concrete physical process in time, the process of 'counting on'. Adding one finger to two fingers is not the same concrete physical process as adding two fingers to one finger.

However, to understand that adding one finger to two fingers is the same as adding two fingers to one finger in the abstract world of mathematics, we need to take a third perspective that can see at least two time-based processes at once. At one time, a child sees that taking two fingers and adding one finger gives three fingers. At a different time, taking one finger and adding two fingers also gives three fingers. In mathematics, processes that occur at different times can be treated as the same if they are considered to be happening in the same 'virtual time'. But what exactly is this 'virtual' time in which different actual concrete times can be brought together?

One clue to the nature of virtual time was found in a study of six-year-olds learning mathematics. This research project was an investigation of the impact of teaching ground rules for talk (Murphy, 2016). In a group of three, two students were working on a magic square activity (see Figure 9.1). They had a square grid and bits of paper with the numbers 1, 2 or 3 on them. They were trying to fill in the square so that each row and column had different numbers, but the numbers in each row and column added up to the same total. As they filled in the magic square, these two students kept saying things like '2 + 1 + 3 = 6' and '3 + 1 + 2 = 6', each time slowly working out the sum on their fingers, and sounding surprised when it always resulted in 6. The third child, let's call her Judy, was looking on and eventually said, 'they are all the same. They all add up to 6' (Wegerif, 2013, p. 55). Because she was not actually counting the numbers herself, but watching the others count, Judy occupied what Bakhtin called the 'witness' position. In any dialogue, Bakhtin wrote, there is always a witness position that listens to and understands the different voices. This counting out loud together was not

| | | |
|---|---|---|
| 1 | 2 | 3 |
| 2 | 3 | 1 |
| 3 | 1 | 2 |

**FIGURE 9.1** 'Counting on fingers' and a 'magic square' grid.

obviously a dialogue. However, the learners had been taught the ground rules of exploratory talk and Judy, at least, might possibly have wanted to turn it into a 'Thinking Together' activity. As outlined in Chapter 8, thinking about the location of the witness position in classroom dialogues led to the development of the idea of dialogic space. But in this example of understanding the concept of commutativity, it is clear this dialogic 'space' is also a 'dialogic time'. In other words, it is a time in which all the different strands of counting can be held together, compared and found to be essentially the same.

It seems almost natural to think of mathematical claims as somehow outside of time or timeless. For example, the claim that $1 + 2 + 3 = 3 + 2 + 1$ is true irrespective of when or where it is stated. Plato was an enthusiastic proponent of the idea of a timeless time, or an eternal realm of truth revealed by mathematics and by philosophy. Perhaps this image of mathematics as outside of time stems partly from the technology used by the ancient Greeks to do mathematics: drawing lines in a sand tray with a stick. This method affords and potentially promotes geometry and geometrical ways of thinking. Think of Pythagoras' famous theorem of $a^2 + b^2 = c^2$, that the sum of the squares on the shorter sides of a right triangle is equal to the square on the longest side called the hypotenuse (the side opposite the right angle). You move a stick in the sand tray to talk through this proof. This happens in horizontal time. Once you have argued this proof and drawn the diagram, you stand back to look upon it as if everything relevant is visible in the defined space of the sand tray (see Figure 9.2). Once made, this kind of proof does

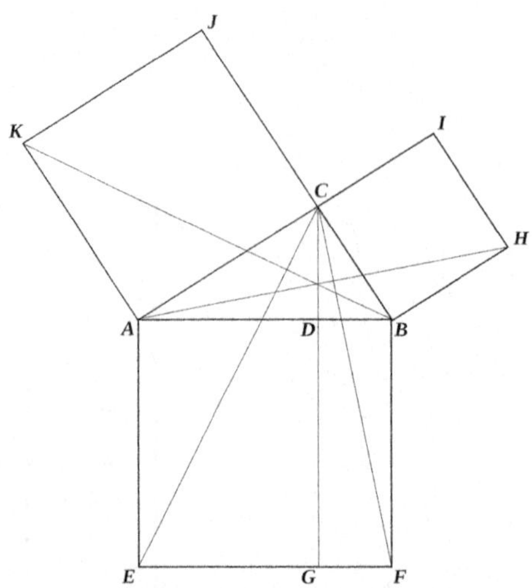


**FIGURE 9.2** Part of Euclid's proof of Pythagorus's theorem.

*Source:* 4C, licensed under CC BY-SA 3.0.

not seem to need the dimension of time at all. It appears to be final, fixed, closed, timeless and eternal.

This sense that the proof is outside of time or 'atemporal' is a product of the material medium used, whether a sand tray or a written parchment. Such an understanding of mathematics as atemporal is unlikely to occur in oral cultures unsupported by any visual representation. This is because, as Ong (1972/2013) and Goody (1986) point out, speaking is always a process in time which means that it is something that occurs within a context. An apparently atemporal view is only made possible if we represent a meaning diagrammatically in a bounded space: for instance, seeing the patterns of lines in a sand tray, marks on a slate, or written notation on paper. When Judy as a witness returned to the concept of addition, she did not just move across horizontal time from one point (*t*1) to another point (*t*2). She also moved into a deeper understanding of addition through journeying into time, from horizontal (*t*1) to vertical time (*t*1+*t*2). The understanding of addition as counting on that is learned at time *t*1 is not disregarded. Rather, it is returned to, preserved and transformed into a deeper understanding at time *t*2, which has now become vertical time.

One way to visualise the material nature of this 'vertical' dimension of time, considered further in the next section, is suggested by Drew Whitworth as a palimpsest (2020a, p. 145). A palimpsest is a manuscript with the original text overwritten with notes and commentaries such that the evolution of meaning can be tracked over time by looking back through all the layers. We refer to the movement into time implicit in education as vertical time to distinguish it from the simple linear movement across time, clock time, which we refer to as horizontal time.[2] We argue that this vertical movement into time is achieved because of education technology, and how we design this technology will shape learners' experience of vertical time.

## Two kinds of vertical time

So far, we have argued that to understand progress in education and conceptual growth, we need to distinguish between vertical time and horizontal time. We also need to make a distinction between two conceptions of vertical time. Plato's idea that concepts exist somehow outside of time, combined with the affordances of print technology (introduced in Chapter 2), can lead to the illusion of monological vertical time. Monological vertical time is the idea that there is a time outside of experienced time that is populated by fixed, eternal truths. The danger of this monological misunderstanding of vertical time in education is that it can lead to a loss of a lived sense of meaning. In the alternative dialogic conception of vertical time, the present is not erased by the perspective of eternity. Instead, it is expanded and enriched by connecting to dialogues at a range of different timescales.

### *Monological vertical time: In the light of eternity*

Baruch Spinoza, a 17th century Jewish-Dutch philosopher, followed Plato in arguing that the goal of intellectual development is to experience everything 'sub specie aeternitatis', or 'in the light of eternity'. Our limited and often confused understanding, Spinoza argued, stems from experiencing things from only a perspective within time (Spinoza, 2006). To see things fully – with all their connections, causes, and consequences – Spinoza claimed is to see them from a point of view outside of time, a vantage point he refers to as the perspective of eternity. Physicist Stephen Hawking (1988) pointed to a similar idea in his book, *A Brief History of Time*, when he famously referred to the aim of physics as to 'know the mind of God'.

Euclid's *Elements*, a book originally written in Alexandria around 300 BCE, was one of the first books printed in large numbers after Gutenberg's development of a printing press in the 15th century. It outlines many geometrical proofs, and is often considered to be one of the most influential textbooks ever written. Just as sand trays were used to make proofs in Ancient Greece, textbooks like Euclid's *Elements* privilege a top-down view from above, as if everything can be seen flat in a diagram on the page. Talking through a proof with others gives a very different impression. In a dialogue, there is uncertainty and openness. When we talk and listen, we are always within time, and it is difficult to imagine standing back and being outside of time (Nikulin, 2010). We can speculate that Spinoza was influenced by the cognitive affordance of textbooks such as Euclid's *Elements* when he proposed his apparently one-way model of education as moving from within time to a viewpoint outside of time, to see everything 'sub specie aeternitatis'.

### *Dialogical vertical time: Expanding and empowering the voice of the present*

In his book *A Secular Age*, Charles Taylor (2009) contrasts two different accounts of vertical time. The first account, from Plato and Aristotle, is the idea of a fixed eternal time. This is suggested as the home of real, eternal ideas such as the truths of mathematics. It is essentially what we refer to above as a 'monological' view of vertical time. An issue with this view of vertical time, Taylor suggests, is that the point of view of eternity, or the 'mind of God', is often seen as the most real or true perspective. This can make all other perspectives or points of view seem less real. For example, the idea (eidos) of a triangle is thought of by Plato as more 'real' than any actual triangle that we might encounter in real life within time: the ideal timeless triangle is always necessarily more perfect than any actual triangle.

Taylor (2009) points to Augustine's writings on time as a source for a different view of vertical time. Like Husserl and Heidegger later, Augustine argued that maintaining awareness of both past and future is always essential to our lived experience of the present. According to Taylor, this idea of 'lived time' or 'gathered time' involves:

> the kind of coherence we find in a melody or a poem . . . There is a kind of simultaneity of the first note with the last, because all have to sound in the presence of the others in order for the melody to be heard.
>
> (p. 56)

Taylor goes on to make a specific link with dialogue, writing that this conception of time:

> involves extended simultaneity of the moment of action or enjoyment, which we see also, for instance, in a conversation which really engages us. Your question, my reply, your rejoinder occur in this sense together, even though like the melody, their ordering in time is of the essence.
>
> (p. 57)

Augustine believed that living in a fragmented and disconnected way can lead to a meaningless life. This is because the significance of each moment of time can be lost. Following from this account, the ideal of education then is to bring everything together into a deeper experience of time. This means experiencing time as a living interconnected whole, in which everything is included, and everything is in resonance with everything else, like the notes of an unbounded symphony. This suggests a 'dialogical' vertical time in which different moments of time are brought together in a way that does not merge them into one, but rather maintains their separateness while still being in dialogue with each other. Taylor gives the example of how we can pattern and move around sounds, words and notes. However, these kinds of human artefacts do not last for long. Other technologies, paintings on cave walls, books and now digital screens, can perhaps sustain a shared dialogic time that is both more inclusive and longer lasting.

## Technology supporting dialogic vertical time

As discussed, Spinoza was perhaps reflecting the cognitive affordances of textbooks when he put forward his apparently one-way model of education as moving from within time to outside of time, a model reflected in some of Vygotsky's writings (1934/1986). But a second, very different model of the role of vertical time in education can also be derived from a different reading of Vygotsky (Derry, 2013). This is a more complex two-way model describing how the mediation of cultural artefacts can bring different timescales into relationship. In this two-way model, the significance of short-term local events and interactions is enhanced through their dialogic engagement with longer-term dialogues of culture, which are mediated by cultural artefacts. This process also works in reverse, as longer-term dialogues of culture are added to and changed by local events and interactions. For example, a classroom dialogue about the technology required for a 'double-slit' experiment, which demonstrates that light and matter can display characteristics of both classically defined waves and particles, can connect the long-term dialogue of science into relation with the lives of students in a way that their experience illuminates the significance of the long-term dialogue of science. The truth of the double-slit experiment demonstrating wave-particle duality is not a timeless truth, but a truth that is located within the global long-term cultural dialogue of science. This dialogue is something that students have access to, and can participate in, through taking up and using the technology.

## Education as expanding dialogic time

That there can be a movement into time (vertical time), as well as a movement in time (horizontal time), can be considered as the essence of education. This idea is perhaps summed up by the well-known quotation at the start of this chapter: 'Those who cannot remember the past are condemned to repeat it' (Santayana, 1905).

One way to re-interpret Vygotsky's famous 'zone of proximal development' is that a teacher or more experienced partner leads a learner from seeing things only within one time context (that of a short-term in-person dialogue apparently contained within a physical present), to being able to see the same things also from the point of view of another time context (that of the longer-term 'virtual' dialogue of academic discourse). Material equipment, such as a graphical calculator, can make it possible to perform a dispersed practice, such as calculating, in a specific practice setting at a particular time and place (Schatzki, 1996). Using material artefacts such as technical words, slide rules, videos and electronic whiteboards can help to expand the significance of the present moment in education.

Science does not provide timeless truths, no more than does religion or art. It is rather an ongoing, fallible dialogue between real people. This dialogue is only possible over large spaces and lengthy periods of time due to the role of mediating technologies such as printed letters, articles, books and increasingly the internet supported by AI language assistants. For instance, Newton's theory of gravity (that posited gravity as a force) was improved (some say replaced) by Einstein's Theory of General Relativity which presented the idea of curved space time. Despite Einstein's theory persisting now for over 100 years, many speculate that it is likely to be soon superseded by a better theory – a theory of quantum gravity – that is currently being discussed and developed in virtual dialogical spaces supported by the internet.

The role of a science teacher is arguably therefore not to teach the finished truth of things, how things might look 'sub specie aeternitatis', but to weave together the very large time-space perspective of science with the smaller and narrower time-space perspective of a face-to-face dialogue with a learner in a classroom (Phillipson & Wegerif, 2016). It is one thing to observe a feather and metal ball fall at the same rate in a vacuum chamber (on a YouTube video perhaps); it is quite another thing to derive from this an understanding of the concept of gravity. Knowledge arises in science as the answer to questions that are asked within a dialogue. For a learner to acquire conceptual understanding, they first need to be a participant in the long-term dialogue of science. This means to link the time-space of the classroom or other learning arena to the time-space of past scientific discoveries, such as Galileo dropping different objects from the leaning tower of Pisa, as well as linking to the time-space of current scientific experiments, such as those being conducted at the CERN collider which might determine our future understanding of gravity.[3]

In addition to connecting the present to the larger time-space perspective of science, it is also important to connect the different concepts and ideas that students learn during a scheme of work, which might occur over multiple lessons or a semester. Mercer (2008) describes the role of time in classroom dialogue using transcripts to illustrate how teachers and groups of learners build up a more complex understanding of a topic over time. He highlights how learners frequently refer back to relate what is being learnt 'now' in a lesson to what has been learnt in previous lessons. Mercer refers to an article by Lemke (2000) which describes a series of timescales. Lemke, a physicist turned science educator, introduces the concept of 'heterochrony' to understand the role of vertical time in education. Borrowing this concept from physics, Lemke defines this in an educational context as the interaction between different timescales mediated by a material-semiotic object. A simple example of heterochrony is the way in which a student taking notes in a notebook can mediate between the short timescale of a small-group collaborative activity, and the longer-term cumulative trajectory of an inquiry-based project carried out over a school term or semester. Lemke links this relating together of different timescales to the idea of dialogue, and more specifically to the formation of personal identity in dialogue. Heterochrony mediated by cultural artefacts is also, amongst other things, about the expansion of the identity of the student. Or, at least, an expansion of the student's capacity to identify with processes that last longer than the perceptual present moment.

Vygotsky, a fan of Spinoza, sometimes seems to present education as a one-way ladder (Van der Veer & Valsiner, 1991). This ladder leads learners away from what he calls false 'participatory' concepts embedded within time, replacing these concepts with what he calls a true understanding derived from a conceptual system that is essentially atemporal or outside of time. In this, Vygotsky is reproducing a fairly common 'enlightenment rationalist' view of education (Wertsch, 1996). One possible criticism of formal education on this one-way ladder model – a danger articulated by Paulo Freire, Ivan Illich, Seymour Papert, bell hooks and others – is that it can disempower learners by removing their own truth,[4] the truth of their experience in the present moment, and replacing it with someone else's truth, a truth that might empower some but leave others feeling disempowered. However, the ideal of education as a journey into time could also arguably be about learners finding more meaning in their present moments, and not less. Another way to think about such an approach is to see it as a way of expanding the reach and the power of the present moment. This means that the present moment is not subordinate to a larger scale of time, eternity for example. Instead, the present moment is a time of growth and becoming, where the whole of time is experienced in the act or movement of time (Merleau-Ponty, 1945/2013, p. 489).[5]

Bakhtin used the term 'chronotope' to refer to the combination of space and time in experience. He argued how the chronotope (time-space) of readers was brought into a dialogic relationship with the chronotope (time-space) of texts. For Bakhtin, a dialogic relationship is a two-way relationship in which mutual understanding can arise from an inter-illumination of perspectives. Bakhtin believed education to involve a journey from the chronotope of 'Small Time' to what he called 'Great Time'. Small Time is characterised by the short-term everyday concerns that we 'fuss about' (Shepherd, 2006). Great Time, on the other hand, is characterised by the unbounded dialogic space in which all cultures and all times can communicate together (Bakhtin, 1986, p. 169). This vision of education as a journey into time is not about abandoning the present moment. Instead, it is about expanding and deepening our participation in the present moment. Aline Nardo points to a similar idea when referring to the educational significance of the distinction between Chronos and Kairos (Marramao, 2007; Nardo, 2023). In Greek mythology, two words are used for time. Chronological time, or the time we have been calling clock time or horizontal time, is personified by Chronos. Complementing Chronos is Kairos, which is the interruption of 'normal time', and is sometimes described as 'deep time'. Kairos refers to time experienced as potentiality or a kind of opening from out of which new things, new understandings and a new sense of self can emerge.

## Technology weaving different timescales together

As previously described, the cognitive and pedagogical affordances of print literacy make it easier to privilege the monological version of a one-way ladder journey into time (monological vertical time). Digital educational technology, however, potentially offers new cognitive and pedagogical affordances that can more evidently support the dialogic two-way model of a journey into time (dialogic vertical time). Specifically, this can be used to augment and expand the potential for meaning in a teaching and learning moment. The mechanism proposed here for developing knowledge is to use digital tools to mediate between different timescales. This can be achieved in the form of what Hennessy (2011) has called 'digital knowledge artefacts'. These offer interim records of past and ongoing collective group activities, which could be potentially social, cognitive or physical. In this way, digital knowledge artefacts can be used to externalise and embody dialogue, thinking and decision-making processes. They may also provisionally represent evolving knowledge as it connects together different timescales. As suggested by Drew Whitworth mentioned earlier, this can already be done with palimpsests, or manuscripts with layers of meaning. However, digital technology enables us to take this affordance for simultaneously holding together two or more times much further than is possible with a palimpsest or a chalk board.

Hennessy's digital knowledge artefacts are linked to an understanding of 'improvable' objects (Wells, 1999) and 'objects of inquiry' (Bereiter, 2005; Scardamalia & Bereiter, 2014); they are supportive devices for learners' emerging thinking and continuous collaborative development of ideas, rather than finished products of dialogue. This notion is also in keeping with conceptions of dialogue as unfinalisable as outlined by Bakhtin (1986). Artefacts provide physical (including digital) records of collaborative activity and ideas. They may remain accessible and be usefully revisited or referenced during subsequent activity. These objects of joint reference can valuably support learning and dialogue to continue over time because they make learning trajectories more visible, and as they connect reasoning in the present to evidence of prior reasoning (Hennessy, 2011).

Looking at the role of interactive whiteboards (IWBs) in classrooms, Hennessy and others show how this technology can be used to enable a collective dialogic space that maintains and supports continuity and development of ideas over time (Mercer et al., 2010). Their findings have potential implications for the implementation of other emergent classroom-based technologies. One example given involves students writing comments on an IWB about a topic at the beginning of their course on that topic. Students can then revisit their comments at the end of the course to see how their understanding of the topic has changed. Revisiting or comparing digital knowledge artefacts like this can make evident differences or agreements between perspectives, in a way not possible without the support of the technology. Further, the need to externalise ideas can prompt students to offer deeper explanations in a collaborative inquiry (Hakkarainen, 2004; Lipponen, 2000). These shared objects of activity 'materialise' the interaction between individual expertise and communal knowledge (Paavola & Hakkarainen, 2021). Their material permanence of form affords greater stability than oral utterances which are normally transient, helping to underpin 'the recursive reflection and revision that is so important a characteristic of knowledge building' (Wells, 1999, p. 116). Further digital knowledge artefacts bring in new modes of interaction with others' ideas. This includes potentially moving beyond verbal language, as a wide range of graphical and other representations – such as images, diagrams, graphs, drawings, multimedia presentations, simulations, animations, concept maps – become possible modes of communication within a multimodal dialogue (Hennessy, 2020). Importantly, the malleable nature of digital artefacts can support a two-way relationship between timescales. This means that longer-term cultural dialogues embedded in objects can enter into local 'small time' dialogues, and vice versa.

## Technology and time

All cultures live in time and anticipate the future. However, there is also evidence that the way we learn to live in shared modern time is shaped by education and how we use time measuring tools (Sinha & da Silva Sinha, 2022). In his book *Technics and Time*, philosopher Bernard Stiegler (1998) argues that our sense of time is mediated by technology. That how we experience time is shaped by technology is perhaps especially true of those tools that measure, and at the same time create, our experience of time. For instance, tools like clocks, calendars and timelines printed in school textbooks.

Returning to the scientific exploration of where the human sense of time originally came from, Stiegler posits that learning to use tools, especially the creation of flint axe heads, involved anticipation of the future. On this model, time did not come into being suddenly. Instead, it emerged as a side effect of a slow co-evolution of humans and their technology. For Stiegler, the use of tools leads to a kind of memory that is not individual, but impersonal and collective. This memory is made up of traces, which are conservations of past interactions, preserved within the way that tools function. The externalisation of our memory in technology is a third type of memory. This is separate from the individual, internal memory of our brain (epigenetic) and the biological, evolutionary memory inherited from our ancestors (phylogenetic). Stiegler calls this third kind of memory technologically mediated memory or epiphylogenetic. He refers to epiphylogenesis to explain how our experience of time emerged and continues to develop. The process of epiphylogenesis is how we, through technology, create shared time.

Let us reconsider the experience of Judy discussed earlier. We can now tentatively claim that Judy was only able to step out of the concrete process of addition as counting on, and see it in a more abstract and formal way, because she was able to take the perspective of the technology, the written addition of numbers that was in front of her on the table, and use this as a kind of lever (see Figure 9.1). In doing this Judy moved, Stiegler might claim, from epigenetic animal time, which is a horizontal time of doing things without much awareness of them, to the epiphylogenetic time of mathematics, which is a neutral, impersonal time mediated by technologies such as mathematical notations. In other words, vertical time is, and always has been, a creation of technology or what Stiegler prefers to call 'technics'.

## Digital technology and the evolving time of education

Tomasello and colleagues (2005) argue, by contrast, that culture, including what Stiegler refers to as 'technic', is only possible because of the human capacity for dialogic pedagogy.[6] Other apes can, like humans, transmit cultural innovations. A well-known example is macaque primates teaching their children how to wash sweet potatoes in the sea to remove sand before eating them (Watson, 1979). However, according to Tomasello and colleagues, humans are unique in what they call the dialogic nature of cultural transmission. By 'dialogic', the shared attention involved in teaching is referred to. Humans do not just focus on the objects being taught, such as how to wash potatoes. They also focus on each other, including their eyes, gestures and eventually the stories that transmit the culture. This capacity for intersubjectivity leads to what Tomasello and colleagues call a 'ratchet effect', in which new discoveries are incorporated into a body of knowledge and culture that endures and evolves over time. This suggests that progress and learning in cultures requires a combination of opening up dialogic space through shared attention and the reification of dialogic processes through the use of material-semiotic means, such as words and pictures, so that the insights of the moment can be reified into forms that can support cumulative knowledge building. The knowledge is not to be found in the objects, but in their affordances or action potentials when they are re-animated in each new context.

Cultural evolution tends to develop slowly through chance innovations. These innovations then get taken up and added to the education curriculum, which is used to transmit knowledge to new generations. Some have claimed that the scientific revolution associated with the European Enlightenment of the 17th century can be seen as speeding up cultural evolution by instituting social processes that actively seek to create useful innovations, instead of just waiting for them to happen (Deutsch, 2011). But although 'science', understood in this way as the process of testing and justifying beliefs implemented in an education system, is a more rapid and flexible way for a culture to respond to changes in the environment, it still ends up sustaining a past-oriented transmissional form of education. Education in both traditional and modern print-literate societies tends to focus more on transmitting knowledge of how to solve only those problems that have been faced in the past, instead of focusing on equipping students with skills needed to face new challenges in the future. In more 'traditional' societies, children learn from stories about how the ancestors overcame challenges and built the world around them. In more 'modern' societies, the school curriculum repeats the trials and experiments of past heroes such as Galileo, Newton and Marie Sklodowska-Curie.

By the time new claims to knowledge had been printed in journals, subject to sufficient peer review and reflection to become the accepted consensus view and so transmitted into encyclopaedias and textbooks, it was always already knowledge of the past. In this way, the timescales of print literacy enforced the dominance of a past-focused orientation in education or 'looking backwards'. However, it is possible that we now can see the emergence of a new relationship to time in education. New digital technology, especially that related to the AI-enhanced internet, enables the possibility to induct learners directly into those dialogues that are creating knowledge in an ever-expanding global present or 'looking forwards'.

The cultural ratchet effect is the process by which new discoveries are made, and then preserved in a fixed material form, so that they are not lost and can be passed on to future generations. Science can be understood as a kind of double ratchet effect, in which ground rules that help scientists actively seek new discoveries are implemented in a material form using print literacy, and articles are written about both methods and discoveries. What could perhaps be called the treble ratchet effect – or the dialogic flow effect – is the technology-supported process by which new discoveries are made and then shared and improved upon in real time through digital media, such as the internet and AI assistants. This is not so much about how we hang onto and transmit the past, but instead how we move into a continuously self-correcting and improving real-time dialogue. The materiality of the digital media used is not about preserving the past (a kind of past-oriented ratchet), but about supporting a continuous flow of meaning-making through participation in creative collective real-time dialogue.

What Bereiter (1994) calls the 'progressive discourse' of science is no longer only found in the slow cycles of print-mediated dialogue, but also live on the internet. This means that students can be inducted into virtual participation in these living dialogues to learn about science in a more authentic and engaging way.[7] Knowledge Forum, the environment to support progressive discourse developed by Scardamalia and Bereiter described in Chapter 4, is now being used to link students debating scientific questions in schools with experts who can participate in the dialogue online, even if they are not physically present (Chan et al., 2019). The internet also makes it easier for students and lifelong learners to engage in real science projects asking cutting-edge questions (e.g., the Khan Academy's Khanmigo edubot and nQuire, as reported in Scanlon et al., 2020). Jane McGonigal, the futurist and game designer whose work we discussed in Chapter 5 and below, argues that online multi-user simulation games offer a powerful new form of education. She argues that these can teach students not only content knowledge, but more importantly how to work together to form a collective intelligence to solve complex distributed problems in real time (McGonigal, 2007). This may be achieved by inducting students into solving problems together on the internet – either real-world problems (Scanlon et al., 2020) or game simulations of problems (Zhonggen, 2019) – and represents a new relationship between education and time. McGonigal also goes further in some massive multiplayer online games to induct players not only into the present, but into a dialogue with alternative versions of the future.

### Case study: Computer-supported education into the future through Superstruct

In 2008, Jane McGonigal was the lead designer for a six-week future-forecasting simulation called Superstruct, created as a research project with the Institute for the Future in Palo Alto, California. The goal was to map out the full range of economic, political, social and emotional impacts of global threats like pandemics. The game was set to occur in the autumn of 2019, which was then 11 years in the future. During this game, around 10,000 people worldwide simulated living through five threats. These included, prophetically, a global outbreak of a fictional virus remarkably similar to Covid-19 (which in the game was called Respiratory Distress Syndrome or ReDS). The game asked people to predict how they would feel, and what they would do, during this kind of rapidly spreading outbreak. How would they change their habits? What social interactions would they avoid? Would they be able to work from home? Would they choose to self-isolate?

The game participants told thousands of stories about what they, personally, would do during such a pandemic. McGonigal comments that[8]:

> When the novel coronavirus first came to global attention in early 2020, I thought the most important findings to share with the world from our massive multiplayer simulation would be the predictions that people had made.

In later work, she gives many examples of useful predictions resulting from the game. While she is proud of this, McGonigal also comments that the game had a more profound and useful purpose than predicting the future:

> I no longer believe that the most important work of a large-scale social simulation like Superstruct is to accurately predict what people will do. Instead, the most important work of a future simulation is to prepare our minds and stretch our collective imagination, so we are more flexible, adaptable, agile, and resilient when the 'unthinkable' happens. . . .
>
> In January 2020, I started receiving emails and Facebook messages from people who participated in the pandemic simulation. They wrote things like, 'I'm not freaking out, I already worked through the panic and anxiety when we imagined it ten years ago'. They said, 'Mask up!' and

> 'Time to start social distancing!' and 'I'm starting to prepare for this now', weeks before it hit mainstream consciousness outside of China that we needed to start making serious changes to our habits and plans. Simulation participants kept telling me, in their own ways, that pre-feeling the future helped them pre-process the anxiety, the overwhelming uncertainty, and the sense of helplessness, so they could move more rapidly to adapt and act resiliently when the future actually arrived.
>
> (McGonigal, 2022, pp. xvii–xviii)

### *Commentary on the Superstruct case study*

Although not specifically intended to be an educational game, it seems that Superstruct had a powerfully positive educational effect in helping players prepare for an uncertain future. Having lived through a simulation of a pandemic made a difference to their response during an actual pandemic. Jane McGonigal's mostly anecdotal evidence here is backed up by research on future-oriented educational approaches (Miller, 2018). For instance, Nardo and Gaydos (2021) have applied a related approach to education in ethics, stimulating students to think the unthinkable by projecting them into contexts beyond their normal experience. Education that focuses on the future instead of the past might help students to work more effectively with change, seeing the positive opportunities, and reducing levels of anxiety. This kind of education expands the shared field of time within which people live, and with which they might become more comfortable through developing a larger extended sense of collective identity. In this way, education for the future is also education that deepens and expands the present moment, arguably helping learners to appreciate the present and experience time as Kairos or the constant creative potential for new beginnings.

## Discussion

As we are writing, pictures from the James Webb[9] telescope are in the news and being shared around the internet. These pictures, from a space telescope set in orbit around the sun, claim to show new features of the early universe shortly after its creation some 15 billion years ago. The new knowledge being discovered is not static; the significance of the information received is being debated in continuous dialogues between experts. New patterns and ideas are adding to and expanding the collective dialogic space. This kind of cutting-edge research expanding the field of what we can see, think and talk about is also part of education.

The James Webb Space Telescope's ability to expand our vision to see both space and time is a dramatisation of the temporal aspect of dialogic space, which we call dialogic time in this chapter. Education, we argue, is and always has been a journey into time. Educational artefacts like cave paintings, textbooks and online science experiments connect the short timescale of in-person experience and small group dialogues with the long timescale of culture. Understanding this role of educational technology can help us to design for the combination of new digital technologies and pedagogies that will more effectively induct students into participation in long-term cultural dialogues. These dialogues in every area of our collective life, not only science and technology but also in music, sport, bread-making and space technology, are living dialogues. Our case study gives a hint as to how education can now be designed such that students can be inducted directly into participation in these living dialogues online.

Discussion of Bernard Stiegler's ideas suggests that educational technology has a role to play in the expansion of time. Stiegler claims that our awareness of time as something outside of our own lived experience is a product of our involvement with technology. It is this shared time, the technologically mediated time of anticipation, that enables the ratchet effect of learning. This involves us taking a step back to become aware of what we have learnt, to mark it with a tool such that we can retrieve it in collective memory, repeat it and teach it forwards. This kind of technological ratchet effect weaving together moments of time is an essential part of the temporal process of education. For example, technology can be used to help students revisit and develop what they learned during the previous school term or university academic year, and to link their learning to the larger timeframe of the progressive discourse of humanity. Each such ratchet move does not just occur in time, it also actively expands our collective time horizon. This use of technology for the expansion of dialogic time through education is an expansion of individual and group identity to become an active participant in a bigger drama. This drama features an expanded living present including the dawn of space and time, as observed by our new telescopes, and the long-term future challenges of life for future generations. We need to engage with these challenges now through forward-facing education that empowers students to thrive in a constantly changing world.

### *Prompts towards a dialogic foundation for the design and use of educational technology*

We have argued in this chapter that it is fruitful to think about education as different ways of expanding dialogic time. Educational technology helps with this; it has the role of linking together dialogues at different scales of time.

One study by Sara Hennessy clearly illustrates how digital educational technology can be used to bring together several different timescales: local short-term dialogues, a scheme of work over a period of a school term, and also a more cultural-historical timescale. In this example, a history teacher began teaching about the Tudors with portraits of two important queens on the electronic whiteboard. Students were invited to the front of the classroom to annotate these representations of historical artefacts with their own thoughts and emotional responses concerning what the portraits signified about the era (see Figure 9.3).

After a term of teaching about the historical context of the portraits, the stored images with annotations were revisited to explore together how students' understanding and feelings had changed because of what they had learnt (Hennessy, 2011). This is interesting in that it uses the large screen to create a shared 'dialogic space' in the short term of an activity annotating the images together. In addition, it can also link together that activity with the longer timescale of the scheme of work, and serve as a bridge to the

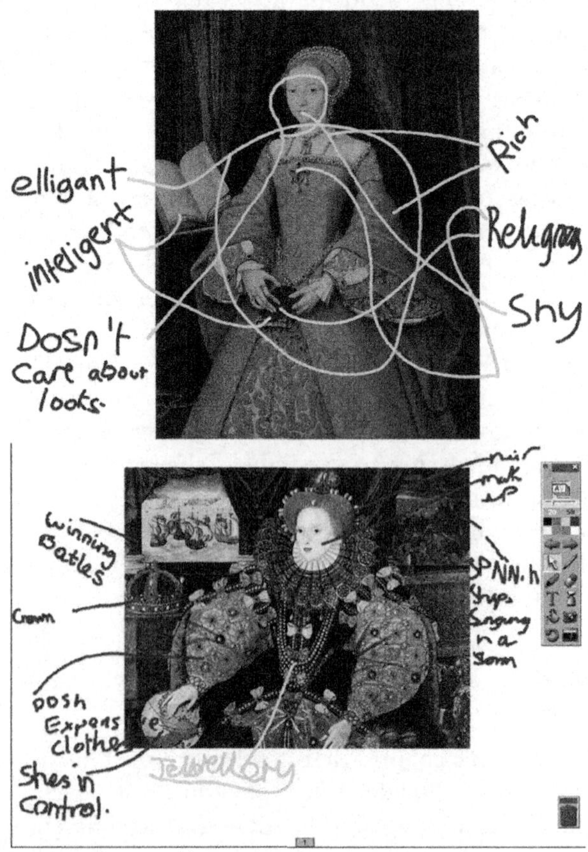


**FIGURE 9.3** Annotated history on an interactive whiteboard.

*Source:* Sara Hennessy.

engagement of students' voices in the longer timescale of cultural history represented by the works of art. Physically adding their own speech and thought bubbles to historical artefacts dramatised a personal participation, and even possession of the cultural history being taught. The use of colourful images, and collecting and developing emotional as well as cognitive responses, illustrates how the multimodal nature of digital media can facilitate a broader vision of education than the use of print literacy alone.

Various software tools exist to support exploring the future through scenario planning. These tools collate together various views on how significant different drivers, such as global warming or advances in space travel, might be. Students working in pairs or small groups can generate key drivers together, before discussing and rating their significance. Software tools can then produce a map of the range of views for further small group and collective discussion (Whitworth, 2020b). Educational technology used in this way to support induction into collective thinking about the future might be of benefit in reducing anxiety about the passage of time, and increase a sense of constructive engagement in taking responsibility for shaping the future (Miller, 2015).

Whereas students annotating and discussing the significance of historical artefacts helps to bring the past into the dialogue, using software to help anticipate the range of possibilities is a way to bring the future into the dialogue. Both illustrate ways that educational technology can be used to expand dialogic time.

# 10

# RESEARCHING EDUCATIONAL TECHNOLOGY

*We do not obtain knowledge by standing outside of the world; we know because we are of the world. We are part of the world in its differential becoming.*

Karen Barad (2007, p. 128)

*We situate ourselves in ourselves and in the things, in ourselves and in the other, and at the point where, by a sort of chiasm, we become the others and we become the world.*

Merleau-Ponty (1968, p. 160)

## Introduction

To explore and develop the theory of educational technology in this book so far, we have often referred to research evidence. Theory, whether explicitly named and articulated theories like connectivism, or the implicit theories implied behind unquestioned assumptions, is necessary to inform research. This is because theory inspires the research questions asked, and shapes the methods used to address these questions. It is therefore important that research findings can also loop back to inform theory, whether to confirm, strengthen, develop or challenge it.

We began the last chapter which focused on dialogic time, Chapter 9, with the well-known quotation: 'Those who cannot remember the past are condemned to repeat it'. This book is in part a response to the concern that the field of educational technology research has not been learning from the past due to a lack of theory. Theory plays a key role in supporting the ability of any field to learn from the past. Practice alone is not enough for cumulative learning, as this might just tell us if something works or not. Theory on

DOI: 10.4324/9781003198499-10

the other hand provides an often tentative and provisional story as to *why* things work or do not work. Educational technology design and use should be informed by theory, and theory can be tested and developed by looking at the consequences of specific designs and uses.

One way to improve the design of future systems is to start with research on what has worked in the past. By studying evidence on what has worked and what has not, we can try to understand when, how and why something worked to determine effective design principles that can be taken forward. To better understand how research might impact the development of educational technology theory, we begin this chapter with a critical review of the history of research on educational technology so far, locating this within the larger field of research on education in general.

One of the main arguments in this book is that new digital technology not only makes new ways of doing education possible, but it also changes how we understand the nature of education. In this chapter, we argue that the same is true of research. New technology not only makes new ways of doing educational research possible, but it also changes how we should think about the purpose and nature of educational research.

## A short history of educational research

The history of educational research has been punctuated by exasperated calls from policy makers and others asking why it cannot be more straightforward, like medical research into whether a new 'treatment' pill works better than 'placebo' in treating a medical condition such as allergic hayfever for example. They claim there should be a simple, scientific way to find out what works and what does not in education. James Paul Gee, whose influential work on video games in education is amongst the highest cited educational technology research, explains why this is not so easy in a foreword to a book written by David Williamson Shaffer (2017). Gee writes that education as a discipline is not a 'hard science' (like the natural sciences), but rather a 'hard hard science'. This is because education as a research area tackles not only hard problems, but also throws into the mix the additional complexity of human beings. Humans (both as individuals and groups) are complex systems in their own right. Put them inside other complex (educational) systems, and that complexity grows. As Gee states:

> Scientists who study their fellow humans are interpreting beings that can interpret right back and can change their interpretive frameworks in the bat of an eye . . . it is as if the cells in a petri dish could plan with each other how to surprise the scientist studying them.
>
> (p. ii)

Despite this inherent complexity of education, the field of educational research has grown considerably since the turn of the 20th century, and rapidly since the start of the 21st century. However, the idea that educational decision making and practice should be informed by research was first advocated in the 19th century. Prompted by the success of the scientific method in the natural sciences, seminal works such as Alexander Bain's *Education as a Science* (1879) argued that rigorous empirical research could be used to potentially transform educational standards. Prior to this, educational practice was, according to its critics at least, largely based on tradition and authority, especially the authority of the Bible, or Aristotle or other classical writers. Critics argue that the validity of an idea was judged more by the authority of its source than by the quality of the research evidence (Nisbet, 2005).

In the early 20th century, educational research textbooks began to appear in Germany that were based on experimental psychological research. This is noteworthy given that the publication of textbooks is often a sign that a topic is beginning to be recognised as a discipline (Nisbet, 2005). The launch of highly regarded educational research journals such as *Educational Review* (1891), the *Journal of Experimental Pedagogy* (1911) and the *Journal of Educational Research* (1920) corroborate this sense of an emerging field. From 1900 onwards, three educational research movements can be identified (De Landsheere, 1993): (1) the child study movement, where educational research was associated with applied psychology; (2) the progressive movement, where philosophy took precedence over science, and life experience over experimentation; and (3) the scientific movement, with a positivist approach and statistical control studies. To a surprising degree, these three different perspectives are still reflected in the main divisions found in discussions amongst educationalists today on social media and in other public spaces.

In her 100-year analysis, Lagemann (2002) argues that influential forces adversely shaped the early field of educational research in a way that would be felt for decades. She describes how a focus on quantification and 'scientism' inadvertently resulted in educational research becoming detached from policy and practice. This promoted a perception of the field as a marginal one, commonly criticised by public policy makers, and side-lined to the fringes of academia. Abandonment of promising pragmatic work by John Dewey and others in favour of that by quantitative psychologists such as Edward Thorndike was, Lagemann argues, pivotal to this marginalisation. The early enthusiasm for student measurement and testing, particularly in the United States, also 'did little for education . . . it measured but it did not analyse' (Travers, 1983, p. 507).

Quantitative research can be broadly characterised as the process of collecting and analysing numerical data. This typically involves analysing statistical correlations found in data, and attempting to isolate causal processes by controlling confounding factors through randomisation. Savenye and Robinson (2013) define qualitative research as developing an understanding of human systems. These systems can be small, such as one student learning with a tablet and an app, or large, such as the culture of education in a country. Qualitative research is typically conducted in a naturalistic setting without intentionally manipulating the environment. It involves detailed, rich descriptions of human behaviours and opinions, collected through using methods such as interviews, in contexts where the researcher may be part of the study as a participant observer.

During the 1950s, the dominance of positivist quantitative research began to be challenged by qualitative and ethnographic approaches, typically developed in other emerging fields such as sociology. The 1960s saw epistemological debate surface across the social sciences, partly motivated by Thomas Kuhn's (1962) account of scientific change. In education, it has been claimed, this debate may have been a reaction to the quantitative empiricism that dominated the field in its formative stages. Coupled with greater funding, and closer alignment with the needs of practitioners and policymakers, it was increasingly acknowledged that adhering to a rigid experimental scientific research ideal could not account for all aspects of education and its many contextual nuances (De Landsheere, 1993). For a while in the 1970s and 1980s, there was a tendency for education researchers to form closed camps as either quantitative or qualitative researchers. The argument was made, usually citing Kuhn's idea of 'incommensurable' paradigms, that the quantitative and qualitative research approaches were incompatible (Maxwell, 2010). The quantitative or more positivistic camp often claimed to be looking for causal explanations using statistical methods. They assumed that the explanatory mechanisms they found from correlations over time were valid and reliable, like the model of causation in the physical sciences. While there are many divisions within the qualitative camp, proponents tended to claim that the goal of research is to understand, rather than explain, human behaviour. They argued that the best way to do this was through 'thick description', which involves understanding why people do what they do and the meanings that experiences have for them.

The reality of most educational research can be argued to not fit either of these two paradigms very well. Experimental quantitative studies controlling variables to test hypotheses like 'if *x* then *y* under conditions *c*' can be of limited value in complex educational contexts that are constantly changing. This is because it is difficult to control for all variables that could affect the outcome of an experiment in a real-world setting. Hence, although experimental studies are often used to identify causal relationships that can be generalised to other settings, the complexity of education can make this difficult. And while 'deep' qualitative descriptions of educational software, such as interviews with teachers and students, may be interesting, they are not always the most efficient way to identify the factors that contribute to whether the software works or not.

To some extent, these considerations have led to a new consensus emerging in the educational research literature that sound inquiry develops in a spiral way, combining different methods and approaches that might previously have been considered incompatible (De Landsheere, 1993; Hammersley, 1996). Nonetheless, qualitative and quantitative research approaches are still treated by many researchers as if they are opposed constructs. In practice, this often means that such research is conducted by different people and research groups. Ironically, this sense of theoretical incompatibility between the quantitative (explanatory) and the qualitative (interpretative) research paradigms can be reinforced by so-called 'mixed methods' approaches to research. This is because the very idea of combining or mixing different methods can itself implicitly reinforce the conceptual difference between these methods (Symonds & Gorard, 2010).

In Chapter 1 we outlined our view, inspired by Diana Laurillard, Mike Sharples and others, that education as an academic discipline is best thought of as a design science. This means viewing education as being concerned with changing the world, rather than with describing or explaining it, in a manner akin to engineering, architecture or computing. If this view is accepted, then it follows that practical education research involves intervening in systems to improve them. This, of course, involves understanding how the systems work and what it would mean for them to improve in the given context of the research. First developed by Kurt Lewin in the 1940s, action research is relevant to education understood as a design discipline. As we consider later, this adopts a pragmatic approach to knowledge and problem solving, and so potentially avoids the supposed incompatibility between quantitative and qualitative approaches.

Starting in the late 1990s, there has been a revival of quantitative experimental approaches in education, in part a response to renewed demands for more 'evidence-based' evaluations. These calls seem remarkably similar to those calling for greater quantification and 'scientism' which dominated in the USA around 100 years ago. This includes a return of the idea that rigorous randomised control trials (RCTs) are the 'gold standard' of good education research (Torgerson & Torgerson, 2012). RCTs can of course offer valuable insights, typically in a quite narrowly specified set of cases. Treating these as the gold standard, however, can be problematic. The fact that this kind of experimental science has been tried before over decades, and was previously abandoned, is also often largely ignored by governments and policy makers (Thomas, 2022).

This brief history, focusing mainly on Europe and the USA, suggests that educational research is still being influenced by methods from other disciplines, even though these methods are not always appropriate for the design-oriented approach that education needs. The influence of research ideals stemming from the natural sciences on the one hand, and from the humanities and descriptive social sciences on the other, has led to a version of what Merleau-Ponty refers to in the context of philosophy as a 'bad dialectic': an unproductive oscillation between supposedly 'objective' so-called 'quantitative' approaches and supposedly 'subjective' so-called 'qualitative' approaches (Merleau-Ponty, 1968, pp. 94 and 116). This bad dialectic effect can be seen both diachronically, as different approaches replace each other over time in a repeating cycle, and also synchronically, as many education research faculties are riven down the middle into quantitative and qualitative research camps, which often do not work together or even understand each other because they speak quite different languages. Later in this chapter we revisit this problem to suggest a way forward. Theory, we argue, needs to be a living voice that continuously emerges out of the dialogic tension that unites these alternative, apparently incompatible and opposed perspectives. Before we do so, however, we look briefly at the history of the more specific strand of educational research that is research on educational technology.

## A short history of educational technology research

In 2019, the 50th Anniversary Volume of a leading educational technology research journal – the *British Journal of Educational Technology* (*BJET*) – was published. Reflecting on the journal's history, the *BJET* editors discuss how the cover of the first issue depicts a focus on audio-visual (AV) technologies, framing educational technology as including slide projectors, film, radio and television (Hennessy et al., 2019). While the centrality of these technologies to the broader field of educational technology has been displaced today, the first editor's statement about the journal's focus remains surprisingly contemporary despite being written in 1970:

> The journal is concerned with the theory, applications and development of educational technology and communications. This definition includes work in the fields of the psychology of learning, audio and visual means of presentation, educational planning and organisation, curriculum development and course design, the production of teaching and learning materials, the storage, retrieval, and dissemination of information, the allocation of resources, the costs and effectiveness of media in education, the design of learning spaces and the problems of innovation.

A thematic review of articles published in the decades since reveals the evolution of educational technology research (Bond et al., 2019): from a focus on multimedia and distance learning (1970–79), to AV technologies and the design of computer-based learning (1980–89), the evolution of distance education and rise of interactive learning (1990–99), implementing and designing online collaborative learning and ICT in schools (2000–09), to investigating the role of learning analytics and mobile collaborative learning (2010–). These shifts reflect the new technologies coming into education, as well as associated developments in the ways in which educational technology is framed, as discussed in Chapter 4.

The history of educational technology has been described as waves of research stimulated by new technologies, such as CD-ROMs, the internet, mobile devices, and AI assistants. Each new wave apparently aims to rediscover educational technology without any sense of a cumulative development (An & Oliver, 2021). It has been argued that consistent weaknesses in educational technology research may have prevented it from becoming a fully established field (Hennessy et al., 2019). These weaknesses include frequent adoption of an uncritical, techno-evangelical outlook. This had led to educational technologies often being promoted as a 'panacea' (or 'solution' or 'cure') through research focused primarily on the digital tools themselves, at the expense of considering the wider learning environment or how to effectively integrate technology into learning design. Arguments that new technology will rapidly transform education and potentially replace teachers are also often articulated throughout the educational technology research literature (Bozkurt, 2020). As discussed in Chapter 4, these claims go back to the mechanical teaching machines tried as far back as the 1920s and again by Skinner in the 1950s (Watters, 2021). Similar claims are still regularly made for each new advance, most recently about the transformative potential of AI in education, repeating almost word-for-word claims made when this field first emerged in the 1980s (Disessa, 1987; O'Shea & Self, 1986).

The rapid pace of technological change, the fact that negative research findings tend to be underreported, and the uneven geographical distribution of research emanating from some regions (with fewer contributions from Africa, the Middle East and South America) are all challenges for the field. Favouritism of the positivist paradigm, and a constant quest to 'prove' whether educational technology is effective, also appears to endure. One problem with this is that it is difficult to define what we mean by 'effective' when the nature of education is also being changed by technology. Hew and colleagues (2019) suggest that this attitude of 'naïve empiricism' might explain why research on educational technology routinely ignores theory. Data collection and analysis tends to take precedence over theory, with researchers mainly describing what they did and sharing what they found – usually that their new 'EdTech' intervention worked – rather than using theory to explain and understand those results in a larger context. This naïve empiricism has restricted development. For the last 50 years at least, studies have repeatedly claimed that new forms of educational technology can either lead to better learning gains within the existing education system, or that it will disrupt and transform that system. Yet, despite this, many commentators claim that very little seems to have changed (Cuban, 2018; Reich, 2020). On the other hand, potentially, this story about a failure to disrupt might now be changing. The global Covid pandemic which forced many schools to close and much education to go online has led to a renewed interest in, and engagement with, digital education (Zancajo et al., 2022).

## New technology suggesting new methods of theory development

We have previously argued that the way we frame the concept of knowledge, and so also the concept of education, is influenced by developments in technology. For example, we suggested that Spinoza's 17th century attempt to write philosophy in a more 'geometrico' style was influenced by the success of Euclid's *Elements*, the highest selling textbook printed by Gutenberg. Toulmin argues that the printing press led to a shift in the way truth was conceptualised. Before Gutenberg, truth was often seen as a kind of dialogue, requiring nuance and interpretation. After Gutenberg, truth began to be seen as a matter of proof, based on Euclid's examples. There is a direct line of evolution from this print-influenced way of thinking about truth and what many still think of as a 'scientific' worldview. Just as Euclidian mathematics appears to work by deduction from a few universal atemporal axioms or statements regarded as self-evidently true, so scientism tends to hold that all real physical events can be explained by subsuming these events as instances of universal 'laws of nature'.[1] Hypothetico-deductive experimental science is often seen as a way of producing knowledge that is similar to the 'geometrico' way of producing knowledge. First you propose a theory, from which you deduce a claim on the lines of *x* causes *y*. Then you design experiments that try to disprove this hypothesis. If you fail to disprove the hypothesis, then you can claim that the theory is supported.

This 'geometrico' way of imagining knowledge worked well for Galileo and Newton. However, it only seems to work well in the context of relatively simple and closed systems. Educational technology, as we claimed at the beginning of this chapter, is part of a highly complex system. For example, understanding how students learn with digital devices requires us to consider the interactions of multiple voices. These voices include the educator, the students, the prompts on the screen, the technology itself and all other voices that impact on the learning situation. Once multiple agents dynamically adapt to each other, the circular feedback loops involved create a level of complexity that makes reduction to a monological or linear model (of the kind *a* causes *b* under conditions *x*, *y*, *z*) not all that useful.

Advances in computing power have made it possible to study complex systems in new ways. John Casti, a mathematician who worked at the Santa Fe Institute for the Study of Complex Adaptive Systems for over a decade, argued that simulation modelling of the interactions of multiple agents is a new scientific method distinct from experimental and linear mathematical modelling. As these methods were developed to study closed, relatively simple systems, Casti argues that they are not well-suited for studying highly complex systems (Casti, 1997).

One way to study complex adaptive systems is to create simulations in which multiple agents are given a set of rules of behaviour, and possibly also rules on how to adapt those rules. These agents are then allowed to interact with each other. When many agents follow even simple rules, this can sometimes result in the 'emergence' of new self-organising systems that cannot be predicted by the rules themselves. Sugata Mitra is perhaps the most well-known researcher to have applied this metaphor of emergent self-organisation to education, proposing the concept of 'self-organised learning environments' (SOLEs) that features learners using the internet to learn independently (Mitra & Dangwal, 2010). But while some studies have applied agent-based modelling simulations to education systems (e.g., Gu & Blackmore, 2015), for the moment at least, the process of teaching and learning is too complex to model effectively (Osberg & Biesta, 2008). Nonetheless, research into complex adaptive systems using computer simulations of multiple agents interacting illustrates how emergence in complex adaptive systems may be researched. For instance, rather than observing the system from the outside, the system can be allowed to run to explore patterns of growth and change that emerge when internal rules governing interactions are tweaked. What we can learn from such research on technologically driven change, using techniques made possible by new technology, is the importance of methodologies that enable us to study the process of how new things emerge. While experimental methods in the social sciences often assume things to be static, there is a need to assume change in order to investigate the processes which support and which hinder growth (Power et al., 2023).

## Research that develops theory with big data

Research methods have evolved over time, often in response to changes in available technology. For instance, commentators have pointed out that the development of cognitive science in the 1950s and 1960s is hard to imagine without the advent of computing enabling the testing of information processing models of cognition (Bruner, 1984). More recent developments in digital communications technology, which enable the collection and processing of vast amounts of 'big' data, can be argued as challenging traditional distinctions between qualitative and quantitative data. Indeed, it is now possible for AI to analyse the emotional tones of a spoken interview without any human qualitative coding (Suen et al., 2020). As previously discussed, most common definitions of quantitative data state that they are numerical, while interviews are typically seen as representative of qualitative data. Yet data gathered and processed by an AI interviewer is numerical in form, a series of '0's and '1's in binary machine code. AI can also convert quantitative data such as the number of clicks a student makes in an online environment to generate qualitative insights into how students feel about a course. As discussed in Chapter 7, such developments suggest the need to move away from a humanist ontology that contrasts the subjective and the objective, towards an ontology that is based on the theory of information and systems of information.

Traditional quantitative methods are often used to show 'learning gains' because of an intervention. However, Shaffer argues that the kind of learning occurring in online educational role-play simulations developed by his team (e.g., featuring playing a bio-scientist or a diplomat), requires a more traditional ethnographic analysis of shifts in epistemology, social identity and values. Since these 'epistemic games' were played in largely digital environments, Shaffer had access to large datasets. His work reveals how traditionally more qualitative aspects of learning – such as shifts in identity, increased collaboration and increased innovation – can be identified in big data. His innovative computer-based methods for undertaking what he calls quantitative ethnography (QE), and particularly tools such as 'epistemic network analysis', have spawned a growing research community with annual conferences and many new examples of rigorous education research in a new vein.

In Chapter 6 we offered the illustration of Generation Global in which classes of young people engaged in dialogue with others from different cultures. We discussed how participants were asked to write about the other group they encountered before and after meeting, following which these two texts were compared using corpus linguistic methods. An analytical approach called the 'dynamic inverted pyramid' (DIP) developed through classroom-based research in Mexico (Wegerif et al., 1999) was used. DIP is a method that allows for the interaction of 'inside' (more qualitative) and 'outside' (more quantitative) views, a concept which can be applied to research on educational technology more generally wherever big data is available.

Exploring patterns in the data from the perspective of the learners, the research team generated conjectures about what these patterns meant for learning. They then tested these conjectures by looking at all the contexts in which these patterns appeared in the data. This not only revealed whether something was relevant, but also why it was relevant. For example, a statistical difference was found between the use of personal pronouns in the 'pre' data when compared to the 'post' data. Then, the context was analysed in more detail to develop a theory about what this meant in relation to different constructions of personal and collective identity: 'I', 'they' and 'we'. Circling back, the data was then analysed again in greater detail to look for statistical patterns, including collocations or word combinations linked to pronouns, to see if the patterns confirmed or disconfirmed the emerging theories.

A similar circling between qualitative and quantitative data was a feature of the Argunaut case study offered in Chapter 7. Maps of student interaction in a dynamic concept-mapping environment (Wegerif et al., 2010) were hand-coded for features like creativity and reasoning, before being fed into a data-mining algorithm which used big data to code all maps automatically in real time. The intention was to use this method to intervene in online dialogues in a way which would iteratively improve the relevance of the coding, with feedback from teachers and students on the value of these interventions leading to the system learning about the most relevant data to code. As is often the case, limited research funding meant this virtuous machine plus human learning circle remained as a pilot. Nonetheless, the idea remains viable. The dynamic iterative exploration of patterns in the data described produces more than only a numerical figure of the statistically significant difference in language use between one group and another. It also includes a detailed narrative explaining why this difference is educationally significant.

We mentioned earlier that there is a growing consensus in education that qualitative and quantitative methods can be combined in a virtuous spiral. This approach starts with exploratory, 'inductive' (bottom-up) research that generates theories. These theories can then be tested in a second stage of 'deductive' (top-down) research. This combination of bottom-up induction and top-down deduction, in a virtuous spiral, is central to the DIP method. Using digital tools can drastically accelerate the rapidity of this virtuous research spiral. This rapidity is important in bringing both sides, the quantitative and the qualitative, together in one dialogic space. The monological illusion that research can be divided into separate, self-contained stages is a powerful and persistent one. This illusion can lead researchers to treat the bottom-up elicitation of meaning and the top-down measuring move as separate methods and separate research projects, even though they are inextricably linked. New technology-supported research approaches such as QE and DIP reveal how research can be conceptualised as a more 'wholistic' dialogue that generates theory, one that goes beyond the separate two research 'voices' model.

## Educational design-based research (EDBR)

Kurt Lewin described action research as 'comparative research on the conditions and effects of various forms of social action and research leading to social action' (Lewin, 1946, p. 35) that uses 'a spiral of steps, each of which is composed of a circle of planning, action, and fact-finding about the result of the action' (p. 38). Action research has been widely applied to educational research. However, perhaps one reason why its influence has been limited in university-based educational research is because it came to be associated with the politics of empowering teachers as researchers of their own practice. This focus on teacher-led research was criticised in the USA by Hodgkinson (1957) and later in the UK by Hammersley (1993). The main point made by both critiques is that teachers are quite busy being professional teachers. As a result, they usually have neither the time nor skills to also be good professional researchers. Doing educational research that can challenge old theories and develop new theories implies reading relevant literature, being experienced in appropriate research methods and contributing effectively to cumulative scientific knowledge through talks and publications. Teacher-led research can be good for personal professional development, these critics imply, but it is not the most effective way to build a cumulative body of theoretical knowledge about teaching and learning.

The term 'design research' is used for a family of approaches that feature design as an integral part of the research process. Importantly, the intention of such design is not only to solve 'real-world' educational problems, or to help learners to achieve goals. It is also to advance scientific knowledge. In design research, design and research are complementary and intertwined: the design is research-based, and the research is design-based (Bakker, 2019, p. 4; Philippakos et al., 2021).

EDBR is a form of action research that avoids some of the problems of teacher-led research pointed to by critics. This can systematically inform the development of educational 'products' (including both technology and/or associated pedagogy) by employing theory and research findings in combination with iterative use in real settings, data collection, analysis and evaluation, and redesign and adaptation (Smørdal et al., 2021). At the outset, a systems analysis is needed to determine the nature of the problem to be investigated. This requires for instance exploratory observations and interviews with lecturers or teachers, students and any other relevant voices. The implementation of any educational intervention developed as a result usually involves close collaboration between specialist researchers and specialist practitioners working together as co-researchers. This important research partnership element of EDBR can be difficult to manage (Cukurova et al., 2019). But despite this difficulty, educational practitioners are very often a necessary part of the research team. This is because EDBR is about knowledge that works in a context, and experienced practitioners have expertise in how to work within that context. Participatory design workshops to gain the views of all, or at least as many as possible, potential users of the system are an important way to build robust designs that stand the best chance of working sustainably in the 'real world'.

Using EDBR for researching educational technology has similarities with the methods that software developers now routinely use, approaches such as 'Agile'. Agile offers an iterative approach to project management and software development. Instead of betting on a 'big bang' launch of a product or service, Agile teams work in small increments (Smith-Nunes & Shaw, 2022). Requirements, plans and results are evaluated continuously. The main difference between this and EDBR is that the latter focuses on developing close-to-practice theory. This theory is generated in the form of design principles that are tried and tested and can be transferred, as a framework for design, to new contexts (Disessa & Cobb, 2016). Mike Sharples (2002) also argues that EDBR is driven by what, following Darke (1978), he calls a 'prime generator', meaning an overarching question or problem that drives the design. For example, the focus of educational research might not directly be to generate 'higher' results on standardised maths and science tests, although this may be a side effect. Rather, such research may focus on developing a set of guidelines for teachers to support learning through students talking effectively together in small groups around digital devices (as was the case in some of our own research: Wegerif, 2007; Wegerif & Dawes, 2004).

## 'Double-loop' EDBR

EDBR has been criticised for being another positivist approach to research in which variables are adjusted and tested to deliver a predetermined goal with no significant development of theory (Engeström, 2011). This is an important criticism. EDBR enables us to tweak designs until they work. But if that is all that EDBR does, then it can potentially be characterised as a form of positivist or monological research that assumes a single supposedly 'correct' perspective on reality. Further, this perspective may be applied in ways that ensure its basic assumptions cannot be questioned by the results.

Sometimes it might be entirely appropriate that EDBR only solves a problem. If a curriculum goal is clear, and teachers and researchers want to work together to design technology and pedagogy to deliver that goal, at the same time developing close-to-practice theory about how to deliver the goal, that is something EDBR can support. But it is also important that the EDBR allows space for reflection on, challenge to, and improvement of the theoretical assumptions that underlie the initial goal. Such reflection and development of theory is exactly what pioneers of EDBR intended (Disessa and Cobb, 2016).

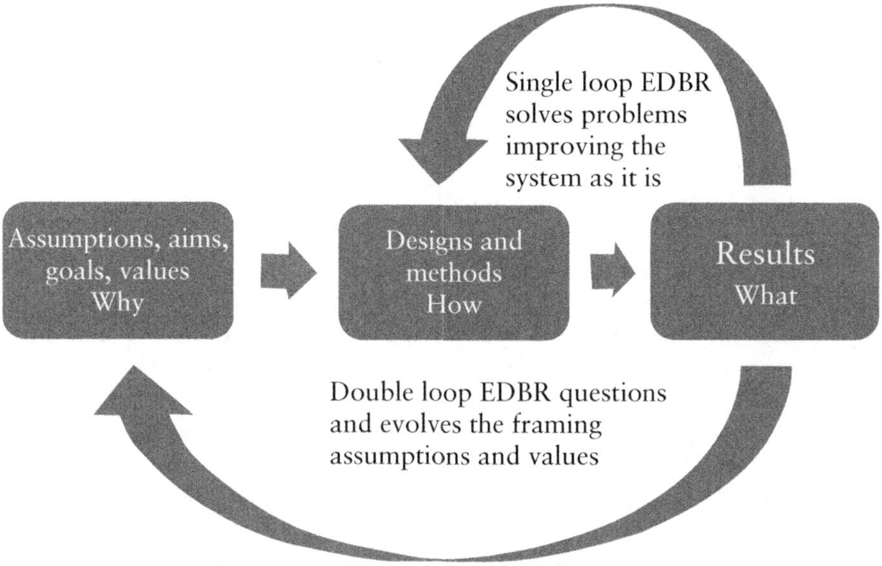


**FIGURE 10.1** Double-loop EBDR.

As Engeström's critique brings out, however, in practice this requirement for reflection on assumptions is not always observed. To evoke the kind of spinning out to larger cultural dialogues that is involved in this process, inspired by Argyris's (2002) related 'double-loop' account of learning, we propose 'double-loop' EDBR (see Figure 10.1).[2]

Educational goals imply values. While these values are often challenged and debated, they should not be seen as intrinsically arbitrary or subjective. The values underpinning educational programmes emerge from, and are part of, a long-term interdisciplinary debate about the nature of human flourishing within communities. In the discipline of education, we do not only study the most efficient way for individual learners to score highly in exams. We also consider indicators relating to well-being, and consider the long-term effects of education as we continually discuss what the goals of education should be and how assessments should be made. Everybody with a stake in education, meaning everybody, should have a voice in this debate.

## An example from research: Creating the construct of 'dialogic space'

Research designs and research programmes reflect the values of the researchers who create them. Indeed, research often makes many assumptions about what is of educational relevance and what is not. However, these assumptions can be challenged by the findings of the research itself. Consider the case of our own research involving the examination of students' classroom talk around digital devices, in particular explicit reasoning (Wegerif & Dawes, 2004). Values can be seen in the chosen focus on explicit reasoning, the research method used, which was mainly discourse analysis of transcribed talk, and in how findings were interpreted, specifically the claim that teaching a more explicitly rational type of 'exploratory talk' leads to better learning outcomes. We are not questioning this claim that more exploratory forms of talk lead to better learning outcomes. Like many others, we believe the 'robustness' of this research is somewhat evidenced by it being widely cited by other researchers and because other studies that used a similar approach produced similar results. Our point is only that, like all research, this claim is based on a set of assumptions. These assumptions can also be questioned and improved as part of the research process.

As is often the case in educational research, not all findings fit easily within a theoretical frame. As discussed in Chapter 8, we observed how students 'thinking together' solved problems through apparent creative leaps that did not involve the co-construction of arguments using explicit reasoning visible in the talk. Sometimes shared pregnant pauses and expressions of uncertainty seemed more relevant to the solutions of problems than any words spoken. Some groups that talked less, but had better emotional rapport, also did better at solving problems and learning together. All this experience led to questioning and developing the assumptions behind the goals of the programme (Wegerif, 2008). Experimental studies also suggest that a more creative computer-based task (e.g., co-writing a short text) benefited from teaching ground rules for talk, but not from the use of explicit reasoning (Rojas-Drummond et al., 2008). Ground rules were then developed to promote playful and creative talk as well as reasoning talk more explicitly. The concept of 'dialogic space' (see Chapter 8) was developed to provide a more comprehensive view of 'exploratory talk', one which does not simply assume a modernist view of reason based on co-construction through explicit argumentation, but also includes creativity and metaphorical resonance as important aspects of collective thinking. From aiming at developing more exploratory talk, the aim switched to expanding dialogic space (Wegerif, 2008).

### *Commentary on this example from research*

The example of the birth of the construct 'dialogic space' as a creative response to a problem builds on and goes beyond a relatively focused research study which was successful in achieving its educational aims, establishing close-to-practice theory that can be used to improve learning gains from group work by students around digital devices. However, even though it worked in practice the evidence gained from the project challenged the main theory being used and this fed back to question and develop the assumptions behind those educational aims, which in turn led to an evolution of both the assumptions and the aims. A process of creative reasoning (or 'abduction') connected the single loop of what was effectively an EDBR study to the larger cultural dialogue relevant to education (mainly philosophy in this case). This enabled an improved design framework for delivering the initial aim to increase exploratory talk and learning in mathematics and science. In addition, it also led to an improved theory or foundation for design, which led to a changed understanding of the initial aim and of what learning in this context meant. A dialogic theoretical framework and programme of research resulted. The aim switched from better talk for thinking to expanding dialogic space. This new aim was not a rejection of the original aim, but rather a way to build on it. This also added a focus on playfulness and on relationship forming, which were not explicitly part of the original aim. As described already in Chapter 8, this new aim of expanding dialogic space is an empirical concept that also implies a certain value: the educational value of opening, widening and deepening dialogic space. Such a notion depends on adapting ideas from the larger dialogue of humanity relevant to education. This includes ideas from philosophers such as Buber and Merleau-Ponty as well as work in the sciences such as complexity theory (e.g., Kauffman, 1995), quantum theory (authors such as Barad, Penrose and Rovelli discussed in previous chapters), and neuroscience (Damasio & Carvalho, 2013). In this way the small loop of empirical learning theory research, and the big loop of dialogue about who we are and what the purposes of education should be, were brought together within the process of an expanding EDBR-focused inquiry into how to design effective classroom pedagogy for collaborative learning around digital devices.

### The significance of double-loop EDBR with digital data: A potential framework for educational technology design

In the introduction to this book, we proposed that education as a discipline is concerned with two central questions: 'what should we teach and learn?' and 'how should we teach and learn it?' Trying to answer these questions inevitably poses a third perhaps even more fundamental question: 'why?' For instance, 'why should we teach and learn this curriculum of knowledge, skills and dispositions as opposed to any other alternative curriculum?' These are different questions from those usually asked in other disciplines including those often seen as close to education such as medicine, psychology and sociology. In general, the research methods, methodologies and paradigms that we use tend to be aligned with the type of questions that we are trying to answer. Someone might say that the question of *what* we should teach and learn is too big for any science to answer. And it is indeed difficult to answer such a question given there are many factors to consider, such as the needs of learners, society and the nature of knowledge itself. However, we do not have any choice but to attempt to answer it. Education is happening anyway: choices must be made about how we teach. In a sense, we always already find ourselves within education. In this situation, the best we can do is monitor what is going on, record the choices made and their consequences, and revise and learn as we go along. This is essentially the kind of design thinking that should be used for any technology development.[3] We are proposing extended that design-focused method for education technology design and use.

The theory of education as expanding dialogic space and dialogic time presented in Chapters 8 and 9 suggests that research is part of the larger social system of education. Research which develops and tests theories is also about learning and teaching. At its best, it is about collective learning and collective teaching. Education involves increasing the power we have to act in the present moment. This is achieved through expanding the space and time of dialogue, and in turn the number of perspectives and depth of understanding that can be applied to solve problems and design ways forward.

## Towards a dialogic research paradigm

The proposal of EDBR as a valuable methodology does not reject the value of the many methods that have been successfully applied in research on educational technology. Indeed, these research methods are routinely implemented as part of the EDBR process. Rather, EDBR intends to provide a better interpretative 'high level' framework for conceptualising educational technology research. For example, RCTs might offer an excellent way to evaluate educational technology once they are taken to scale, perhaps after a phase of EDBR (Connolly, 2009). However, while RCTs can only show what happens in a specific context, they are often interpreted as offering a kind of universal causal law applicable to all contexts. Similarly, phenomenological analysis and other interpretative methods can be very useful as a way of finding out how teachers and students respond to interventions. But interpretative methods alone are often not enough to fully understand all aspects of educational technology design given the well evidenced disparities between what teachers and students think works best for learning, and what actually works best for learning, insofar as this can be measured (Hattie, 2023).

A key ontological assumption here is that knowledge is shaped by perspectives and is situated, and hence it is often useful to generate as many perspectives as possible. Another ontological assumption is that things do not stay the same. The goal of research then is not to find reality as it is eternally, but to observe processes of growth and to generate understandings that can help us to steer that process of growth.

These key ontological assumptions share similarities with the Bakhtinian dialogic theory outlined in Chapters 1, 7 and 8. Words mean, Bakhtin said, not by how they are defined in the dictionary nor by what they are intended to mean by whoever speaks them. Rather meaning is generated by the difference that these words make in a dialogue.[4] However, dialogues are never finished. We might think that they are finished, like the written down dialogue of Socrates with Phaedrus that we quoted in Chapter 2. However, even as we return to look at them, we interpret them anew thereby continuing the dialogue (Bakhtin, 1986, p. 146). And in science, for example, dialogues certainly seem to make progress but do not lead to fixed and final truths. We might think we have found the truth of things, only for the next utterance in this dialogue to completely re-interpret everything that has gone before. There are always multiple voices, perspectives and possibilities in play, with no final conclusion – no 'last word' as Bakhtin put it.

### Chiasm: The 'outside-in' and 'inside-out' nature of research

When discussing the problems of paradigms in educational research earlier, we referred to Merleau-Ponty's idea of a 'bad dialectic'. His claim is that our external more objective views in research, and our internal more subjective views, have become stuck in opposition preventing growth and progress. Merleau-Ponty's proposed solution to the 'bad dialectic' problem is a methodology of 'sur-reflexion' or 'hyper-dialectic' that he linked to his account of ontology as 'chiasm'. Chiasm is a term borrowed from rhetoric that reverses the order of subject and object in a sentence. The sentence: 'I see the world: the world sees me' is a chiasm. Merleau-Ponty used chiasm to describe a relationship between two perspectives, an inside and an outside perspective, in which each perspective includes the other in what he called a 'mutual envelopement'. The world defines the datum or smallest unit of data while at the same time the datum, as 'a difference that makes a difference', defines the world (see Chapter 7). Sur-reflexion, is, Merleau-Ponty wrote, a kind of reflection on things that: 'would also take itself and the changes it introduces into the spectacle into account'[5] (1968, p. 38).

In dialogue, we see not just two separate voices interacting, but also an outside perspective looking in and an inside perspective looking out. To see clearly is not just to inhabit one body looking out at the world, or to see oneself located and defined as if from the outside. Instead, to see clearly is to 'rise above' this dichotomy, seeing as if from the 'point of view' of the dialogic space that unites these two apparent opposites. Educational progress in dialogic terms then is about learning to take both sides of a dialogue into account, and holding this contradiction together at once to potentially produce useful sparks of insight.

For example, finding meaning in big data from user interactions in a MOOC is not just about taking an 'outside' view to identify statistically significant patterns. However, nor is it just taking an 'inside' view to consider the lived meaning of the data, words written in text chats for example. Instead, it is the iterative oscillation between these two perspectives: inside-out and outside-in, recognising that valuable design insights come from the dialogic creative tension of juxtaposing these two aspects without reducing either one. In reality, we can only make meaning of these studies through an implicit dialogue between 'outside' and 'inside' perspectives. If the meaning we seek in research is only to be found as something that emerges in the dialogic creative tension between an inside and an outside perspective, then it follows that we should try to design empirical research in such a way as to bring these two perspectives into a fruitful or mutually illuminative relationship without allowing the generative tension to collapse (see further discussion about a 'chiasm' research methodology in Kershner et al., 2020, Chapter 8).

## Discussion

This chapter is about research as the collective dialogue through which theory is developed, challenged and refined. Theory, we claimed in Chapter 1, is essential for any field of practice to be able to learn from the past. However, our brief history suggested some problems with the way in which research has been working in the field of education technology. We diagnosed part of the problem as being that of a stuck dialectic or an opposition that had become fixed such that learning was no longer happening. Connecting to our analysis of the cognitive affordances of print literacy in Chapter 2, we related the false alternatives of quantitative and qualitative research paradigms to the dualism of a fixed objective world confronting a separate world of human experience. New digital technology, we suggested, might offer ways forward with new methods that dynamically integrate the quantitative with the qualitative: the supposedly objective with the supposedly subjective. The new dialogic research paradigm we proposed is not just the juxtaposition of different methods, but their integration in a dialogic ontology which is both relational and open, meaning that it assumes that everything is interconnected in a continuous process of growth and change. A key assumption of this dialogic ontology which, following Merleau-Ponty, we named as 'chiasm' is that there is no 'inside' without an 'outside' and no 'outside' without an 'inside'. The general epistemology that follows from this ontology is knowledge construction as part of an open-ended dialogue oscillating rapidly between inside (more qualitative or subjective) and outside (more quantitative or 'objective') perspectives. We illustrated briefly, for example, how AI-supported data analysis can be used to support a rapid cycle between theory generation from student experiences, and theory testing from objective learning data. Without rejecting any methods, the methodology we proposed as most appropriate for this dialogic conception of theory development in educational technology was what we called 'double-loop' educational design-based research or EDBR. This is a vision of how educational technology designs can be researched and developed by implementing theories in designs, trying them out to see what happens, rethinking and refining the theory, and trying them out again in a repeating cycle.

### *Prompts towards a dialogic foundation for the design and use of educational technology*

Any development of a new technology system, including educational technology systems, requires moving between the 'outside' view (or views) of the designer and the 'inside' view (or views) of the user. First you design it, then you try it out, then you refine the design in the light of experience and so on. We propose that educational technology designs should always be informed by a growing body of theory about how to teach and learn with technology. And, as far as is possible, it would be beneficial if the findings of each design project could be used to update and improve that body of theory.

A project management methodology called Agile is now perhaps the most popular way to develop and continuously improve software. This approach includes iterative cycles of testing design conjectures, reflecting on the outcomes and learning from this. EDBR shares similarities with Agile. However, it goes further in the direction of emphasising learning and the development of the kind of theory that can transfer across contexts. This kind of research is not just about evaluating the impact of systems in terms of pre-determined learning gains. It is also concerned with generating insights into how and why educational technologies work that can transfer to inform other projects and initiatives. Additionally, 'double-loop' EDBR is not only about testing and developing design principles and design frameworks. It uses designs to embody theories from the larger dialogue of educational theory and educational technology. The outcomes of implementing these designs in systems that work (or that do not work for reasons we can determine) can shed light on, challenge and develop those theories. Ideally, double-loop EDBR could be used to link theory and practice in cycles of inquiry within an online community of practice to continuously improve our knowledge of how to make education work in addition to expanding our understanding of why we are making education work.

While EDBR is still somewhat considered to be a 'methodological newcomer' (Bakker, 2019), it is increasingly being used to support a range of educational technology research. For instance, EDBR has successfully underpinned a range of ambitious studies in low- and middle-income countries through the work of the EdTech Hub (https://edtechhub.org/), as well as studies by individual researchers including doctoral students (e.g., Igglesden, 2022).

# 11

# TOWARDS A DIALOGIC FOUNDATION FOR THE DESIGN OF EDUCATIONAL TECHNOLOGY

*The current search for new educational funnels must be reversed into the search for their institutional inverse: educational webs which heighten the opportunity for each one to transform each moment of his living into one of learning, sharing, and caring.*

Ivan Illich (1971) in 'Deschooling society'

*For years we've been calling for curriculum for life, a curriculum which will see us leaving school with a greater understanding of the world around us, we are pleading for more emphasis on employability, communication skills and personal well-being. Isn't the foundation of education creating well-rounded, well informed young people ready for the future? So why do I, after spending 14 years in countless classrooms, feel so unsure about what's to come?*

Izzy Garbutt, MYP for Wigan, speaking to UK Youth Parliament, 4 November 2022

## A summary of the argument so far

Technology is normally understood as a supplement and support for the main business of education. We began this book with a history of education that reversed this relationship, suggesting that technology has been central to education from the beginning and that education systems have often developed to serve the interests of technology. For example, we looked at the work of Comenius to suggest that perhaps the pedagogy of modern schooling is as much about expanding the reach and impact of print literacy as it is about servicing the human need for education. Given that technology is embedded at the heart of education, it follows that the 'voices' of technology need to be

DOI: 10.4324/9781003198499-11

taken more seriously in our understanding of education. If the arguments in this book about the importance of technology in education are accepted, then it follows that any theory of education must also be a theory of educational technology.

One way to take technology seriously is by examining the affordances of different technologies. At its most basic, the idea of affordance is hard to dispute. After all, it seems obvious that different designs 'afford' different manipulations: some door handles afford turning, some tea-pot handles afford lifting and pouring, and so on. But when we apply this idea of affordances beyond physical manipulations to meaning making it becomes more controversial. Do different kinds of educational technology afford different types of learning? We investigated this issue in Chapter 3, concluding that a user's response to technology depends also on what can be described as the cultural tradition or the genre-expectations of the user. This means it is important to think not only about designing technology, but to combine this with the design of pedagogy that might influence the way in which the technology is used. We illustrated this with the iterative design cycle of Talkwall, a tool to support learning through dialogue in combination with pedagogy designed to promote exploratory talk.

In Chapter 4 we delved deeper to further explore the history of how educational technology has been thought about and used. Following Wittgenstein, and a strand of thinking in the recent empirical philosophy of technology, we called these ways of using technology in education 'grammars'. Education technology can be seen and designed to act as a teaching machine, a tool to think with or a learning environment. In Chapter 5 we looked at the more recent grammars of online learning communities of practice, educational multi-user role-play games and learning by network building.

Heidegger's account of how the use of tools extends human agency and human experience is valuable, we argued, for understanding how educational technology works. However, Heidegger failed to extend this insight to our involvement with modern networked technology. This was because, it seems, Heidegger could only relate to modern technology from the outside, without the empathy that comes from living something from 'within'. As a result, Heidegger mainly saw modern technology, technology which was already then forming a global network around him, as a threat to the human essence or to human 'being'. We used Levinas to help us take Heidegger's general approach further to suggest that embracing modern digital networked technology might be the key to a transformation of what it means to be human in an ethically positive direction, enabling all humans to be in relationship to each other even when separated by different countries and traditions.

Simondon and Stiegler helped us to understand how the 'human' and the 'technological' have co-evolved. Building on their work, we argue that education has been the bridge connecting the psychological individuation of persons with technological objects. We suggest that this produces what Simondon calls 'transindividuations', or persons who are both individual and collective, like voices in a dialogue. For example, as in the case study in Chapter 2, linking otherwise remote communities of farmers via mobile phones and a platform for sharing peer-learning. This project did not only lead to learning, it also created a new community and an expanded sense of self around the use of the education technology.

We gave the example of ELIZA, one of the first chatbots, to show that technology can serve as an effective dialogue partner. A more contemporary example could be ChatGPT, or another 'Conversational AI', if used as an online tutor able to guide students through the stages of solving maths problems or writing educational essays.[1] This capacity of technology to support educational dialogues challenges those definitions that insist dialogue requires the interaction of at least two separate human consciousnesses.

Dialogue in education is often described as humanistic and contrasted to more 'mechanistic' and 'instrumental' views of education (e.g., Biesta, 2016; Robinson, 2019). Against this contrast and 'othering' or marginalisation of technology, we argue that good (dialogic) education is not human as opposed to technological, but hybrid. We defined dialogue as interaction that supports learning by opening up a shared dialogic space of reflection, within which new insights and understandings can emerge. Building on the cybernetic learning theory of Gordon Pask, we argued that learning is both intrinsically dialogic and intrinsically technological. The two aspects, dialogue and technology, are so entangled and intertwined that they cannot be separated. Dialogues are learning conversations, and while learning often takes the immediate form of a lightning strike of insight or intuition, if it is to be cumulative then then there has to be some trace or record of what has been learnt carried forward in the ongoing dialogue. Cumulative learning occurs when a new idea or perspective is given a form that can be encapsulated, built upon and revisited: perhaps a written sign, a phrase, a picture or video. We described this process as the 'ratchet effect' in Chapter 9. The same process is exemplified in the use of the 'rise above' button which is a design feature of Scardamalia and Bereiter's 'Knowledge Forum' introduced in Chapter 4. This same ratchet effect was found in the talk of groups solving analogical reasoning test problems together as described in Chapter 8. To solve these problems groups needed to share virtual manipulations and so they created phrases – like 'taking the circle out', 'turning the square clockwise' or 'adding another diamond' (Wegerif, 2007) – that served as markers and tokens to be shared and sometimes carried forward in solving the next problem (Fernández et al., 2001). This is a technological process that is also fully 'human'. Learning occurs when biological organisms join together with technology to form larger self-organising systems. Furthermore, we argued that learning in dialogues occurs because the dialogue itself becomes a self-organising system uniting humans with technologies such as sign systems. As a self-organising system, the dialogue takes on agency, anticipates possible futures, focuses in on what seems to be the best solution and so, like a kind of vortex, draws participants forward, often unexpectedly, into new understandings that were not available to them before entering into the dialogue.

In Chapters 8 and 9 we developed a theory of education with technology as expanding dialogic space and dialogic time. For this account to work, we must stop thinking of learners as primarily biological bodies whose brains need to be filled with 'cognitive structures' and 'long-term memories'. Instead, we suggest a need to think of people as primarily dialogical beings who participate in a range of shared meaning spaces, some of which need to be widened and deepened. The dialogues that learners actively participate in can vary in their level of exclusivity, inclusivity, monoglotism, cosmopolitanism, focus and expansiveness. The role of the educator becomes to induct students into new dialogic spaces and to help them to navigate those spaces. Educational technology, the design of pedagogy and technology, becomes a way to link together the short-term local dialogues of the classroom or other learning space with longer-term and more global dialogues of culture. This could be as technologically simple as teaching students how to use a sign for the concept of 'zero', developed in India many centuries ago, or as complex as asking their AI-powered edubot to identify immersive virtual reality experiences that animate the concept of a cosmic black hole.

## The idea of a 'foundation for design'

Educational technology requires design, not only in terms of technological design (e.g., software and hardware features), but also in terms of pedagogical or instructional design (i.e., how such technology is effectively integrated into the teaching and learning process). Yet, all design implies philosophical assumptions about who we are, how we know and what we ought to do. Those assumptions have to come from somewhere. Some educational technology designs might make assumptions that are superficial, contradictory and ethically suspect. In this book, we have explored sources of some of the underlying assumptions of educational technology design to identify strategies that might better inform a future foundation for design. Inevitably, we may have only partially succeeded. Looking at educational technology in any one way means not looking at it in all other possible ways, other ways which might also prove valuable if pursued. This is why we put forward our dialogic theory of educational technology, in a spirit of intellectual humility, as a contribution to a much larger continuing discussion. While necessarily provisional and tentative, this theory is nonetheless grounded in the rich theory and research discussed throughout our journey to this, the final chapter of our book.

In Chapter 10, we argued for the value of educational design-based research (EDBR) as a way of developing better educational technology as well as associated pedagogy and theory. We suggest that this methodological framework can help educational institutions find a way to use digital technologies to enhance students' learning and engagement, and address potential tensions between policy, practice and research (Erstad & Silseth, 2022). The EDBR cycle begins with a primary generator or driving question. Higham and Booth (2018) for example, working with school leaders to design more ethical schools, worked with the question: 'how should we live together?' After an exploratory phase, an initial design framework is then developed. This first design framework is a set of provisional conjectures as to what the designer or designers think is going to work, conjectures which are then tested by implementing them in practice and observing what happens. This initial design framework, however tentative, has a particular view of reality embedded within it. It is inevitable that any design framework will make implicit assumptions about what education is, the role of technology in education and the nature of reality. What we mean by a 'foundation for design' is a theory of educational technology that is not yet fully developed and so not yet at the level of specificity needed to produce the kind of claims that can be directly tested with experiments, but that nonetheless can be used to inform the development of a preliminary design framework which can produce such a set of claims. A 'foundation for design', therefore, is a philosophical world view that guides the questions asked during the exploration phase of the design process, and informs the creation of the initial design framework. Although this foundation for design is not directly tested, it is indirectly tested and so is not arbitrary. It is based on reflection and debate, and it will be revised if it is successfully challenged by the findings of research. In Chapter 10, we describe how founding assumptions can also evolve through dialogue as part of the larger research process. We called this 'double-loop' EDBR. Ultimately, the larger research process is open-ended and does not have any fixed boundaries. We offer this theory of educational technology as a contribution to the collective dialogue of educational theory and as a potential part of a larger education design process that seeks to build a better future for humanity, technology and the world. This means that, even though the theory is too broad to be directly tested in any one iteration, it can be indirectly tested and developed over time by evaluating whether it inspires designs that contribute to human flourishing.[2]

## A practical foundation for design

The theory of educational technology that we propose as a foundation for design involves designing for expanding dialogue. This theory is more a foundation for design than it is a design framework. It is a way of thinking about education which will inform the development of different design frameworks in different contexts.

Most chapters in this book end with quite practical design implications. We have also provided many example case studies which might inspire ideas for design. Rather than repeat all our suggestions here, we summarise the core themes. We suggest that educational technology should be designed to engage learners, connect them in peer-to-peer inquiry, expand dialogic space and identity through induction into long-term cultural dialogues, and finally engage learners and communities in productive dialogue with the open-ended horizon of the unknown.

### *1) Design for engagement*

If education is about drawing students into meaningful dialogues mediated by digital technology, then a key step is to get them interested and to hook them into participation. Once dialogues start-up, they develop their own contagious agency that motivates everyone involved. However, the moment of first stepping into dialogue can be delicate. In classroom dialogues, in particular small-group dialogue, it appears important to create a warm and trusting environment where students are invited to share ideas and are listened to with respect. In online education, things can be more difficult. AI-powered online tutors are rapidly developing and could potentially prove compelling dialogue partners for educational journeys. Others report that getting students to asynchronously produce short videos of their interests using tools such as 'Flipgrid' (or Padlet or Miro) works well to promote engagement in online classes (Bartlett, 2018). In a higher education context, using an edubot to match new students with others who share their interests has been shown to increase their sense of belonging to the university (Abbas et al., 2022). While the importance of 'promoting engagement' might sometimes be overlooked or taken for granted, we suggest it as a foundational step in our emerging dialogic foundation for design.

### *2) Design for connection*

A new powerful form of education made possible by digital technology is peer-to-peer learning that connects people to learn together in online communities. This book provides various examples of how relationships and communities can inspire and sustain learning. These examples include mobile mediated peer-to-peer learning (Chapter 2), the MIT Scratch community (Chapter 5), and an online role-playing game exploring the future (Chapter 9). Scratch was originally developed as an online community that could be used as an alternative to school, but is now widely used to supplement school teaching and learning in the computing curriculum. The same could be true in many other subject areas, especially where teachers with relevant subject expertise are in scarce supply. One could imagine a near future where online communities of inquiry in many areas, perhaps supported by volunteers, do not replace schools but augment them.

### *3) Design for expansion*

Education involves expanding the space and the time of learning, using technology to link the small time and place of face-to-face interactions with the larger and longer-term dialogues of scientific communities and communities of practice of every kind. In the case study of Kevin Martin's research in Kenya in Chapter 2, it is noticeable that the peer-to-peer resources of farmers in a local region were augmented by imported open education resources that document the latest expert knowledge on issues of value to the community. In a similar way the case study of Shengpeng Shi's research in China (Chapter 8) demonstrates a focus on 'teaching the dialogue so far' in addition to support for peer-to-peer dialogue. 'Teaching the dialogue so far' looks much like a traditional transmissional approach to knowledge, but it teaches that all knowledge is fallible and part of an ongoing dialogue. Students are expected to actively participate in this dialogue by articulating their positions.

### *4) Design for dialogue with the future and with the unknown*

Using technology to teach and transmit knowledge, even when we do this in the form of 'teaching the dialogue so far' in a way that encourages participation, still carries with it the danger that we assume we know everything that is important in advance. In Chapter 6, Heidegger reminded us that the point of education is to bring learners into dialogue with a mystery that is outside of, or beyond, everything that we can know in advance. In Chapter 9, we looked at the importance of education that engages with the unknown and the open-ended potential of the future. This suggests the need to design educational technology not only for the expansion of knowledge, but also in a way that supports opportunities for open encounters with the genuinely unexpected. The case study offered in Chapter 6 gives one example of technology designed to support dialogue with different others where the outcome is uncertain. The case study offered in Chapter 9 is of using a digital online role-play game to project learners into an encounter with the challenge of an unknown and uncertain future.

## Building dialogic ethics into the design process

From the first chapter of this book, we have argued that education is at least partly about how we design the future. This includes, perhaps controversially, the idea that education is about designing future people. This raises the very important and difficult question: who decides on the design?

We have sometimes referred to the potential of new communications technology to facilitate global dialogues as if these inevitably lead to progress. However, many exchanges on the internet are not of any obvious educational value. Even if we take the long-term and global dialogue of science as our example, there are many times when this dialogue is distorted by interests that do not seem to align with the collective good. In a situation where there are multiple views, but a decision needs to be taken, then what is the best way to decide? In our view, dialogue is the only ethical way forward, even though it may be imperfect in practice. A dialogic ethics is not about particular ethical claims, but rather focuses on the process of making decisions together. As explored throughout this book and particularly in Chapters 8 and 10, dialogue is much more than explicit verbal reasoning. It is also about possessing the intellectual humility to be open to learning from the perspective of the other, and being able to empathise with different perspectives as well as seeing from different perspectives. Dialogic ethics is a 'meta-ethics'. It is not a specific value system competing on the same level with other value systems. Instead, it is about how we can learn to rise above differences. The ideal of making decisions based on dialogue is that everyone can potentially benefit from the outcome, even if this means giving up some of their freedom of action. When dialogue succeeds, all participants feel more empowered and more expanded. In the language of Simondon explored in Chapter 7, a successful dialogue around a technological design builds a new community as a cybernetic 'transindividual', which means that this is not merely an external community but also a new expanded internality or sense of identity for each participant.

As we have considered, evidence from educational research indicates that such mutually expansive dialogue is possible. We also hope that many readers will have some evidence from their own experience that enables them to give context to our claim that dialogue can sometimes be a good way to make design decisions. Nonetheless, we also know (as can be seen most days on the internet) that in practice dialogue often fails. Sometimes this failure seems to be because of reasons that are structural and hard to address by individual action (Spohr, 2017). Our claim is not that dialogue is easy, but only that it is possible. Actual dialogues in real contexts will never be perfect. That is why we propose taking a design-based research approach as discussed in Chapter 10. Continuous monitoring and feedback as to why dialogues are not working well can inform new interactions and new designs for interactional spaces. Continuous critique from multiple voices is essential to ensure that educational technology designs are as effective, responsive and ethical as possible. The idea of dialogic ethics is not a simple answer to the problem of how to decide on the design of educational technology and pedagogy. Rather, it is more of a promise to keep trying to do better, guided by the dialogic principle of openness to the other and the possibility of learning from the other. In response to the many concerns about the impact of technology in education we believe that dialogic ethics should be the foundation for all educational design decisions. We also suggest it should be a central part, perhaps the most important part, of what we teach and what we expect students to learn.

## The challenge we face

Like lightning-strikes or the formation of snowflakes, our education systems and technology are responses to tensions, drivers and constraints in the larger environment. The main difference between the evolution of human technology and natural technology, such as Beaver's dams or spiders' webs, is that the mechanism of dialogue enables humans to anticipate more desirable futures. As such, humans can generate designs motivated by a longer-term creative vision, in addition to resolving immediate tensions (Heylighen, 2022b).

In the introduction to this book, we raised the challenge of the Digital Age and the spread of the internet, now increasingly enhanced with AI language assistants (Brubaker, 2022). Initial hopes for improved access to democracy have been replaced with concerns about the effects of AI-generated 'fake news' and 'deep fakes' that could distort collective decision-making. The similar initial hope that increased transparency and access to decision-making would lead to greater community cohesion is now also widely seen as unrealistic. The internet was intended as a global medium with the potential to reduce tensions between different countries. Yet, there seem to be more conflicts now than before the advent of the internet. Indeed, some aspects of this increased sense of conflict appear to be linked to the way algorithms on social media sites keep users engaged and amplify the impact of more angry and violent voices (Fisher, 2022).

We linked the challenges of the transition to the Digital Age, an age of hyper-connectivity, in a cultural-historical timescale to the increasing awareness of the Anthropocene, a geological epoch characterised by human impact on the planet, in the much larger geological timescale. The Anthropocene, we argued, offers challenges to the future. These challenges require collaboration across different countries and cultures to understand and address problems such as global warming, which cannot be solved by any one country or culture acting alone.

Research that begins with the question of 'why does education need educational technology?' might be missing the real question which is perhaps: 'why does technology need education and what kind of education does it need?' The history of technological innovations shows that technology sometimes calls education into being to mitigate its threats and to realise its potential.

Literacy, including mathematics, is the most obvious example. This technology has led to the mass compulsory formal schooling that we now tend to take for granted as part of modern life. Literacy can only create a collective culture with cumulative learning if people can read. For literacy to function optimally, mass compulsory education is required. Perhaps the same is true of our new digital media. Without appropriate regulation and education, the internet and AI linked to the internet might be destructive. But when combined with dialogic education into how to use this technology to learn together with others, it might provide an effective medium for solving problems peacefully together. We will only find out if we try.

We suggest that the 'voices' of new technologies ought to be included in the dialogue about how we design the future. Indeed, with the many media stories about the potential educational impact of social media like TikTok, and powerful Generative AI, it seems that the voices of new technologies may already be muscling their way into the dialogue. Many of the case studies and research evidence in this book show that it is possible to use education to design the next generation of tools and, indeed, the next generation of learners to be more dialogic. We think it would be a good idea if the next generation of learners are equipped with the skills and knowledge required to participate in the kinds of global collective intelligence that we so evidently need now, and will probably need even more in the future.

Simondon's concern with overcoming the alienation of humans from machines is relevant to the big challenges that education faces today. The advent of the Digital Age in a cultural-historical timescale, and the advent of the Anthropocene in a geological timescale, raise serious threats to the continued flourishing of humanity. These threats are both side effects of growth in technology that is alienated from the collective interests of humanity. Adequately responding to challenges such as mass migration, warfare and the polarisation of wealth probably means that we need to build a more collective dialogic self-identity together. We can do this by using technology to build shared dialogic spaces. Educational technology to support the conscious dialogue of humans with machines, in order to eventually create a more planetary-wide collective intelligence, is demanded of us now as a response to the many challenges of our time.

# NOTES

## Chapter 1: Introduction: Why we need a theory of educational technology

1 See www.filmsforaction.org/watch/schooling-the-world-2010/, which is a powerful documentary describing the damaging impact of literacy education on many oral cultures.
2 https://nepc.colorado.edu/blog/i-gave-my-students-ipads
3 www.codingpirates.dk
4 AECT Definition and Terminology Committee: https://aect.org/news_manager.php?page=17578
5 The idea of a dominant mode of communication is inspired by Mark Poster (2001, 2018). This posits that technologies of communication like oracy, literacy, print literacy and the internet are significant markers of historical phases in a similar way to modes of production such as feudalism and capitalism. This is because developments in technologies of communication are as much a driver of change as developments in the technology of production.
6 https://ourworldindata.org/internet
7 The theory of Manuel Castells that the Digital or Information Age involves a change in space and time as we transition to a more internet-mediated social form remains relevant. Although this thesis is challenged by some critics, it is supported by evidence of the emergence of some new social practices and new social identities based around the internet (e.g., Castells, 2020; Kui, 2019; Slavina & Brym, 2020).
8 This idea that education as a discipline should be characterised through asking distinctly educational questions was influenced by conversations with Gert Biesta. See, for example, Siegel and Biesta (2022) in addition to Saeverot and Biesta (2013).
9 Our theory of dialogic education is influenced also by the educationalist, philosopher and activist Paulo Freire (1970). It is related to the more recent work of bell hooks that is influenced by Freire as well as by Buddhism, particularly the activist Buddhist monk Thich Nhat Hanh (hooks, 2014).

## Chapter 2: An alternative history of educational technology

1 Henri Breuil popularised the theory of Paleolithic cave paintings as hunting magic, intended to increase the number of animals and to ensure successful kills by means of magical images. See Giedion (1953).
2 The cultural aspect of technology adoption can perhaps be illustrated by one explanation that has been offered for the relatively slow uptake of print in Islamic countries. Between 800 and 1400, books were in demand in the Islamic world and many scribes made a good living in Baghdad by copying texts. This golden age of literacy was in part caused by improved paper-making techniques originating in China. However, the style of writing developed involved flowing lines that joined letters together as if imitating the lines of fire that Mohammed saw when the words of the Quran were first revealed to him in a cave. Seeking new markets, a Venetian entrepreneur called Paganini printed the Quran in 1537. Despite being cheaper, these copies of the Quran did not compare well in perceived quality to the hand-crafted calligraphy version most Muslims preferred. As a result, it is claimed by some historians, the printing of Arabic texts did not really take off until the early 19th century (Van Dijk, 2005).
3 Our analysis focuses on Europe. Some have argued that the understanding of reason in the West as involving abstract and general claims is linked to the decontextualising nature of the alphabet (Logan, 2004 building on McLuhan, 1964). However more recent neurological studies of reading suggest that the main cognitive impacts of writing are common across different scripts (Bolger et al., 2005) and the claims about the link between the alphabet and abstract thinking have been challenged as a product of ethnocentric bias (Lau, 2014). Nonetheless it is evident that the nature of Chinese logographic writing had an impact on the way in which printing developed in China (Tsien, 1985) and it is not implausible that this more concrete and contextual style of writing had some impact on why ways of thinking in China have been and remain generally less monologic than the dominant ideology of rationalism that some claim developed in the West after Gutenburg and the spread of alphabetic print literacy (Nisbett, 2004).
4 Adapted from the PhD thesis of Dr Kevin Martin (2022).

## Chapter 3: Affordance theory

1 https://pol.is/home
2 'The paper seen and the seeing of it are only two names for one indivisible fact which, properly named, is the datum, the phenomenon, or the experience. The paper is in the mind and the mind is around the paper, because paper and mind are only two names that are given later to the one experience, when, taken in a larger world of which it forms a part, its connections are traced in different directions. To know immediately, then, or intuitively, is for mental content and object to be identical' (James, 1895, p. 110).
3 Katherine Hayles (2012, 2021) explores the importance of the process between touching the keyboard and generating code on a screen suggesting that perhaps the 'gap' could also be seen between, for example, the touch of a finger on the 'A' key, and the appearance of the letter 'a' on the screen. Hayles compares the complexity of the technological processes involved in electronic text to the complex physiological processes involved in perception. The implication of this might be that any bio-technical collaboration like a web designer creating a new website cannot adequately be described by binaries like body and world, but consists of many systems interacting with each other over boundaries. Awareness of this added complexity and depth does not take away from the value of

Merleau-Ponty's insight that these interactions between systems do not so much occur within space and time, as create the space and time within which they are perceived to occur.

4 The point apparently being made by Merleau-Ponty was perhaps expressed more clearly by the popular philosopher Alan Watts (1999, p. 28) who wrote: 'Really, the fundamental, ultimate mystery – the only thing you need to know to understand the deepest metaphysical secrets – is this: that for every outside there is an inside and for every inside there is an outside, and although they are different, they go together'.

5 Zavota (2018) brings out the similarities between the ontologies of Barad and the late Merleau-Ponty arguing that his approach fits with and can usefully augment Barad's 'agential realism'.

6 The use by Gibson of the word 'man' here signals the issue of who exactly has designed the technology that shapes the world of experience. In much recent work in the field of science, technology and society (STS), Gibson, Merleau-Ponty and others have been criticised for not taking into account the diversity of experiences and the power-relations involved in the design and use of technology. Alternative narratives can be found under the headings, 'feminist technoscience', 'Crip technoscience' and 'queer STS'.

7 Here Merleau-Ponty raises a theme since taken up and elaborated in a way which has been influential on technology design under the headings of 'extended cognition' (Clark & Chalmers, 1998; Cukurova, 2019) and 'embodied cognition' (Foglia & Wilson, 2013).

8 The Digitalised Dialogues Across the Curriculum (DiDiAC) project was funded by the Research Council of Norway (FINNUT/Project No: 254761).

9 Acknowledging this reality of educational design enables us to address more consciously the political and ethical issues raised by the idea of designing people. Education has always been about designing people but is not always comfortable about admitting this (Wegerif, 2018). We address the ethical issues raised by design more in Chapter 7 and Chapter 10 where, influenced by Simondon, we propose, as far as possible, a design process that is inclusive, participatory and dialogic, such that design is something we collectively do to shape ourselves and our lives rather than something that one group, the designers, imposes on another group, the designed.

## Chapter 4: The 'grammar' of educational technology

1 What Wittgenstein (1953/2009) says about language in *Investigations* – that language use is related to activities, games and a form of life – can also be said about the use and meaning of technology: technologies are embedded in games, which have rules but also require a tacit understanding of them, and all this provides a grammar for technology use and meaning (Coeckelbergh & Funk, 2018). Coeckelburgh writes that: 'The point is not only that language shapes how we deal with technology, but that the transcendental structure of language is similar to the transcendental structure of technology. Both are deeply embedded in the social-cultural world. The meaning of words and the meaning of things is not a matter of word-objects or of things-objects alone; what words and things mean and do depends on larger structures such as games and a form of life, which render use and meaning possible. Just as linguistic grammar provides a structure that renders possible and constrains our use of language, there is language and other transcendental grammars that make possible and govern the use of (other) technologies. Moreover, technology can change the game. It is phenomenologically

and hermeneutically "active", so to speak. Culture is not a matter of a kind of (virtual?) things, but is performed and enacted. There is no form of life separate from *how we do things*' (Coeckelbergh, 2022, p. 252).

2 Many other examples of using digital devices as a teaching machine or tutor could have been chosen. For instance, in Europe, CenturyTech is an adaptive teaching approach that also claims to get good results (www.century.tech/our-impact/). In China, Squirrel AI offers online adaptive tutoring and also has evaluations that suggest it can accelerate learning in maths (Wang et al., 2023; see also Knox, 2020).

3 https://schoolsnortheast.org/marketplace/case-study/sparx-st-james-case-study/12462/

4 https://eidu.com/

5 Readers further interested in constructionism-related developments in the field of educational technology may be interested to view a 2021 special section titled 'Constructionism moving forward' edited by Jake Byrne and colleagues (2021) which appeared in the *British Journal of Educational Technology*.

## Chapter 5: Steps towards a 'dialogic' grammar

1 Wenger later acknowledged problems with this concept of a 'community'. Individual learning journeys can be complex, involving many communities, and there are types of learning in schools that do not end and are not intended to end in expert status within any clearly defined community. What we are describing here is more the 'ideal type' of community-based learning as this is outlined by Lave and Wenger in their 1991 book *Situated Learning: Legitimate Peripheral Participation*.

2 The reification mechanism described by Wenger relates to the more general collective intelligence mechanism of 'stigmergy', first developed to describe how non-human social animals like ants coordinate behaviour through traces left in the environment. This is described in detail by Rolf Baltzersen in his 2022 book *Cultural-Historical Perspectives on Collective Intelligence*.

3 www.ted.com/talks/jane_mcgonigal_gaming_can_make_a_better_world

4 https://janemcgonigal.com/2014/01/06/transcript-games-can-make-a-better-world/

5 https://halfanhour.blogspot.com/2007/02/what-connectivism-is.html

6 Many thanks to Steve Higgins for this formulation.

## Chapter 7: The 'meaning' of technology

1 'La valeur du dialogue de l'individu avec l'objet technique est donc de conserver l'effort humain, et de créer un domaine de transindividuel, distinct de la communauté, . . .'

2 This common interpretation is not quite correct because Heidegger did not write about the human so much as about 'dasein' or 'being there'. This suggests human experience is a modality of Being as a whole. In other words, to be human for Heidegger already implies being more than human.

3 The connection made by Heidegger between modern technology and a loss of human meaning can still be found in contemporary educational technology literature. Many studies that apply theory to educational technology adopt a critical stance that, whether they cite Heidegger or not, resonates with his critique of modern technology (Selwyn, 2017; Williamson, 2018). These echoes of Heidegger are possibly mediated by other writers influential in the field of critical sociological theory of technology, who, whilst very clearly distinct from Heidegger in their

political positions, may nonetheless have been influenced by his writings in their philosophical outlook. Marcuse, for example, associated what he called 'technological rationality' with a closed system of domination and control limiting human freedom (Marcuse & Kellner, 2013). Habermas, who criticised Marcuse as being too negative about technology, nonetheless associated technical reason with instrumental reason or what, following Weber, he called 'zweckrationalität' (means-ends rationality) in contrast to communicative rationality (Habermas, 1970). While the zweckrationalität associated with technology seeks the most efficient way to achieve predetermined ends, communicative rationality is concerned with the ethical quality of reasoning understood as a dialogue across different perspectives seeking mutual understanding. As Feenberg brings out, Habermas's account of how technological rationality is taking over the lifeworld and driving out more communicative (i.e., more human) reasoning is similar to the critique of technology by Heidegger in 'The question concerning technology' (Feenberg, 2012). Foucault also appears to channel the spirit of Heidegger when he uses the term 'technological power' to refer to systems of surveillance and control that shape people in ways that reduce their freedom and their experience of meaning (Foucault, 1975).

4 Although a more reflective position contrasting technologically mediated learning with human relationships in education is elaborated in Biesta (2016).

5 In the interest of balance, we should acknowledge here some significant work on the 'non-human systems' of education. Bruno Latour's Activity Network Theory (ANT) gives an active role to material objects and the materiality of technology and has been widely applied to studies of education and education technology (Fenwick & Edwards, 2019). There is also, even more recently than ANT, a growing strand of post-humanist theorising in education technology summarized by Sian Bayne (2018) and exemplified by Jeremy Knox's study of MOOCs (2016). We have not focused very much on Latour and Post-Humanism in education technology research as this literature is often focused on sociological concerns that are, arguably, only indirectly related to education rather than directly focusing on the role of technology as a part of the project of education.

6 We experience present moments of time, for example, not in isolation but in the context of many moments that have gone before including those not experienced by us personally. This larger flow of collective time, Stiegler claims, is possible because our experience is never in fact immediate but is always already mediated by the use of shared artefacts including a shared language with its use of tenses and shared calendars and clocks (Stiegler, 1998). Meaning comes from beyond the horizon of that which is present to consciousness. Meaning also comes to us already shaped by our collective involvement with technology. Not only do we use technology in the form of a hammer and nails to fix the fence, we use technology in the form of the language we use to plan the event and describe the event and the marks we perhaps made in a calendar to clear time for the task. If this argument is valid then phenomenology alone is not enough to ground the meaning of meaning, we also need the study of technology.

7 The claim that 'a thing is what it is and not another thing' is the essential claim of identity sometimes referred to by the formula 'A=A'. This claim is one bulding block of classical logic. It was first articulated clearly by Leibniz who attributed it to Aristotle. (Leibniz, 1973, p. 185)

8 The idea of self-organisation has been widely applied to social systems, including education, by Luhmann (and those influenced by Luhmann) using the closely related concept of 'autopoiesis', Greek for self-making (Luhmann, 1986). The theory of autopoiesis was originally developed by two Chilean biologists Humberto Maturana and Francisco Varela as an answer to the question: What is life? Or: What distinguishes the living from the non-living? Their answer was: A living system reproduces itself (Varela et al., 1991). They defined the

autopoietic system as a system that recursively reproduces its elements through its own elements. Although autopoietic systems, single-celled organisms for example, interact with their environment, they are said to be 'organisationally closed' in the sense that they both produce, and are produced by, themselves.

9 Sugata Mitra, a computer scientist with a PhD in theoretical physics, conducted the famous 'hole-in-the-wall' experiments that placed computers with access to the internet into walls in Indian slums and observed how children taught themselves many things. He won the TED Prize for his talk about this approach to education in 2013, referring to this 'minimally invasive' approach to education. This idea relates to the theme from Geary that education into complex skills that are recent in evolutionary terms, skills like literacy, mathematics and computer science, is often experienced by children as difficult (see Chapter 2). Mitra seems to agree with Papert's claims that digital technology can make learning even complex content easy and natural (see Chapter 4). However, Mitra's approach is not based on programming computers, but on unguided exploration of the internet by children working together. The claims Mitra makes for the value of this educational approach are controversial. We do not wish to engage with that debate. Relevant for our argument here is Mitra's interesting use of the term 'self-organisation'. By quoting a study of traffic patterns (Kumar & Mitra, 2006) within this education paper (Mitra & Dangwal, 2010), Mitra makes clear that he is inspired by using simulations to model complex systems. He also seems to suggest by using this metaphor of self-organisation that, whereas in traditional classrooms the 'meaning' of the activity is determined by the curriculum in advance and imposed upon children, in SOLEs meaning emerges from minimally guided interactions of children with each other and with the internet.

10 The ontological equivalence of self and agency at the individual biological unit level and at the collective social level is also one of the findings of recent social psychology summed up in Self-Categorization Theory (Reicher et al., 2012).

11 www.aldebaran.com/en/pepper

12 https://info.flip.com/en-us.html

13 www.tinkerplots.com/

## Chapter 8: Technology and expanding dialogic space

1 Innis (1950/2022) makes a distinction between communications technologies that primarily serve to extend time like rock carvings and those that primarily expand space like lightweight papyrus documents.

2 In fact, as we argue elsewhere, all dialogues have a potentially unlimited or infinite space of resonance and this is certainly true of dialogues in oral societies. What we are trying to get at here are what could be seen as two levels of superposition in a dialogue, the first level is the immediate community of the dialogue and the meanings made within that community, and the second level is the 'cosmos' or more unbounded background to the dialogue. The expansion of dialogic space refers only to the first level, the immediate community and the immediate reference of words can be made to expand through technologies like writing.

3 It is interesting that bell hooks (2014), inspired by critical educational theory of Paulo Friere but also by Buddhism, revisits many of the same themes as the liberal tradition, especially the importance of educating to expand freedom and understanding as increasing the potential to act in new ways.

4 See for example suggestions of use in: www.iesalc.unesco.org/wp-content/uploads/2023/04/ChatGPT-and-Artificial-Intelligence-in-higher-education-Quick-Start-guide_EN_FINAL.pdf

## Chapter 9: Technology and expanding dialogic time

1 Perhaps linking to the term 'clock time' gives too smooth and linear an image for horizontal time. This time is also structured by materiality; the timetable is structured by the available teaching spaces for different activities and punctuated by times of transition, students spilling out of a classroom into the corridor when the break bell goes for example. The ideas of horizontal and vertical time are idealised abstractions from the reality of time which is always in practice a complex combination of both dimensions.
2 This metaphor is not perfect: horizontal chronological or clock time is a one-way movement constrained by the arrow of time, whereas vertical time is two-way – it is possible to move up or down the timescales of vertical time.
3 https://home.cern/news/news/experiments/new-antimatter-gravity-experiments-begin-cern
4 The issue here is not just about individual experiences of what gives meaning in life being overridden by someone else's truth, but also about culturally mediated ways of finding meaning being removed by a colonising perspective from a different cultural perspective which, under the guise of teaching 'truth' in the abstract, actually subordinates one cultural and historical perspective to that of another, thereby undermining and disempowering some students at the expense of others.
5 See also William Blake, 'Auguries of Innocence': 'To see a World in a Grain of Sand / And a Heaven in a Wild Flower / Hold Infinity in the palm of your hand / and Eternity in an hour' (www.poetryfoundation.org/poems/43650/auguries-of-innocence) and Nietzsche, whose whole work could be described as urging humans to go beyond resentment against time in order to learn how to live fully in the already eternal and infinite present: 'The "kingdom of God" is not something that men wait for – it had no yesterday and no day after tomorrow, it is not going to come at a "millennium" – it is an experience of the heart, it is everywhere and it is nowhere . . .' (The Antichrist, aphorism 34, www.gutenberg.org/files/19322/19322-h/19322-h.htm).
6 To be clear we are not disagreeing with Stiegler here, but rather pointing out that it is not just technology that creates human time but technology in combination with dialogic relations around technology and also supported by technology. This combination of technology and dialogue is needed for progress: the process of collective learning whereby dialogic tensions between perspectives lead to the creative emergence of new designs that are then recorded in some form in order to be transmitted to each new generation.
7 These positive claims about the internet refer to the potential of the internet to sustain self-improving global dialogues and are not intended as a description of the current reality. The many problems of the quality of dialogue on the internet are well known including the fragmentation that comes from the varied ownership and control of the different internet platforms. However, despite these problems we can see signs of the kind of ideal referred to here. The global scientific and policy dialogue around how to respond to the Covid-19 pandemic, for example, was certainly more effective because of the internet than the global dialogue and response to the Spanish Influenza pandemic about 100 years earlier.
8 https://medium.com/institute-for-the-future/during-a-pandemic-we-all-need-to-stretch-our-imagination-a9295cfcd1f8
9 www.nasa.gov/webbfirstimages

## Chapter 10: Researching educational technology

1 The trouble with this approach is not only that many systems we are involved with are complex and open but also that it is descriptive rather than explanatory,

noting regular correlations in data without explaining them and so confusing epistemology, or what we know, with ontology, what is really there and what is really going on (Bhaskar, 2013).

2 See also Luckin and Cukurova (2019) for a related argument about the role of the interdisciplinary learning sciences in the education technology design research process.

3 The idea that we should apply systems analysis and engineering to redesigning education systems is not new. It has been advocated by Hugh Burkhardt for decades; see, for example, Burkhardt and Schoenfeld (2021). Our chiasm approach accepts this and augments it with added dialogic reflection.

4 This might, on the face of it, appear like a return to Hegelian dialectics. Hegel claimed that things cannot be understood separately from the system that defines them. To understand a thing is to understand its origin and its future. In many ways Bakhtin agreed with Hegel although he also went further. Hegel suggested, since everything is related to everything, the truth is the Whole. To understand any event, including an act of teaching and learning, is to locate it within the historical unfolding of the whole system. Bakhtin agrees with Hegel that the truth is the whole. The true meaning of an utterance, he writes, is found in the whole dialogue. The problem is that for Bakhtin the dialogue is never finished. This open-endedness means also that the meanings of words can never be fixed once and for all but are always in play (Bakhtin, 1986, p. 146). Bakhtin therefore contrasts his dialogics to Hegel's dialectics, accusing Hegel of trying to close down the real differences between voices which are essential for meaning.

5 This relates to the idea of 'second-order cybernetics', developed by Heinz von Foerster (1995) and others, with key inspiration coming from Margaret Mead. Second-order cybernetics took the role of the observer into account. It was influential on Pask's development of a cybernetic theory of learning as conversation. Foerster differentiated first-order cybernetics as 'the cybernetics of observed systems' and second-order cybernetics as 'the cybernetics of observing systems'.

## Chapter 11: Towards a dialogic foundation for the design of educational technology

1 www.khanacademy.org/khan-labs

2 We are aware that some find the concept of 'flourishing' vague and hard to convert into clear measures. Nonetheless making educational decisions is necessary and in making such difficult and always uncertain decisions we are inevitably guided by some sort of concept of flourishing which, while never perfect, can be subject to self-criticism and self-improvement through the educational research process. As Kristjansson (2017, p. 104) points out, 'any effort deserving of the name "education" must be characterised as education for flourishing'.

# REFERENCES


Abbas, N., Whitfield, J., Atwell, E., Bowman, H., Pickard, T., & Walker, A. (2022). Online chat and chatbots to enhance mature student engagement in higher education. *International Journal of Lifelong Education*, 1–19. Available online at: https://doi.org/10.1080/02601370.2022.2066213

Agalianos, A., Noss, R., & Whitty, G. (2001). Logo in mainstream schools: The struggle over the soul of an educational innovation. *British Journal of Sociology of Education*, *22*(4), 479–500.

Alexander, H. (2015). *Reimagining liberal education: Affiliation and inquiry in democratic schooling*. Bloomsbury Publishing.

Alexander, R. (2020). *A dialogic teaching companion*. Routledge.

Alexander, V. N., Bacigalupi, J. A., & Garcia, Ò. C. (2021). Living systems are smarter bots: Slime mold semiosis versus AI symbol manipulation. *Biosystems*, *206*, 104430.

An, T., & Oliver, M. (2021). What in the world is educational technology? Rethinking the field from the perspective of the philosophy of technology. *Learning, Media and Technology*, *46*(1), 6–19.

Anderson, B. (2008). Imagined communities: Reflections on the origin and spread of nationalism. In S. Seidman & J. C. Alexander (Eds), *The new social theory reader*. Routledge.

Arastoopour, G., Shaffer, D. W., Swiecki, Z., Ruis, A. R., & Chesler, N. C. (2016). Teaching and assessing engineering design thinking with virtual internships and epistemic network analysis. *International Journal of Engineering Education*, *32*(2), 1492–1501.

Argyris, C. (2002). Double-loop learning, teaching, and research. *Academy of Management Learning & Education*, *1*(2), 206–218.

Aristotle. (1925). *Nichomachean ethics: Book 6*. (W. D. Ross, Trans.). The Internet Classics Archive. Available online at: http://classics.mit.edu/Aristotle/nicomachaen.6.vi.html (Original work published 350 BCE).

Arnseth, H. C., Hanghøj, T., & Silseth, K. (2018). Games as tools for dialogic teaching and learning: Outlining a pedagogical model for researching and designing game-based learning environments. In H. C. Arnseth, T. Hanghøj, T. Duus Henriksen, M. Misfeldt, R. Ramberg & S. Selander (Eds), *Games and education: Designs in and for learning*. Brill.

Ashby, W. R. (1957). *An introduction to cybernetics*. Chapman & Hall Ltd.

Bain, A. (1879). *Education as a science*. D. Appleton.

Bainbridge, W. S. (2008). Cognitive expansion technologies. *Journal of Evolution and Technology*, *19*(1), 8–16.

Bakhtin, M. (1986). *Speech genres and other late essays*. University of Texas.

Bakker, A. (2019). *Design research in education: A practical guide for early career researchers*. Routledge.

Bakker, A., & Derry, J. (2011). Lessons from inferentialism for statistics education. *Mathematical Thinking and Learning*, *13*(1–2), 5–26.

Bakker, A., & van Eerde, D. (2015). An introduction to design-based research with an example from statistics education. In A. Bikner-Ahsbahs, C. Knipping & N. Presmeg (Eds), *Approaches to qualitative research in mathematics education: Advances in mathematics education*. Springer.

Baltzersen, R. K. (2022). *Cultural-historical perspectives on collective intelligence*. Cambridge University Press.

Barad, K. (2007). *Meeting the universe halfway: Quantum physics and the entanglement of matter and meaning*. Duke University Press.

Barsky, C. K., & Glazek, S. D. (2014). 21st century ergonomic education, from little e to big E. *arXiv: 1403.0281*. Available online at: https://arxiv.org/abs/1403.0281.

Bartlett, M. (2018). Using Flipgrid to increase students' connectedness in an online class. *Elearn*, *2018*(12). doi:10.1145/3302261.3236703.

Bateson, G. (1972). *Steps to an ecology of mind*. Jason Aronson Inc. Available online at: https://ejcj.orfaleacenter.ucsb.edu/wp-content/uploads/2017/06/1972.-Gregory-Bateson-Steps-to-an-Ecology-of-Mind.pdf

Bayne, S. (2015). Teacherbot: Interventions in automated teaching. *Teaching in Higher Education*, *20*(4), 455–467.

Bayne, S. (2018). Posthumanism: A navigation aid for educators. *On Education: Journal for Research and Debate*, *1*(2), 10–17899.

Beauchamp, G., Joyce-Gibbons, A., McNaughton, J., Young, N., & Crick, T. (2019). Exploring synchronous, remote collaborative interaction between learners using multi-touch tables and video conferencing in UK primary schools. *British Journal of Educational Technology*, *50*(6), 3214–3232.

Beigi, S., & Heylighen, F. (2021). Collective consciousness supported by the web: Healthy or toxic? In *International Conference on Computational Collective Intelligence*, 29 September – 1 October, Rhodes, Greece. Springer.

Benner, J. A. (2021). *The Ancient Hebrew lexicon of the Bible*. Ancient Hebrew Research Center.

Bereiter, C. (1994). Implications of postmodernism for science, or, science as progressive discourse. *Educational Psychologist*, *29*(1), 3–12.

Bereiter, C. (2005). *Education and mind in the knowledge age*. Routledge.

Bereiter, C., & Scardamalia, M. (2003). 'Learning to work creatively with knowledge'. In E. Corte, L. Verschaffel, N. Entwistle & J. Merrienboer (Eds), *Powerful learning environments: Unravelling basic components and dimensions*. Elsevier Science, Advances in Learning and Instruction Series.

Bergson, H. (1932/1977). *The two sources of morality and religion* (Audra, R. A., Brereton, C., Trans.). University of Notre Dame Press.

Bhaskar, R. (2013). *A realist theory of science*. Routledge.

Biemann, A. D. (2022). Humanizing the it: Martin Buber on technology and the ethics of things. *Religions*, *13*(2), 137. https://doi.org/10.3390/rel13020137

Biesta, G. (2016). The rediscovery of teaching: On robot vacuum cleaners, non-egological education and the limits of the hermeneutical world view. *Educational Philosophy and Theory*, *48*(4), 374–392.

Biesta, G. (2022). School-as-institution or school-as-instrument? How to overcome instrumentalism without giving up on democracy. *Educational Theory*, *72*(3), 319–331.

Bloomfield, B. P., Latham, Y., & Vurdubakis, T. (2010). Bodies, technologies and action possibilities: When is an affordance? *Sociology*, *44*(3), 415–433.

Boddington, G. (2021). The Internet of Bodies – alive, connected and collective: The virtual physical future of our bodies and our senses. *AI & Society*. Available online at: https://doi.org/10.1007/s00146-020-01137-1

Bodily, R., Leary, H., & West, R. (2019). Research trends in instructional design and technology journals. *British Journal of Educational Technology*, *50*(1), 64–79.

Bolger, D. J., Perfetti, C. A., & Schneider, W. (2005). Cross-cultural effect on the brain revisited: Universal structures plus writing system variation. *Human Brain Mapping*, *25*(1), 92–104.

Bond, M., Zawacki-Richter, O., & Nichols, M. (2019). Revisiting five decades of educational technology research: A content and authorship analysis of the British Journal of Educational Technology. *British Journal of Educational Technology*, *50*(1), 12–63.

Bower, M. (2008). Affordance analysis – matching learning tasks with learning technologies. *Educational Media International*, *45*(1), 3–15.

Bozkurt, A. (2020). Educational technology research patterns in the realm of the digital knowledge age. *Journal of Interactive Media in Education*. Available online at: http://doi.org/10.5334/jime.570

Brubaker, R. (2022). *Hyperconnectivity and its discontents*. John Wiley & Sons.

Bruner, J. (1984). Notes on the cognitive revolution. *Interchange*, *15*(3), 1–8.

Buber, M. (1937). *I and thou* (Smith, R. G., Trans.). T. & T. Clark.

Bullock, C. S., & Bullock, S. M. (2020). Re-imagining history teaching by challenging national narratives. In C. W. Berg & T. M. Christou (Eds), *The Palgrave handbook of history and social studies education*. Palgrave Macmillan.

Burkhardt, H., & Schoenfeld, A. (2021). Not just 'implementation': The synergy of research and practice in an engineering research approach to educational design and development. *ZDM – Mathematics Education*, *53*(5), 991–1005.

Byrne, J. R., Girvan, C., & Clayson, J. (2021). Constructionism moving forward. *British Journal of Educational Technology*, *52*(3), 965–968.

Cao, Y. (2022). *Developing teachers' contingent responsiveness in dialogic science teaching via mixed-reality simulations: A design-based study*. PhD Thesis, Faculty of Education, University of Cambridge. https://doi.org/10.17863/CAM.90530.

Carrigan, M., & Porpora, D. V. (2021). Introduction: Conceptualizing post-human futures. In M. Carrigan & D. V. Porpora (Eds), *Post-human futures*. Routledge.

Castells, M. (2020). Space of flows, space of places: Materials for a theory of urbanism in the information age. In R. L. Gates & F. Stout (Eds), *The city reader*. Routledge.

Casti, J. L. (1997). *Would-be worlds: How simulation is changing the frontiers of science*. John Wiley & Sons, Inc.

Cayari, C. (2011). The YouTube effect: How YouTube has provided new ways to consume, create, and share music. *International Journal of Education & the Arts*, *12*(6), n6.

Chalmers, D. J. (2022). *Reality+: Virtual worlds and the problems of philosophy*. Penguin UK.

Chan, C. K., Tong, Y., & van Aalst, J. (2019). Progressive dialogue in computer-supported collaborative knowledge building. In N. Mercer, R. Wegerif & L. Major (Eds), *The Routledge international handbook of research on dialogic education*. Routledge.

Chang, A. W. S. (2021). Making our best move with Audrey Tang and Taiwan's digital democracy. *American Quarterly*, *73*(2), 363–369.

Chemero, A., & Käufer, S. (2016). Pragmatism, phenomenology, and extended cognition. In R. Madzia & M. Jung (Eds), *Pragmatism and embodied cognitive science: From bodily intersubjectivity to symbolic articulation*. De Gruyter.

Chesler, N. C., Arastoopour Irgens, G., D'Angelo, C. M., Bagley, E. A., & Shaffer, D. W. (2013). Design of a professional practice simulator for educating and motivating first-year engineering students. *Advances in Engineering Education*, July. Available online at: https://advances.asee.org/publication/kjhjkh/

Chong, I., & Proctor, R. W. (2020). On the evolution of a radical concept: Affordances according to Gibson and their subsequent use and development. *Perspectives on Psychological Science*, *15*(1), 117–132.

Churcher, K., Downs, E., & Tewksbury, D. (2014). 'Friending' Vygotsky: A social constructivist pedagogy of knowledge building through classroom social media use. *Journal of Effective Teaching*, *14*(1), 33–50.

Clark, A. (2004). 'We have always been . . . cyborgs'. *Metascience*, *13*(2), 169–180.

Clark, A., & Chalmers, D. (1998). The extended mind. *Analysis*, *58*(1), 7–19.

Coeckelbergh, M. (2017). *Using words and things: Language and philosophy of technology*. Routledge.

Coeckelbergh, M. (2020). *Introduction to the philosophy of technology*. OUP.

Coeckelbergh, M. (2022). The grammars of AI: Towards a structuralist and transcendental hermeneutics of digital technologies. *Technology and Language*, *3*(2), 148–161.

Coeckelbergh, M., & Funk, M. (2018). Wittgenstein as a philosopher of technology: Tool use, forms of life, technique, and a transcendental argument. *Human Studies*, *41*, 165–191.

Comenius, J. A. (1657/1967). *The Great Didactic [Didactica Magna] of John Amos Comenius* (Keatinge, M. W., Trans.). Russell & Russell.

Connolly, P. (2009). The challenges and prospects for educational effectiveness research. *Effective Education*, *1*(1), 1–12.

Conole, G., & Dyke, M. (2004). What are the affordances of information and communication technologies? *ALT-j*, *12*(2), 113–124.

Cook, V., Warwick, P., Vrikki, M., Major, L., & Wegerif, R. (2019). Developing material-dialogic space in geography learning and teaching: Combining a dialogic pedagogy with the use of a microblogging tool. *Thinking Skills and Creativity*, *31*, 217–231.

Cormier, D., & Siemens, G. (2010). The open course: Through the open door – open courses as research, learning, and engagement. *EDUCAUSE Review*, *45*(4), 30–39.

Craig, T. K., Rus-Calafell, M., Ward, T., Leff, J. P., Huckvale, M., Howarth, E., . . . Garety, P. A. (2017). AVATAR therapy for auditory verbal hallucinations in people with psychosis: A single-blind, randomised controlled trial. *The Lancet Psychiatry*, *5*(1), 31–40.

Crilly, N. (2021). The evolution of 'co-evolution' (part II): The biological analogy, different kinds of co-evolution, and proposals for conceptual expansion. *She Ji: The Journal of Design, Economics, and Innovation*, 7(3), 333–355.

Cromwell, J. (2019). *'Schoolboy, where have you been going so long?': The Old Babylonian student and school*. Papyrus Stories. Available online at: https://papyrus-stories.com/2019/09/23/schoolboy-where-have-you-been-going-so-long-the-old-babylonian-student-and-school/

Csikszentmihalyi, M. (1990). *Flow: The psychology of optimal experience*. Harper & Row.

Cuban, L. (1986). *Teachers and machines: The classroom use of technology since 1920*. Teachers College Press.

Cuban, L. (2009). *Oversold and underused*. Harvard University Press.

Cuban, L. (2018). *The flight of a butterfly or the path of a bullet? Using technology to transform teaching and learning*. Harvard Education Press.

Cukurova, M. (2019). Learning analytics as AI extenders in education: Multimodal machine learning versus multimodal learning analytics. In T. Mitchell (Ed.), *Proceedings of AIAED 2019*. AIAED.

Cukurova, M., Luckin, R., & Clark-Wilson, A. (2019). Creating the golden triangle of evidence-informed education technology with EDUCATE. *British Journal of Educational Technology*, *50*(2), 490–504.

Daltry, B., Major, L., Jordan, K., Otieno, M., Otieno, K., Kaye, T., & Friedberg, A. (2022). Evaluating digital personalised learning in Kenya: An exploratory analysis of integrating an adaptive learning tool into classroom instruction. In *Proceedings of British Association for International & Comparative Education (BAICE)*, Edinburgh, UK, 13–15 September.

Damasio, A., & Carvalho, G. B. (2013). The nature of feelings: Evolutionary and neurobiological origins. *Nature Reviews Neuroscience*, *14*(2), 143–152.

Darke, J. (1978). The primary generator and the design process. In W. E. Rogers and W. H. Ittelson (Eds), *New Directions in Environmental Design Research* (Proceedings of EDRA, 9). EDRA.

Daskolia, M., & Kynigos, C. (2012). Applying a constructionist frame to learning about sustainability. *Creative Education*, *3*(6), 818.

Dawes, L., Mercer, N., & Wegerif, R. (2000). *Thinking together: A programme of activities for developing thinking skills at KS2*. Questions Publishing Company.

de Barros, A., & Ganimian, A. J. (2023). Which students benefit from computer-based individualized instruction? Experimental evidence from public schools in India. *Journal of Research on Educational Effectiveness*. https://doi.org/10.1080/19345747.2023.2191604.

De Laat, M., Chamrada, M., & Wegerif, R. (2008). Facilitate the facilitator: Awareness tools to support the moderator to facilitate online discussions for networked learning. In *Proceedings of the 6th International Conference on Networked*

*Learning*, 5–6 May, Halkidiki, Greece. www.networkedlearningconference.org.uk/past/nlc2008/

De Landsheere, G. (1993). History of educational research. In M. Hammersley (Ed.), *Educational research: Current issues* (Vol. 1). Paul Chapman.

Dede, C. (2008). Theoretical perspectives influencing the use of information technology in teaching and learning. In J. Voogt & G. Knezek (Eds), *International handbook of information technology in primary and secondary education*. Springer.

Dehaene, S. (2009). *Reading in the brain*. Penguin.

Dehaene, S., Cohen, L., Morais, J., & Kolinsky, R. (2015). Illiterate to literate: Behavioural and cerebral changes induced by reading acquisition. *Nature Reviews Neuroscience*, *16*(4), 234–244.

Deleuze, G. (1968/1994). *Difference and repetition*. (Patton, P. Trans). Columbia University Press.

Derrida, J. (1968). La différance. In *Théorie d'ensemble*. Éditions de Seuil.

Derrida, J. (1989). *Of spirit: Heidegger and the question*. University of Chicago Press.

Derry, J. (2013). *Vygotsky: Philosophy and education*. John Wiley & Sons.

Deutsch, D. (2011). *The beginning of infinity: Explanations that transform the world*. Penguin.

Disessa, A. A. (1987). The third revolution in computers and education. *Journal of Research in Science Teaching*, *24*(4), 343–367.

Disessa, A. A., & Cobb, P. (2016). Ontological innovation and the role of theory in design experiments. *Journal of the Learning Sciences*, *13*(1), 77–103.

Donnelly, R., & Patrinos, H. A. (2021). Learning loss during COVID-19: An early systematic review. *Prospects*, *51*, 601–609.

Downes, S. (2012). Connectivism and connective knowledge: Essays on meaning and learning networks. Available online at: www.downes.ca/files/books/Connective_Knowledge-19May2012.pdf

Dron, J. (2022). Educational technology: What it is and how it works. *AI & Society*, *37*(1), 155–166.

Engeström, Y. (2011). From design experiments to formative interventions. *Theory & Psychology*, *21*(5), 598–628.

Erstad, O., & Silseth, K. (2022). Transformations and unresolved tensions. In K. Kumpulainen, A. Kajamaa, O. Erstad, Å. Mäkitalo, K. Drotner & S. Jakobsdóttir (Eds), *Nordic childhoods in the digital age*. Routledge.

Fawns, T. (2022). An entangled pedagogy: Looking beyond the pedagogy-technology dichotomy. *Postdigital Science and Education*, *4*, 711–728.

Feenberg, A. (2012). *Questioning technology*. Routledge.

Fenwick, T., & Edwards, R. (Eds) (2019). *Revisiting actor-network theory in education*. Routledge.

Fernández, M., Wegerif, R., Mercer, N., & Rojas-Drummond, S. (2001). Reconceptualizing 'scaffolding' and the zone of proximal development in the context of symmetrical collaborative learning. *The Journal of Classroom Interaction*, *36/37*(2/1), 40–54.

Fisher, M. (2022). *The chaos machine: The inside story of how social media rewired our minds and our world*. Hachette UK.

Flecha, R. (2000). *Sharing words: Theory and practice of dialogic learning*. Rowman & Littlefield.

Foglia, L., & Wilson, R. A. (2013). Embodied cognition. *Wiley Interdisciplinary Reviews: Cognitive Science*, *4*(3), 319–325.

Foucault, M. (1975). *Discipline and punish: The birth of the prison*. Random House.

Frankel, S., & Kerr, M. (2020). Math as social endeavor: Groupwork and the blackboard. *Notices of the American Mathematical Society*, *67*(9), 1357–1358.

Freire, P. (1970/2000). *Pedagogy of the oppressed* (30th edn) (Ramos, M. B., Trans.). Continuum.

Friedberg, A. (2022). Introducing EIDU's solver platform: Facilitating open collaboration in AI to help solve the global learning crisis. In *Artificial Intelligence in Education. Posters and Late Breaking Results, Workshops and Tutorials, Industry and Innovation Tracks, Practitioners' and Doctoral Consortium: 23rd International Conference, AIED 2022, Durham, UK, July 27–31, 2022, Proceedings, Part II*. Springer International Publishing.

Fujita, T., Doney, J., Flanagan, R., & Wegerif, R. (2021). Collaborative group work in mathematics in the UK and Japan: Use of group thinking measure tests. *Education 3–13*, *49*(2), 119–133.

Gadamer, H. G. (1989). *Truth and method* (Weinsheimer, J., & Marshall, D. G., Trans.). Continuum.

Geary, D. C. (2008). An evolutionarily informed education science. *Educational Psychologist*, *43*(4), 179–195.

Gee, J. P. (2003). What video games have to teach us about learning and literacy. *Computers in Entertainment (CIE)*, *1*(1), 20. Available online at: https://doi.org/10.1145/950566.950595

Geeng, C., Yee, S., & Roesner, F. (2020). Fake news on Facebook and Twitter: Investigating how people (don't) investigate. In *Proceedings of the 2020 CHI conference on Human Factors in Computing Systems*. April 25–30, 2020, Honolulu, USA.

Gibson, J. J. (1977). The theory of affordances. In R. Shaw & J. Bransford (Eds), *Perceiving, acting, and knowing: Toward an ecological psychology*. Erlbaum.

Gibson, J. J. (1979). *The ecological approach to visual perception*. Houghton Mifflin.

Giedion, S. (1953) Abbé H. Breuil, *Four Hundred Centuries of Cave Art*, tr. by Mary E. Boyle, realized by Fernand Windels. *College Art Journal*, *12*(4), 381–383, doi:10.1080/15436322.1953.11465808.

Gilman, D. C., Peck, H. T., & Colby, F. M. (Eds) (1905). 'Comenius, Johann Amos'. *New International Encyclopaedia* (1st edn). Dodd, Mead.

Gilombe, M. M., & Yeoman, J. (2010). The essence of the Mbuya Mask: Immediate function and beyond. *Art in Translation*, *2*(1), 55–78.

Goody, J. (1986). *The logic of writing and the organization of society*. Cambridge University Press.

Goody, J., & Goody, J. R. (1977). *The domestication of the savage mind*. Cambridge University Press.

Gray, M. P. (2010). *Cave art and the evolution of the human mind*. Masters Thesis, Victoria University of Wellington, New Zealand.

Gu, X., & Blackmore, K. L. (2015). A systematic review of agent-based modelling and simulation applications in the higher education domain. *Higher Education Research & Development*, *34*(5), 883–898.

Habermas, J. (1970). *Toward a rational society* (Shapiro, J. J., Trans.). Beacon.

Haig, D. (2020). *From Darwin to Derrida: Selfish genes, social selves, and the meanings of life*. MIT Press.

Hakkarainen, K. (2004). Pursuit of explanation within a computer-supported classroom. *International Journal of Science Education*, *26*(8), 979–996.

Hammersley, M. (1993). On the teacher as researcher. *Educational Action Research*, *1*(3), 425–445.

Hammersley, M. (1996). The relationship between qualitative and quantitative research: paradigm loyalty versus methodological eclecticism. In J. T. Richardson (Ed.), *Handbook of qualitative research methods for psychology and the social sciences*. BPS Blackwell

Harari, Y. N. (2014). *Sapiens: A brief history of humankind*. Random House.

Haraway, D. (1991). A cyborg manifesto: Science, technology, and socialist-feminism in the late twentieth century. In *Simians, cyborgs and women: The reinvention of nature*. Routledge.

Haraway, D. (1997) You are cyborg. *Wired*, interviewed by Hari Kunzru, February 1, 1997. www.wired.com/1997/02/ffharaway/

Harman, G. (2011). *Heidegger explained: From phenomenon to thing*. Open Court.

Harris, R. (1986). *The origin of writing*. Open Court Publishing Company.

Hattie, J. (2023). *Visible learning: The sequel: A synthesis of over 2,100 meta-analyses relating to achievement*. Taylor & Francis.

Hawking, S. (1988). *A brief history of time: From the Big Bang to Black Holes*. Bantam Books.

Hayles, N. K. (2012). *How we think: Digital media and contemporary technogenesis*. University of Chicago Press.

Hayles, N. K. (2021). *Postprint: Books and becoming computational*. Columbia University Press.

Heidegger, M. (1957). *Identität und Differenz (Identity and difference)* (Stambaugh, J., Trans.). Harper & Row.

Heidegger, M. (1966). *Discourse on thinking* (Anderson, J. M., & Freund, E. H., Trans.). Harper & Row.

Heidegger, M. (1969). *Identity and difference* (bilingual edn, Stambaugh, J., Trans.). Harper & Row.

Heidegger, M. (1977). The question concerning technology. In *The question concerning technology and other essays* (Lovitt, W., Trans.). Harper & Row.

Heisenberg, W. (1958). *Physics and philosophy: The revolution in modern science*. Penguin Classics.

Hennessy, S. (2011). The role of digital artefacts on the interactive whiteboard in mediating dialogic teaching and learning. *Journal of Computer Assisted Learning*, *27*(6), 463–586.

Hennessy, S. (2020). Methods for researching technology-mediated dialogue. In R. Kershner, S. Hennessy, R. Wegerif & A. Ahmed (Eds), *Research methods for educational dialogue*. Bloomsbury Publishing.

Hennessy, S., Mavrikis, M., Girvan, C., Price, S., & Winters, N. (2019). BJET editorial for the 50th anniversary volume in 2019: Looking back, reaching forward. *British Journal of Educational Technology*, *50*(1), 5–11.

Hetherington, L., & Wegerif, R. (2018). Developing a material-dialogic approach to pedagogy to guide science teacher education. *Journal of Education for Teaching*, *44*(1), 27–43.

Hew, K. F., Lan, M., Tang, Y., Jia, C., & Lo, C. K. (2019). Where is the 'theory' within the field of educational technology research? *British Journal of Educational Technology*, *50*(3), 956–971.

Heylighen, F. (2022a). Relational agency: A new ontology for co-evolving systems. Manuscript submitted for publication. In P. Corning (Ed.), *Evolution 'on purpose': Teleonomy in living systems* (Vienna Series in Theoretical Biology). MIT Press.

Heylighen, F. (2022b). The meaning and origin of goal-directedness: A dynamical systems perspective. *Biological Journal of the Linnean Society*. Available online at: https://doi.org/10.1093/biolinnean/blac060

Higham, R., & Booth, T. (2018). Reinterpreting the authority of heads: Making space for values-led school improvement with the Index for Inclusion. *Educational Management Administration & Leadership*, *46*(1), 140–157.

Hinton, G. E. (1990). Connectionist learning procedures. In J. Shavlik & T. Dietterich (Eds), *Readings in machine learning*. Morgan Kaufmann.

Hodgkinson, H. L. (1957). Action research – A critique. *The Journal of Educational Sociology*, *31*(4), 137–153.

Hof, B. (2021). The turtle and the mouse: How constructivist learning theory shaped artificial intelligence and educational technology in the 1960s. *History of Education*, *50*(1), 93–111.

Holmes, W., & Tuomi, I. (2022). State of the art and practice in AI in education. *European Journal of Education*, *57*(4), 542–570.

Holmes, W., Bialik, M., & Fadel, C. (2020). *Artificial intelligence in education*. Center for Curriculum Redesign.

hooks, b. (2014). *Teaching to transgress*. Routledge.

Hui, Y. (2018). On the soul of technical objects: Commentary on Simondon's 'technics and eschatology' (1972). *Theory, Culture & Society*, *35*(6), 97–111.

Hui, Y., & Halpin, H. (2013). Collective individuation: The future of the social web. In G. Lovink & M. Rasch (Eds), *Unlike Us Reader*, *8*. Institute of Network Cultures.

Husserl, E. (1950). *Husserliana: gesammelte Werke*. Nijhoff/Kluwer.

Igglesden, T. (2022). *Designs and affordances for dialogue in Google Classroom: A design-based research study*. PhD Thesis, Faculty of Education, University of Cambridge.

Ihde, D. (2010). *Heidegger's technologies: Postphenomenological perspectives*. Fordham University Press.

Illich, I. (1971). *Deschooling society*. Harper and Row.

Innis, H. A. (1950/2022). *Empire and communications*. University of Toronto Press.

Jabr, F., & Rothschild, A. (2012). How brainless slime molds redefine intelligence. *Scientific American*. Available online at: www.nature.com/articles/nature.2012.11811.pdf?origin=ppub

James, W. (1895). The knowing of things together. *Psychology Review*, 2, 105–124.

Jeong, H., & Hmelo-Silver, C. E. (2016). Seven affordances of computer-supported collaborative learning: How to support collaborative learning? How can technologies help? *Educational Psychologist*, *51*(2), 247–265.

Jordan, K. (2014). Initial trends in enrolment and completion of massive open online courses. *International Review of Research in Open and Distributed Learning*, *15*(1), 133–160.

Jowett, A. J. (1989). Patterns of literacy in the People's Republic of China. *GeoJournal*, *18*(4), 417–427.

Kabudi, T., Pappas, I., & Olsen, D. H. (2021). AI-enabled adaptive learning systems: A systematic mapping of the literature. *Computers and Education: Artificial Intelligence*, *2*, 100017.

Kafai, Y. B., & Burke, Q. (2015). Constructionist gaming: Understanding the benefits of making games for learning. *Educational Psychologist*, *50*(4), 313–334.

Kagohara, D. M., van der Meer, L., Ramdoss, S., O'Reilly, M. F., Lancioni, G. E., Davis, T. N., . . . & Sigafoos, J. (2013). Using iPods® and iPads® in teaching programs for individuals with developmental disabilities: A systematic review. *Research in Developmental Disabilities*, *34*(1), 147–156.

Kant, I. (1803). *Kant on education (über Pädagogik)*. D. C. Heath & Company.

Kaplan, A. (1964). *The conduct of inquiry: Methodology for behavioral science*. Chandler.

Kaplan, R. (1999). *The nothing that is: A natural history of zero*. Oxford University Press.

Kauffman, S. (1995). *At home in the universe: The search for laws of self-organization and complexity*. Oxford University Press.

Kennedy, D. (2014). Neoteny, dialogic education and an emergent psychoculture: Notes on theory and practice. *Journal of Philosophy of Education*, *48*(1), 100–117.

Kennewell, S. (2001). Using affordances and constraints to evaluate the use of information and communications technology in teaching and learning. *Journal of Information Technology for Teacher Education*, *10*(1–2), 101–116.

Keogh, B., & Naylor, S. (1999). Concept cartoons, teaching and learning in science: An evaluation. *International Journal of Science Education*, *21*(4), 431–446.

Kershner, R., Hennessy, S., Wegerif, R., & Ahmed, A. (2020). *Research methods for educational dialogue*. Bloomsbury Publishing.

Knight, S., Shum, S. B., & Littleton, K. (2014). Epistemology, assessment, pedagogy: Where learning meets analytics in the middle space. *Journal of Learning Analytics*, *1*(2), 23–47.

Knox, J. (2016). *Posthumanism and the massive open online course: Contaminating the subject of global education*. Routledge.

Knox, J. (2020). Artificial intelligence and education in China. *Learning, Media and Technology*, *45*(3), 298–311.

Konstantinou, D., Parmaxi, A., & Zaphiris, P. (2021). Mapping research directions on makerspaces in education. *Educational Media International*, *58*(3), 223–247.

Kotsiou, A., Fajardo-Tovar, D. D., Cowhitt, T., Major, L., & Wegerif, R. (2022). A scoping review of Future Skills frameworks. *Irish Educational Studies*, *41*(1), 171–186.

Krippendorff, K. (2005). *The semantic turn: A new foundation for design*. CRC Press.

Kristjansson, K. (2017). Recent work on flourishing as the aim of education: A critical review. *British Journal of Educational Studies*, *65*(1), 87–107.

Kuhn, T. S. (1962). *The structure of scientific revolutions*. University of Chicago Press.

Kui, Y. (2019). Governance change and political identity in the internet age. *Social Sciences in China*, *40*(4), 129–147.

Kumar, S., & Mitra, S. (2006). Self-organizing traffic at a malfunctioning intersection. *Journal of Artificial Societies and Social Simulation*, *9*(4), Paper 3.

Lagemann, E. C. (2002). *An elusive science: The troubling history of education research*. University of Chicago Press.

Lakoff, G., & Johnson, M. (2008). *Metaphors we live by*. University of Chicago Press.

Lantz-Andersson, A., Lundin, M., & Selwyn, N. (2018). Twenty years of online teacher communities: A systematic review of formally-organized and informally-developed professional learning groups. *Teaching and Teacher Education*, *75*, 302–315.

Lau, R. W. (2014). Chinese writing and abstract thought: A historical-sociological critique of a longstanding thesis. *International Journal of Humanities and Social Science*, *4*, 37–54.

Laurillard, D. (2002). *Rethinking university teaching: A conversational framework for the effective use of learning technologies*. Routledge.

Laurillard, D. (2012). *Teaching as a design science: Building pedagogical patterns for learning and technology*. Routledge.

Lave, J. (1977). Cognitive consequences of traditional apprenticeship training in West Africa. *Anthropology & Education Quarterly*, *8*(3), 177–180.

Lave, J., & Wenger, E. (1991). *Situated learning: Legitimate peripheral participation*. Cambridge University Press.

Lefstein, A., & Snell, J. (2013). *Better than best practice: Developing teaching and learning through dialogue*. Routledge.

Leibniz, G. (1973). *Philosophical writings*. (G. H. R. Parkinson, ed., Mary Morris and G. H .R. Parkinson, trans.). London: J. M. Dent & Sons Ltd.

Leiman, M. (2002). Toward semiotic dialogism: The role of sign mediation in the dialogical self. *Theory & Psychology*, *12*(2), 221–235.

Lemke, J. L. (1990). *Talking science: Language, learning, and values*. Ablex Publishing Corporation.

Lemke, J. L. (2000). Across the scales of time: Artifacts, activities, and meanings in ecosocial systems. *Mind, Culture, and Activity*, 7(4), 273–290.

Levinas, E. (1990). Heidegger, Gagarin and us. In *Difficult freedom: Essays on Judaism* (Hand, S., Trans.). Johns Hopkins Press.

Lewin, K. (1946). Action research and minority problems. *Journal of Social Issues*, *2*(4), 34–46.

Lewin, K. (1952). *Field theory in social science: Selected theoretical papers by Kurt Lewin*. Tavistock.

Lewis-Williams., D. J. (2002). *The mind in the cave: Consciousness and the origins of art*. Thames & Hudson.

Lewis-Williams, D. J., & Dowson, T. A. (1990). Through the veil: San rock paintings and the rock face. *The South African Archaeological Bulletin*, 45(151), 5–16.

Lewis-Williams, D. J., & Pearce, D. G. (2004). *San spirituality: Roots, expression, and social consequences*. Rowman Altamira.

Leydesdorff, L. (2021). Evolutionary and institutional triple helix models. In *The evolutionary dynamics of discursive knowledge*. Springer.

Linell, P. (2009). *Rethinking language, mind and world dialogically: Interactional and contextual theories of human sense-making*. Information Age.

Lingis, A. (1994). *The community of those who have nothing in common*. Indiana University Press.

Lipman, M. (2003). *Thinking in education*. Cambridge University Press.

Lipponen, L. (2000). Towards knowledge building discourse: From facts to explanations in primary students' computer mediated discourse. *Learning Environments Research*, *3*, 179–199.

Littleton, K., & Mercer, N. (2013). *Interthinking: Putting talk to work*. Routledge.

Lobo, L., Heras-Escribano, M., & Travieso, D. (2018). The history and philosophy of ecological psychology. *Frontiers in Psychology*, *9*, 2228. Available online at: https://doi.org/10.3389/fpsyg.2018.02228

Logan, R. K. (2004). *The alphabet effect: A media ecology understanding of the making of western civilization*. Hampton Press.

Luckin, R., & Cukurova, M. (2019). Designing educational technologies in the age of AI: A learning sciences-driven approach. *British Journal of Educational Technology*, *50*(6), 2824–2838.

Luhmann, N. (1986). The autopoiesis of social systems. In F. Geyer & J.v.d. Zouwen (Eds), *Sociocybernetic paradoxes*. Sage.

Major, L. (2014). *An empirical investigation into the effectiveness of a robot simulator as a tool to support the learning of introductory programming*. PhD Thesis, Keele University.

Major, L., & Francis, G. (2020). Technology-supported personalised learning: Rapid evidence review. *EdTech Hub*. https://doi.org/10.5281/zenodo.3948175.

Major, L., & Warwick, P. (2019). 'Affordances for dialogue': The role of digital technology in supporting productive classroom talk. In N. Mercer, R. Wegerif & L. Major (Eds), *The Routledge international handbook of research on dialogic education*. Routledge.

Major, L., Warwick, P., Rasmussen, I., Ludvigsen, S., & Cook, V. (2018). Classroom dialogue and digital technologies: A scoping review. *Education and Information Technologies*, *23*(5), 1995–2028.

Major, L., Francis, G. A., & Tsapali, M. (2021). The effectiveness of technology-supported personalised learning in low- and middle-income countries: A meta-analysis. *British Journal of Educational Technology*, *52*(5), 1935–1964.

Major, L., Smørdal, O., Rasmussen, I., Warwick, P., Cook, V., & Vrikki, M. (2022). Investigating digital technology's role in supporting classroom dialogue: Integrating 'enacted affordance' into analysis across a complex dataset. *International Journal of Research & Method in Education*. Available online at: https://doi.org/10.1080/1743727X.2022.2032632

Major, L., Twiner, A., & Wegerif, R. (2022). Simulated internships in schools: Engaging learners with the world of work to promote collaborative creativity. In K. MacCallum & D. Parsons (Eds), *Industry practices, processes and techniques adopted in education*. Springer, Singapore.

Mansour, N., Wegerif, R., Skinner, N., Postlethwaite, K., & Hetherington, L. (2016). Investigating and promoting trainee science teachers' conceptual change of the nature of science with digital dialogue games 'InterLoc'. *Research in Science Education*, *46*, 667–684.

Marcuse, H., & Kellner, D. (2013). The problem of social change in the technological society. In *Towards a critical theory of society*. Routledge.

Marramao, G. (2007). *Kairós: Towards an ontology of 'due time'* (P. Larrey & S. Cattaneo, Trans.). Davies Group Publishers.

Martin, K. (2022). *Using mobile phones to enhance small group dialogic learning: A design based approach to educational innovation in rural East Africa*. PhD Thesis, Faculty of Education, University of Cambridge. Available online at: www.repository.cam.ac.uk/handle/1810/338346

Marx, K., & Engels, F. (1845/1970). *The German ideology* (Vol. 1). International Publishers Co.

Maslow, A. H. (1966). *The psychology of science: A reconnaissance*. Harper & Row.

Matusov, E. (2009). *Journey into dialogic pedagogy*. Nova Publishers.

Matusov, E., & Wegerif, R. (2014). Dialogue on 'dialogic education': Has Rupert gone over to 'the dark side'? *Dialogic Pedagogy: An International Online Journal, 2*. https://doi.org/10.5195/dpj.2014.78.

Mavrikis, M., & Holmes, W. (2019). Intelligent learning environments: Design, usage and analytics for future schools. In S. Yu, H. Niemi & J. Mason (Eds), *Shaping future schools with digital technology: An international handbook*. Springer.

Maxwell, J. A. (2010). Using numbers in qualitative research. *Qualitative Inquiry, 16*(6), 475–482.

McGonigal, J. (2007). Why I love bees: A case study in collective intelligence gaming. *The ecology of games: Connecting youth, games, and learning*. Available online at: https://avantgame.com/McGonigal_WhyILoveBees_Feb2007.pdf

McGonigal, J. (2011). Be a gamer, save the world. *The Wall Street Journal*, 22 January.

McGonigal, J. (2022). *Imaginable: How to see the future coming and be ready for anything*. Bantam Press.

McLoughlin, C., & Lee, M. (2007). Social software and participatory learning: Pedagogical choices with technology affordances in the Web 2.0 era. In *ICT: Providing choices for learners and learning. Proceedings ASCILITE Singapore 2007*. Centre for Educational Development, Nanyang Technological University.

McLuhan, M. (1964). *Understanding media*. Mentor.

Mead, G. H. (1934). *Mind, self, and society*. University of Chicago Press.

Mead, G. H., & Morris, C. W. (1967). *Mind, self, and society, from the standpoint of a social behaviorist* (Introduction and Ed. C. W. Morris). University of Chicago Press.

Meaney, M. J. (2019). The future of social mobility? MOOCs and hegemonic design bias. Available online at: www.researchgate.net/profile/Michael-Meaney/publication/333755888_The_Future_of_Social_Mobility_MOOCs_and_Hegemonic_Design_Bias/links/5d026a27299bf13a3852477b/The-Future-of-Social-Mobility-MOOCs-and-Hegemonic-Design-Bias.pdf

Mercer, N. (1995). *The guided construction of knowledge: Talk amongst teachers and learners*. Multilingual Matters.

Mercer, N. (2008). The seeds of time: Why classroom dialogue needs a temporal analysis. *The Journal of the Learning Sciences, 17*(1), 33–59.

Mercer, N., Hennessy, S., & Warwick, P. (2010). Using interactive whiteboards to orchestrate classroom dialogue. *Technology, Pedagogy and Education, 19*(2), 195–209.

Mercer, N., Wegerif, R., & Major, L. (2019). *The Routledge international handbook of research on dialogic education*. Routledge.

Merleau-Ponty, M. (1945/2013). *Phenomenology of perception*. Routledge.

Merleau-Ponty, M. (1962). *Phenomenology of perception* (Smith, C., Trans). Routledge & Kegan Paul.

Merleau-Ponty, M. (1968). *The visible and the invisible: Followed by working notes*. Northwestern University Press.

Michaels, S., O'Connor, C., & Resnick, L. B. (2008). Deliberative discourse idealized and realized: Accountable talk in the classroom and in civic life. *Studies in Philosophy and Education, 27*(4), 283–297.

Miller, R. (2015). Learning, the future, and complexity: An essay on the emergence of futures literacy. *European Journal of Education*, *50*(4), 513–523.

Miller, R. (2018). *Transforming the future: Anticipation in the 21st century*. Taylor & Francis.

Mingers, J. (2014). *Systems thinking, critical realism and philosophy: A confluence of ideas*. Routledge.

Minsky, M. (Ed.) (1969). *Semantic information processing*. The MIT Press.

Mitra, S., & Dangwal, R. (2010). Limits to self-organising systems of learning – The Kalikuppam experiment. *British Journal of Educational Technology*, *41*(5), 672–688.

Moate, J., Hulse, B., Jahnke, H., & Owens, A. (2019). Exploring the material mediation of dialogic space – A qualitative analysis of professional learning in initial teacher education based on reflective sketchbooks. *Thinking Skills and Creativity*, *31*, 167–178.

Mumford, L. (2010). *Technics and civilization*. University of Chicago Press.

Muralidharan, K., Singh, A., & Ganimian, A. J. (2019). Disrupting education? Experimental evidence on technology-aided instruction in India. *American Economic Review*, *109*(4), 1426–1460.

Murphy, C. (2016). Changing the way to teach maths: Preservice primary teachers' reflections on using exploratory talk in teaching mathematics. *Mathematics Teacher Education and Development*, *18*(2), 29–47.

Nagel, T. (1989). *The view from nowhere*. Oxford University Press.

Nardo, A. (2023). *Teaching beyond Chronos: A philosophical analysis of 'presentless' concepts of teaching, their implications and alternatives*. Manuscript submitted for publication.

Nardo, A., & Gaydos, M. (2021). 'Wicked problems' as catalysts for learning in educational ethics games. *Ethics and Education*, *16*(4), 492–509.

Nikulin, D. (2010). *Dialectic and dialogue*. Stanford University Press.

Nisbet, J. (2005). What is educational research? Changing perspectives through the 20th century. *Research Papers in Education*, *20*(1), 25–44.

Nisbett, R. (2004). *The geography of thought: How Asians and Westerners think differently . . . and why*. Simon and Schuster.

Nørgård, R. T., & Paaskesen, R. B. (2016). Open-ended education: How open-endedness might foster and promote technological imagination, enterprising, and participation in education. *Conjunctions: Transdisciplinary Journal of Cultural Participation*, *3*(1), 1–25.

Norman, D. A. (1988). *The psychology of everyday things*. Basic Books.

Norman, D. A. (1999). Affordance, conventions, and design. *Interactions*, *6*(3), 38–43.

Norman, D. A. (2002). *The design of everyday things*. Basic Books: New York.

Noyes, J. (1983). The QWERTY keyboard: A review. *International Journal of Man-Machine Studies*, *18*(3), 265–281.

Nye, B. D., Graesser, A. C., & Hu, X. (2014). AutoTutor and family: A review of 17 years of natural language tutoring. *International Journal of Artificial Intelligence in Education*, *24*, 427–469.

Nystrand, M. (1997). *Opening dialogue: Understanding the dynamics of language and learning in the English classroom* (Language and Literacy Series). Teachers College Press.

Oakeshott, M. (1959). *The voice of poetry in the conversation of mankind: An essay*. Bowes & Bowes.

Oakeshott, M. (1989). *The voice of liberal learning: Michael Oakeshott on education* (Fuller, T. Ed.). Yale University Press.

OECD. (2015). *Students, computers and learning: Making the connection*. Available online at: www.oecd.org/education/students-computers-and-learning-9789264239555-en.htm.

Oliver, M. (2005). The problem with affordance. *E-Learning and Digital Media*, *2*(4), 402–413.

Oliver, M. (2016). What is technology? In N. Rushby & D. Surry (Eds), *The Wiley handbook of learning technology*. Wiley Blackwell.

Oliver, M. (2020). Infrastructure and the post-truth era: Is Trump Twitter's fault? *Postdigital Science and Education*, *2*(1), 17–38.

Olson, D. R., & Oatley, K. (2014). The quotation theory of writing. *Written Communication*, *31*(1), 4–26.

Ong, W. J. (1969). World as view and world as event. *American Anthropologist, New Series*, *71*(4), 634–647.

Ong, W. J. (1972/2013). *Orality and literacy*. Routledge.

Osberg, D., & Biesta, G. (2008). The emergent curriculum: Navigating a complex course between unguided learning and planned enculturation. *Journal of Curriculum Studies*, *40*(3), 313–328.

Osborne, R. (2014). *An ecological approach to educational technology: Affordance as a design tool for aligning pedagogy and technology*. PhD Thesis, University of Exeter.

Osborne, R., Dunne, E., & Farrand, P. (2013). Integrating technologies into 'authentic' assessment design: An affordances approach. *Research in Learning Technology*, *21*, 21986. https://doi.org/10.3402/rlt.v21i0.21986.

O'Shea, T., & Self, J. (1986). *Learning and teaching with computers: The artificial intelligence revolution*. Prentice Hall Professional Technical Reference.

Paavola, S., & Hakkarainen, K. (2021). Trialogical learning and object-oriented collaboration. In U. Cress, C. Rosé, A. F. Wise & J. Oshima (Eds), *International Handbook of Computer-Supported Collaborative Learning*. Springer.

Palmgren-Neuvonen, L., Littleton, K., & Hirvonen, N. (2021). Dialogic spaces in divergent and convergent collaborative learning tasks. *Information and Learning Sciences*, *122*(5/6), 409–431.

Papert, S. (1986). *Constructionism: A new opportunity for elementary science education*. Massachusetts Institute of Technology, Media Laboratory, Epistemology and Learning Group.

Papert, S. A. (1980/2020). *Mindstorms: Children, computers, and powerful ideas*. Basic Books.

Pask, G. (1976). *Conversation theory: Applications in education and epistemology*. Elsevier.

Pea, R., & Cole, M. (2019). The living hand of the past: The role of technology in development. *Human Development*, *62*(1–2), 14–39.

Penrose, R., & Mermin, N. D. (1990). *The emperor's new mind: Concerning computers, minds, and the laws of physics*. Oxford University Press.

Pérez, J. Q., Daradoumis, T., & Puig, J. M. M. (2020). Rediscovering the use of chatbots in education: A systematic literature review. *Computer Applications in Engineering Education*, *28*(6), 1549–1565.

Peters, R. S. (Ed.) (2010). *The concept of education* (International Library of the Philosophy of Education, Vol. 17). Routledge.

Philippakos, Z., Howell, E., & Pelligrino, A. (2021). *Design-based research in education: Theory and applications*. Guilford Publications.

Phillips, R. (1978). Masking in Mende Sande Society initiation rituals. *Africa: Journal of the International African Institute*, *48*(3), 265–277.

Phillipson, N., & Wegerif, R. (2016). *Dialogic education: Mastering core concepts through thinking together*. Routledge.

Pickering, A. (2009). Beyond design: Cybernetics, biological computers and hylozoism. *Synthese*, *168*(3), 469–491.

Plato. (370BCE / 2008). *Phaedrus* (B. Jowett, Trans.). Forgotten Books.

Poster, M. (2001). *What's the matter with the internet?* (Vol. 3). University of Minnesota Press.

Poster, M. (2018). *The second media age*. John Wiley & Sons.

Power, S. A., Zittoun, T., Akkerman, S., Wagoner, B., Cabra, M. . . . Gillespie, A. (2023). Social psychology of and for world-making. *Personality and Social Psychology Review*. https://doi.org/10.1177/10888683221145756.

Ravenscroft, A., Wegerif, R. B., & Hartley, J. R. (2007). Reclaiming thinking: Dialectic, dialogic and learning in the digital age. *British Journal of Educational Psychology* (Monograph Series, *Learning through Digital Technologies*, J. Underwood & J. Dockrell, Guest Eds), Series II(5), 39–57.

Reich, J. (2020). *Failure to disrupt: Why technology alone can't transform education*. Harvard University Press.

Reicher, S. D., Haslam, S. A., Spears, R., & Reynolds, K. J. (2012). A social mind: The context of John Turner's work and its influence. *European Review of Social Psychology*, *23*(1), 344–385.

Resnick, M. (2017). Fulfilling Papert's dream: Computational fluency for all. In *Proceedings of the 2017 ACM SIGCSE Technical Symposium on Computer Science Education*, March 8–11, Seattle, WA.

Ritella, G., Loperfido, F. F., De Giglio, G., Scurani, A., & Ligorio, M. B. (2022). Adopting educational robotics and coding to open dialogic spaces in lower secondary education. *Dialogic Pedagogy: An International Online Journal*, *10*, DT41-DT58.

Robinson, M. (2019). *Curriculum: Athena versus the machine*. Crown House Publishing Ltd.

Robson, E. (2001). The tablet house: A scribal school in Old Babylonian Nippur. *Revue d'Assyriologie*, *95*(1), 39–67.

Rojas-Drummond, S. M., Albarrán, C. D., & Littleton, K. S. (2008). Collaboration, creativity and the co-construction of oral and written texts. *Thinking Skills and Creativity*, *3*(3), 177–191.

Rommetveit, R. (1992). Outlines of a dialogically based social-cognitive approach to human cognition and communication. In A. Wold (Ed.), *The dialogical alternative: Towards a theory of language and mind*. Scandinavian Press.

Rovelli, C. (2021). *Helgoland: Making sense of the quantum revolution*. Penguin.

Rovelli, C. (2022). The relational interpretation. In O. Freire (Ed.), *The Oxford Handbook of the History of Quantum Interpretations*. Oxford Academic. Available online at: https://doi.org/10.1093/oxfordhb/9780198844495.013.0044

Russell, M. (Ed.) (2006). *Technology and assessment: The tale of two interpretations*. Information Age Publishing.

Russell, S. J. (2010). *Artificial intelligence: A modern approach*. Pearson Education, Inc.

Saadatmand, M., & Kumpulainen, K. (2014). Participants' perceptions of learning and networking in connectivist MOOCs [Massive Open Online Courses]. *Journal of Online Learning and Teaching*, *10*(1), 16–30.

Saeverot, H., & Biesta, G. (2013). On the need to ask educational questions about education: An interview with Gert Biesta. *Policy Futures in Education*, *11*(2), 175–184.

Santayana, G. (1905). *The life of reason*. Charles Scribner's Sons.

Savenye, W. C., & Robinson, R. S. (2013). Qualitative research issues and methods: An introduction for educational technologists. In D. Jonassen (Ed.), *Handbook of research for educational communications and technology*. Taylor and Francis.

Scanlon, E., Herodotou, C., Sharples, M., & McLeod, K. (2020). nQuire: Citizens acting as scientists in massive open online learning. In *Proceedings of the Seventh ACM Conference on Learning@ Scale*, Virtual Conference, 12–14 August.

Scardamalia, M. (2004). CSILE/Knowledge Forum®. In A. Kovalchick & K. Dawson (Eds), *Education and technology: An encyclopaedia*. ABC-CLIO.

Scardamalia, M., & Bereiter, C. (2014). Knowledge building and knowledge creation: Theory, pedagogy, and technology. In R. K. Sawyer (Ed.), *The Cambridge handbook of the learning sciences* (2nd edn). Cambridge University Press.

Schad, M., & Jones, W. M. (2020). The maker movement and education: A systematic review of the literature. *Journal of Research on Technology in Education*, *52*(1), 65–78.

Schatzki, T. R. (1996). *Social practices: A Wittgensteinian approach to human activity and the social*. Cambridge University Press.

Scott, B. (2001). Conversation theory: A constructivist, dialogical approach to educational technology. *Cybernetics & Human Knowing*, *8*(4), 25.

Scribner, S., & Cole, M. (2013). *The psychology of literacy*. Harvard University Press.

Searle, J. R. (1982). The Chinese room revisited. *Behavioral and Brain Sciences*, *5*(2), 345–348.

Seels, B., & Richey, R. (1994). *Instructional technology: The definition and domains of the field*. Association for Educational Communications and Technology.

Seidel, S., Berente, N., Debortoli, S., & Srinivasan, N. (2016). Tweeting Like Taylor Swift? Affordances, status production, and online platforms. In *2016 49th Hawaii International Conference on System Sciences (HICSS)*, Koloa, HI, IEEE.

Selwyn, N. (2017). *Education and technology: Key issues and debates* (2nd edn). Bloomsbury Publishing.

Shaffer, D. W. (2006). Epistemic frames for epistemic games. *Computers & Education*, *46*(3), 223–234.

Shaffer, D. W. (2017). *Quantitative ethnography*. Cathcart Press.

Sharples, M. (2002). *How we write: Writing as creative design*. Routledge.

Sharples, M. (2009). Towards an interdisciplinary design science of learning. In *European Conference on Technology Enhanced Learning*, Berlin, Heidelberg, Springer.

Sharples, M., Taylor, J., & Vavoula, G. (2010). A theory of learning for the mobile age: Learning through conversation and exploration across contexts. In B. Bachmair (Ed.), *Medienbildung in neuen Kulturräumen: die deutschsprachige und britische Diskussion*. VS Verlag für Sozialwissenschaften Wiesbaden.

Shepherd, D. (2006). A feeling for history? Bakhtin and 'the problem of great time'. *The Slavonic and East European Review*, *84*(1), 32–51.

Shi, S. (in preparation). *Designing a dialogic virtual learning environment for teaching, learning, and researching together in higher education*. PhD Thesis, Faculty of Education, University of Cambridge.

Shotter, J. (2008). Dialogism and polyphony in organizing theorizing in organization studies: Action guiding anticipations and the continuous creation of novelty. *Organization Studies*, *29*(4), 501–524.

Sidorkin, A. M. (1999). *Beyond discourse: Education, the self and dialogue*. State University of New York Press.

Siegel, S. T., & Biesta, G. (2022). The problem of educational theory. *Policy Futures in Education*, *20*(5), 537–548.

Siemens, G. (2005). Connectivism: A learning theory for a digital age. *International Journal of Instructional Technology and Distance Learning*, *2*(1), 3–10.

Simon, H. (1969). *The sciences of the artificial*. MIT Press.

Simondon, G. (2005). *L'individuation à la lumière des notions de forme et d'information*. Éditions Jérôme Millon.

Simondon, G. (2017). *On the mode of existence of technical objects*. Univocal Publishing.

Simondon, G. (2020). *Individuation in light of notions of form and information*. University of Minnesota Press.

Sinha, C., & da Silva Sinha, V. (2022). Time and events – In language, mind and world (Review essay). Available online at: https://doi.org/10.31234/osf.io/639vx

Skinner, B. F. (1968). *The technology of teaching*. Appleton-Century-Crofts.

Slavina, A., & Brym, R. (2020). Demonstrating in the internet age: A test of Castells' theory. *Social Movement Studies*, *19*(2), 201–221.

Smith, S. U., Hayes, S., & Shea, P. (2017). A critical review of the use of Wenger's community of practice (CoP) theoretical framework in online and blended learning research, 2000–2014. *Online Learning*, *21*(1), 209–237.

Smith-Nunes, G., & Shaw, A. (2022). Doctoral colloquium – ME++ data ethics of biometrics through ballet and AR. In *2022 8th International Conference of the Immersive Learning Research Network (iLRN)*, 30 May 2022–4 June 2022. IEEE.

Smørdal, O., Rasmussen, I., & Major, L. (2021). Supporting classroom dialogue through developing the Talkwall microblogging tool: Considering emerging concepts that bridge theory, practice and design. *Nordic Journal of Digital Literacy*, *16*(2), 50–64.

Spinoza, B. (2006). *The essential Spinoza: Ethics and related writings*. Hackett Publishing.

Spohr, D. (2017). Fake news and ideological polarization: Filter bubbles and selective exposure on social media. *Business Information Review*, *34*(3), 150–160.

Stahl, G. (2006). *Group cognition: Computer support for building collaborative knowledge (acting with technology)*. The MIT Press.

Stahl, G. (2007). Meaning making in CSCL: Conditions and preconditions for cognitive processes by groups. In *Proceedings of the 8th international conference on computer supported collaborative learning*, New Brunswick, NJ, 16–21 July. International Society of the Learning Sciences.

Stahl, G. (2010). Guiding group cognition in CSCL. *International Journal of Computer-Supported Collaborative Learning*, *5*, 255–258.

Stahl, G. (Ed.) (2021). *Theoretical investigations: Philosophical foundations of group cognition* (Vol. 18). Springer Nature.

Stiegler, B. (1998). *Technics and time: The fault of Epimetheus* (Vol. 1). Stanford University Press.

Stojanov, K. (2017). *Education, self-consciousness and social action: Building as a neo-Hegelian concept*. Routledge.

Street, B. (2006). Understanding and defining literacy (Background Paper for EFA Global Monitoring Report). 2006/ED/EFA/MRT/PI/92. UNESCO.

Suen, H. Y., Hung, K. E., & Lin, C. L. (2020). Intelligent video interview agent used to predict communication skill and perceived personality traits. *Human-centric Computing and Information Sciences*, *10*, 1–12.

Sweller, J. (2005). Implications of cognitive load theory for multimedia learning. In R. E. Mayer (Ed.), *The Cambridge handbook of multimedia learning*. Cambridge University Press.

Sweller, J., Kirschner, P. A., & Clark, R. E. (2007). Why minimally guided teaching techniques do not work: A reply to commentaries. *Educational Psychologist*, *42*(2), 115–121.

Symonds, J. E., & Gorard, S. (2010). Death of mixed methods? Or the rebirth of research as a craft. *Evaluation & Research in Education*, *23*(2), 121–136.

Taylor, C. (2009). *A secular age*. Harvard University Press.

Tennie, C., Call, J., & Tomasello, M. (2009). Ratcheting up the ratchet: On the evolution of cumulative culture. *Philosophical Transactions of the Royal Society B: Biological Sciences*, *364*(1528), 2405–2415.

Terren, L., & Borge-Bravo, R. (2021). Echo chambers on social media: A systematic review of the literature. *Review of Communication Research*, *9*, 99–118.

Thomas, D., & Brown, J. S. (2011). *A new culture of learning: Cultivating the imagination for a world of constant change*. CreateSpace.

Thomas, P. L. (2022). *The Science of Reading movement: The never-ending debate and the need for a different approach to reading instruction*. National Education Policy Center.

Tomasello, M., Carpenter, M., Call, J., Behne, T., & Moll, H. (2005). Understanding and sharing intentions: The origins of cultural cognition. *Behavioral and Brain Sciences*, *28*(5), 675–691.

Torgerson, C. J., & Torgerson, D. J. (2012). The need for randomised controlled trials in educational research. *British Journal of Educational Studies*, *49*(3), 316–328.

Toulmin, S. E. (2003). *The uses of argument*. Cambridge University Press.

Travers, R. M. W. (1983). *How research has changed American school*. Mythos Press.

Tsien, T. T. (1985). *Science and civilisation in China*. Volume 5: *Chemistry and Chemical Technology*. Part I: *Paper and Printing* (J. Needham, Ed.). Cambridge University Press.

Tsui, A., & Tavares, N. (2021). The technology cart and the pedagogy horse in online teaching. *English Teaching and Learning*, *45*(1), 109–118.

Turing, A. M. (1950). Computing machinery and intelligence. *Mind*, *59*(236), 433–460.

Turkle, S. (1996). *Virtuality and its discontents searching for community in cyberspace*. The American Prospect.

Turkle, S. (2011). *Alone together: Why we expect more from technology and less from each other*. Basic Books.

Van der Veer, R., & Valsiner, J. (1991). *Understanding Vygotsky: A quest for synthesis*. Blackwell Publishing.

Van Dijk, A. (2005). Early printed Qur'ans: The dissemination of the Qur'an in the West. *Journal of Qur'anic Studies*, 7(2), 136–143.

Varela, F. G., Maturana, H. R., & Uribe, R. (1991). Autopoiesis: The organization of living systems, its characterization and a model. In G. J. Klir (Ed.), *Facets of systems science*. Springer.

Vedral, V. (2018). *Decoding reality: The universe as quantum information*. Oxford University Press.

Volosinov, V. N. (1986). *Marxism and the philosophy of language*. Harvard University Press.

Von Foerster, H. (Ed.) (1995). *Cybernetics of cybernetics: Or, the control of control and the communication of communication* (2nd edn). Future Systems.

Von Petzinger, G. (2017). *The first signs: Unlocking the mysteries of the world's oldest symbols*. Simon and Schuster.

Vygotsky, L. S. (1934/1986). *Thought and language* (A. Kozulin, Trans.). MIT Press.

Waddington, D. (2013). A parallel world for the World Bank: A case study of Urgent: Evoke, an educational alternate reality game. *Revue internationale des technologies en pédagogie universitaire/International Journal of Technologies in Higher Education*, *10*(3), 42–56.

Wang, S., Christensen, C., Cui, W., Tong, R., Yarnall, L., Shear, L., & Feng, M. (2023). When adaptive learning is effective learning: Comparison of an adaptive learning system to teacher-led instruction. *Interactive Learning Environments*, *31*(2), 793–803.

Watson, L. (1979). *Lifetide: The biology of the unconscious*. Simon & Schuster.

Watters, A. (2021). *Teaching machines: The history of personalized learning*. MIT Press.

Watts, A. (1999). *The Tao of philosophy*. Tuttle Publishing.

Wegerif, R. (2002). *Literature review in thinking skills, technology and learning* (Report Number 2). FutureLab Series.

Wegerif, R. (2004). The role of educational software as a support for teaching and learning conversations. *Computers & Education*, *43*(1–2), 179–191.

Wegerif, R. (2006). A dialogic understanding of the relationship between CSCL and teaching thinking skills. *International Journal of Computer-Supported Collaborative Learning*, *1*(1), 143–157.

Wegerif, R. (2007). *Dialogic education and technology: Expanding the space of learning*. Springer Science & Business Media.

Wegerif, R. (2008). Dialogic or dialectic? The significance of ontological assumptions in research on educational dialogue. *British Educational Research Journal*, *34*(3), 347–361.

Wegerif, R. (2013). *Dialogic education for the internet age*. Routledge.

Wegerif, R. (2018). New technology and the apparent failure of democracy. An educational response. on education. *Journal for research and debate*, *1*(1). https://doi.org/10.17899/on_ed.2018.1.7

Wegerif, R. (2019). Towards a dialogic theory of education for the internet age. In N. Mercer, R. Wegerif & L. Major (Eds), *The Routledge international handbook of research on dialogic education*. Routledge.

Wegerif, R., & Dawes, L. (2004). *Thinking and learning with ICT: Raising achievement in primary classrooms*. Routledge.

Wegerif, R., & Mercer, N. (1997). A dialogical framework for researching peer talk. *Language and Education Library*, *12*, 49–64.

Wegerif, R., Mercer, N., & Rojas-Drummond, S. (1999). Language for the social construction of knowledge: Comparing classroom talk in Mexican preschools. *Language and Education*, *13*(2), 133–150.

Wegerif, R., McLaren, B. M., Chamrada, M., Scheuer, O., Mansour, N., Mikšátko, J., & Williams, M. (2010). Exploring creative thinking in graphically mediated synchronous dialogues. *Computers & Education*, *54*(3), 613–621.

Wegerif, R., Doney, J., Richards, A., Mansour, N., Larkin, S., & Jamison, I. (2019). Exploring the ontological dimension of dialogic education through an evaluation of the impact of internet mediated dialogue across cultural difference. *Learning, Culture and Social Interaction*, *20*, 80–89.

Weizenbaum, J. (1966). ELIZA – A computer program for the study of natural language communication between man and machine. *Communications of the ACM*, *9*(1), 36–45.

Weizenbaum, J. (1976). *Computer power and human reason: From judgment to calculation*. W. H. Freeman & Co.

Weller, M. (2020). *25 years of ed tech*. Athabasca University Press.

Wells, G. (1999). *Dialogic inquiry: Towards a socio-cultural practice and theory of education*. Cambridge University Press.

Wenger, E. (1998). *Communities of practice: Learning, meaning, and identity*. Cambridge University Press.

Wenger, E. (2010). Communities of practice and social learning systems: The career of a concept. In C. Blackmore (Ed.), *Social learning systems and communities of practice*. Springer.

Wertsch, J. V. (1996). The role of abstract rationality in Vygotsky's image of mind. In A. Tryphon & J. N. Voneche (Eds), *Piaget–Vygotsky: The social genesis of thought*. Psychology Press.

Whitworth, A. (2020a). *Mapping information landscapes: New methods for exploring the development and teaching of information literacy*. Facet Publishing.

Whitworth, A. (2020b). Fostering digital skills and competencies through discursive mapping of information landscapes. In A. Curaj, L. Deca & R. Pricopie (Eds), *European higher education area: Challenges for a new decade*. Springer.

Williamson, B. (2018). The hidden architecture of higher education: Building a big data infrastructure for the 'smarter university'. *International Journal of Educational Technology in Higher Education*, *15*(1), 1–26.

Wimmer, A., & Feinstein, Y. (2010). The rise of the nation-state across the world, 1816 to 2001. *American Sociological Review*, *75*(5), 764–790.

Winograd, T., & Flores, F. (1986). *Understanding computers and cognition: A new foundation for design*. Intellect Books.

Wittgenstein, L. (2009). *Philosophical investigations* (4th edn) (Hacker, P. M. S., & Schulte, J. Trans.). John Wiley & Sons.

Wittgenstein, L., Ambrose, A., & Macdonald, M. (1979). *Wittgenstein's lectures, Cambridge, 1932–1935: From the notes of Alice Ambrose and Margaret Macdonald*. Rowman and Littlefield.

Yang, Y., van Aalst, J., Chan, C. K., & Tian, W. (2016). Reflective assessment in knowledge building by students with low academic achievement. *International Journal of Computer-Supported Collaborative Learning*, *11*, 281–311.

Zancajo, A., Verger, A., & Bolea, P. (2022). Digitalization and beyond: The effects of Covid-19 on post-pandemic educational policy and delivery in Europe. *Policy and Society*, *41*(1), 111–128.

Zavota, G. (2018). A feminist approach to the visible and the invisible through Karen Barad's agential realism. *Acta Structuralica*, *2*, 147–169.

Zembylas, M., & Vrasidas, C. (2005). Levinas and the 'inter-face': The ethical challenge of online education. *Educational Theory*, *55*(1), 61–78.

Zhang, J., Scardamalia, M., Reeve, R., & Messina, R. (2009). Designs for collective cognitive responsibility in knowledge-building communities. *The Journal of the Learning Sciences*, *18*(1), 7–44.

Zhonggen, Y. (2019). A meta-analysis of use of serious games in education over a decade. *International Journal of Computer Games Technology*, Article ID 4797032. Available online at: https://doi.org/10.1155/2019/4797032.

# INDEX

Page numbers in *italics* indicate illustrations, **bold** a table

Printed in Great Britain
by Amazon

40124101R00139